Routledge Revivals

Ernest Bevin

First published in 1993, this book presents a biography of a central figure in the development of both the labour movement and British politics in the first half of the twentieth century. This highly accessible account of Bevin's life and career was the first to make use of documents pertaining to his activities during the Second World War and bring together numerous secondary studies to posit an alternative interpretation. The book is split into chronological sections dealing with his early years, his time a trade union leader from 1911 to 1929, the beginnings of his involvement in the labour party during 1929-1939, and his time in office as Minister of Labour and then Foreign Secretary.

Ernest Bevin

Peter Weiler

First published in 1993
by Manchester University Press

This edition first published in 2016 by Routledge
2 Park Square, Milton Park, Abingdon, Oxon, OX14 4RN
and by Routledge
711 Third Avenue, New York, NY 10017

Routledge is an imprint of the Taylor & Francis Group, an informa business

© 1993 Peter Weiler

The right of Peter Weiler to be identified as author of this work has been
asserted by him in accordance with sections 77 and 78 of the Copyright,
Designs and Patents Act 1988.
All rights reserved. No part of this book may be reprinted or reproduced or
utilised in any form or by any electronic, mechanical, or other means, now
known or hereafter invented, including photocopying and recording, or in any
information storage or retrieval system, without permission in writing from the
publishers.

Publisher's Note
The publisher has gone to great lengths to ensure the quality of this reprint but
points out that some imperfections in the original copies may be apparent.

Disclaimer
The publisher has made every effort to trace copyright holders and welcomes
correspondence from those they have been unable to contact.

A Library of Congress record exists under LC control number: 92002494

ISBN 13: 978-1-138-67565-0 (hbk)
ISBN 13: 978-1-315-56049-6 (ebk)

Ernest Bevin

Peter Weiler

MANCHESTER UNIVERSITY PRESS
Manchester and New York

Distributed exclusively in the USA and Canada by St. Martin's Press, New York

Copyright © Ernest Bevin 1993

Published by Manchester University Press,
Oxford Road, Manchester, M13 9PL, UK
and Room 400, 175 Fifth Avenue, New York, NY 10010, USA

Distributed exclusively in the USA and Canada
by St. Martin's Press, Inc., 175 Fifth Avenue, New York, NY 10010, USA

British Library Cataloguing-in-Publication Data
A catalogue record for this book is available from the British Library

Library of Congress Cataloging-in-Publication Data
Weiler, Peter, 1942–
    Ernest Bevin / Peter Weiler.
      p. cm. – (Lives of the left)
    ISBN 0–7190–2178–2 (hardback)
    1. Bevin, Ernest, 1881–1951. 2. Statesmen – Great Britain –
Biography. 3. Labor leaders – Great Britain – Biography. 4. Great
Britain – Foreign relations – 1945– I. Title. II. Series.
DA585.B4W44. 1993
941.085'092–dc20
  [B]   92–2494

ISBN 0 7190 2178 2 *hardback*

Set in Perpetua
by Koinonia Ltd, Manchester

Printed in Great Britain
by Bookcraft (Bath) Limited

Contents

	Preface	vii
1	**Early years**	1
2	**Trade union leader**	8
3	**Social democrat**	53
4	**Minister of Labour**	100
5	**Foreign Secretary**	144
	Conclusion	188
	Notes	195
	Bibliography	216
	Index	227

To Kathleen, Sarah and Emma with love

Preface

To anyone familiar with the history of the British labour movement in this century, Ernest Bevin needs no introduction. Shortly after the First World War, he founded the Transport and General Workers' Union, which was long the largest trade union in Britain. He was, with Trades Union Congress General Secretary Walter Citrine, largely responsible for the direction that the British trade union movement took after the General Strike of 1926. After the financial crisis of 1931, he played a significant role in the reshaping of the Labour Party's policy that became the basis of the programme enacted by the 1945 Labour government. In 1940, aged fifty-nine, he began a new career, overseeing the wartime government's labour policies and in the process contributing to the creation of the postwar welfare state. After the war, in what to many contemporary observers seemed the most surprising move of his long career, Bevin served as Foreign Secretary in the 1945 Labour government, helping to shape the international order that prevailed for the next forty years. In short, Bevin's career was centrally important to the development of both the British labour movement and British politics in the first half of the twentieth century.

A biography necessarily imposes order on the complexity that is any individual's life. In this instance, while trying to do justice to the multifaceted nature of Bevin's career, I have employed two related concepts, labourism and corporatism, used by many other historians to explain the shape taken by the British labour movement. When Bevin began his career in the labour movement at the beginning of the twentieth century, the direction that movement would take was not fixed. Although predominately moderate in outlook, the movement contained tensions between a visionary desire to transform capitalist society and a need to make an accommodation with that society for the sake of immediate economic gains. The drive towards accommodation, which nevertheless went along with a strong sense

vii

PREFACE

of class consciousness and class solidarity, has been called labourism. John Saville has defined it as 'a theory and practice which [accepts] the possibility of social change within the existing framework of society ... [and emphasises] the unity of Capital and Labour'.[1]

These contradictory impulses toward transformation and accommodation also marked the life of Ernest Bevin, particularly his early career. Bevin was deeply conscious of his own subservient position within British society and filled with a corresponding anger at its unfairness. This anger led him at times to a vision of a 'socialist commonwealth' but more often towards a desire for acceptance by society. Bevin's dominant concerns derived from his work as a trade union leader to protect the living standards of his followers and secure recognition of the trade union movement. To accomplish these goals, he became a proponent of a particular labourist strategy that has come to be called corporatism, the arrangement in which trade union leaders explicitly accept the limits of the capitalist economy and work to secure a partnership with capital and the state, trading labour peace for recognition and influence. After the General Strike of 1926, Bevin played a crucial role in turning the labour movement toward a corporatist path and away from direct action, the use of organised working-class power to secure political changes, and the syndicalist ideal of direct workplace democracy.

Since Alan Bullock has written a three-volume biography of Bevin, why write another one? One reason is that Bullock's biography is so massive that only specialists read it. There are no other scholarly biographies of Bevin, only journalistic accounts. Moreover, although Bullock's impressive biography remains definitive as a narrative, it is written very much from Bevin's point of view, since Bullock shared the labourist and corporatist ideals of his subject. Bullock's stance is that of a Labour loyalist from a generation for whom Bevin was a hero.

A second reason is that documents about Bevin's life are now available, particularly for the Second World War, which were still closed when Bullock was writing. In addition, numerous new secondary studies about the period during which Bevin lived have provided additional data for most of the key moments in his career. All of this new information makes possible alternative interpretations of Bevin's life and work. For the sake of brevity, however, I have neither cited all the scholars whose work I have used nor

viii

PREFACE

indicated how I have entered into a number of historical debates about the British labour movement and British political developments. Specialists will recognise both my intellectual debts and the historiographical arguments; for others, it would be an unnecessary distraction.

This is a biography of Bevin's public life. Like most members of the working class, Bevin left no diaries and few personal letters; in fact, we know very little about his early years. Although I wish I had been able to describe the interaction of Bevin's inner emotional concerns and desires and his public life, I have not been able to do so. I do make judgements here and there about Bevin's personality, but by and large I have had no choice but to focus on the public man.

For analytic purposes I have introduced an artificial distinction into Bevin's life. Chapter 2, which discusses the period from 1911 to 1929, focuses on Bevin as a trade union leader, while Chapter 3, which discusses the period from 1929 to 1939, focuses more on Bevin as a social democrat. I found that this division made it easier to show the coherence of Bevin's trade union and political views. It also made sense since Bevin took an active role in Labour Party affairs only after 1929. However, readers should bear in mind that although Bevin was always first and foremost a trade unionist, he was also always a democratic socialist and supporter of Labour. His political and trade union concerns were never totally distinct.

I am very grateful to the friends and colleagues who helped me with this biography. I had an informative discussion about Bevin with Regan Scott, who gave me access to Transport and General Workers' Union records. Richard and Rachel Boulton, Jennifer Davis, John Field and Virginia Hjelmaa provided me with hospitality, helping to make my research trips to England both easy and pleasant. At Warwick University's Modern Records Centre, Alistair Tough was unfailingly patient and helpful. Rodney Lowe pointed me to some interesting Ministry of Labour files. Dick Lourie provided much sound editorial advice. Jon Schneer commented helpfully on Chapter 2. Carolyn Eisenberg, Bob Hannigan and Melvyn Leffler did the same for Chapter 5. Nina Fishman made a number of useful suggestions on the first four chapters. Paul Breines, Jim Cronin, Denis MacShane, John Saville and Deborah Valenze read the entire manuscript in draft. Their perceptive criticisms greatly strengthened

ix

PREFACE

the book. I hope they forgive me for not accepting all of their suggestions. David Howell was a model editor, never impatient and always helpful. Once again, my greatest debt is to my family. My daughters, Sarah and Emma, reminded me about what is really important in life. My wife Kathleen was both my best critic and my strongest support. The dedication only hints at what they mean to me.

Bevin addressing the TUC in 1930

Copyright The Hulton Picture Company.

1 Early years

The entire world noted Ernest Bevin's death in 1951. As the founder and first General Secretary of the Transport and General Workers' Union, he had long been one of the best known trade union leaders in England. In the last decade of his life he had also achieved national fame as Minister of Labour in the wartime Coalition government and world fame as Foreign Secretary in the Labour government of 1945. His ashes were buried in Westminster Abbey. That someone from obscure origins should manage to secure admission to the pantheon of British statesmen, along with Churchill and Pitt, is striking. But although rags to riches stories are unusual, they are not unheard of. What is more interesting to consider is that the socialist Bevin was at the end celebrated as 'mirroring the soul of the English people', as one of his biographers commented, or reflecting 'characteristically British qualities – courage, frankness, shrewdness, and practicality', as *The Times* put it in his obituary.[1] Thus there are two stories to relate here in discussing Ernest Bevin's life. One is about a remarkable man who rose from humble circumstances to great power. The other is about how Bevin's life came to be understood as exemplifying the changes undergone by British society in the first half of this century.

Born in the Somerset village of Winsford on 7 March 1881, Ernest Bevin was the youngest of seven children. His mother, Diana Mercy Tidboald, had married an agricultural labourer, William Bevin, in 1864, when she was twenty-three years old, and moved with him in the early 1870s to South Wales. They were part of a general migration from the economically depressed English country-side that characterised the last decades of the nineteenth century. In 1877, however, Mercy Bevin returned alone to the village, accom-panied only by her six children. Thereafter, she listed herself as a widow. Ernest was illegitimate and never found out who his father was, his mother having left the man's name off the parish register.

1

All we know is that he must have been a big man, since Ernest, though short, was barrel chested, with a massive head and hands so large that they were later described as looking like 'a bunch of bananas'.[2]

Doing what work was available for a single woman in the village, Mercy Bevin just managed to support Ernest and the other children still at home. She served as a midwife, did domestic work both at the village inn, the Royal Oak, and for those of her neighbours who could afford to hire her, and occasionally supplemented her income with relief from the parish. There is no record of what Ernest's life was like in these years, except that it was marked by poverty and insecurity. 'I'm sure', one village contemporary recalled, 'there's no one in this wide world was ever poorer than he and his mother'.[3]

Nine miles from the nearest railway line, Winsford was relatively isolated from the rest of England. Ernest's main contact with the larger world came from his attendance at the village school, although his Methodist mother may not have been pleased that it was run by the Church of England. Independently minded, she passed on her religious nonconformity to her son, whom she sent from an early age to Methodist Sunday school. Ernest was only eight years old when she died of cancer in 1889 at the age of forty-eight.

In spite of her own difficulties, Mercy Bevin seems to have provided an emotionally supportive home for her youngest son, laying the basis for the self-confidence that later made it possible for him to work on equal terms with men who had been bred to command people of his station in life. Her ability to live on her own points to a woman of strong character, as does perhaps her reputation for keeping a 'spotlessly clean' house.[4] It may be the case that Bevin's own sense of order — 'You must have a thing tidy', he was fond of saying — derived from these years. He always kept a picture of his mother on his desk.

After his mother died, the young Ernest moved to Devon where he was taken in by his twenty-five-year-old half-sister Mary and her husband, George Pope, who worked on the railway. For the next three years, he continued his schooling, one year more than required by law. Then, like any other boy of his social class, Bevin had to go to work, in his case for a neighbouring farmer who paid him sixpence a week plus room and board for doing a variety of odd jobs: clearing stones, cutting up turnips for cattle food, mending

EARLY YEARS

fences, etc. The next year he went to work for more money for another farmer, who turned out to be less congenial. Bevin soon quarrelled with him – there are varying accounts in village lore – and left to live in Bristol with his eldest half-brother Jack. Ernest was thirteen years old.

Having to leave school at the age of eleven was for him a source of both bitterness and regret. 'I know the joy that knowledge can bring', he later said. 'When I realise what a higher conception of life knowledge means if rightly used, I hate to think that the Church, the State, the Master Class, the Landlord Class are not content with taking from us the fruits of our toil, but that they must withhold knowledge from us and our forefathers. I hate them for that more than for anything else.'[5]

It seems reasonable to speculate – and since Bevin did not like to discuss these years that is all we can do – that the absence of a father, the early death of his mother and the various moves he made afterwards had a profound influence on him. All we can say is that Bevin made use of these harsh circumstances to build up his own self-confidence. This faith in his own ability grew eventually into a tremendous egotism, often articulated as anger at the traditional wielders of power for not acknowledging his abilities or those of other workers. He later said that the deprivation and imposed deference with which he was raised – 'I had to work at ten years of age . . . and was taught to bow to the squire and touch my hat to the parson' – produced an 'intense hatred' in him that led him to 'direct [his] mind to a policy to give to [his] class a power to control their own destiny and labour'.[6] Perhaps we can also say that his ability to endure, to fight back against life's blows and remain confident of his own ability exacted a price – in the form of a somewhat solitary nature, an increasingly work-driven personality, and a harshness to those who disagreed with him.[7] Although Bevin could be generous to those who worked for him, he was not a kind or easygoing man.

Besides Jack, another of Ernest's half-brothers, Albert, also lived in Bristol, training to be a pastrycook. Albert secured Ernest a job in the same bakehouse, where he was paid 6 shillings plus meals for working at odd jobs for seventy-two hours a week. Ernest soon tired of this work and drifted into a series of other jobs over the next few years, working for the longest period of time for the tramway company. He made no attempt that we know of to acquire

3

ERNEST BEVIN

any specific skill or to apprentice himself to a skilled trade. But in 1900 he settled down as a mineral water delivery man, a job that must have provided him some satisfaction since he maintained it for all but one year until 1911. The job allowed him to work outdoors at his own pace, and although the hours were long, the pay was relatively good, 18 shillings a week plus a commission to start. Through extra work, he was able to build up his income to almost £2 per week.

The most significant developments in Bevin's life during these years came not at work but in his growing political concerns and in his personal life. In these years he married Florence Townley, the daughter of a Bristol wine taster, a change that may have made him a shade less serious. Henceforth, he attended music hall performances on Saturday night, rather than a sermon or political lecture. His marriage seems to have been a perfectly conventional one. Florence Bevin stayed at home, tending the house, of which she was quite proud, and their only child, Queenie, who was born in 1914; she was not active in any of her husband's political or trade union causes. His brothers, whom one might have expected to remain of some importance in his life, 'gradually lost touch with him'.[8]

Throughout this period, Bevin maintained his attachment to the nonconformist religion first instilled in him by his mother. Eventually, he joined the Manor Hall Baptist Church, becoming baptised by full immersion in January 1902. He remained an active member of the church until 1905, distributing tracts and often speaking at its open air meetings. As with so many in his generation of labour leaders, chapel-going clearly exerted a formative influence. In the dominant view, a natural hierarchy ran from God through the local squire or business owner to the vicar and down to the lowly labourer. In place of this, nonconformity taught the equal dignity of all men, and the worthiness of the humble. Although in many ways quite conservative politically, stressing an individual moral response to social problems and opposing any form of political radicalism, it did provide a basis of self-respect for workers. In the chapel, they could control their own spiritual lives, independent of traditional leaders, and arrive at their own understanding of life's travails. For some, too, and certainly for Bevin, the chapel provided an initial forum, a place where they could learn to speak in public and to respond to the often unspoken needs of their audience.

4

EARLY YEARS

Gradually, however, and in ways that we do not know in any detail, Bevin came to find nonconformity inadequate, particularly as a response to the injustice that characterised a society in which a third of the working class, even measured by the most strict standard, lived in poverty; where unemployment was a constant fear; and where 10 per cent of the population owned virtually all wealth in the country. One source of this expansion of his horizon was his own self-education. Throughout these years, Bevin attended different adult schools and discussion classes, such as those conducted by the then famous pacifist minister James Moffatt Logan. He also read what he could on his own: Jack London's *People of the Abyss*, Leo Chiozza Money's *Riches and Poverty* (a critique of the maldistribution of wealth in Edwardian England) and Bryce's *English Constitution*. But we do not know what else Bevin read or how exactly he came to find nonconformity inadequate. What we do know is that he began to attend meetings of the Bristol Socialist Society during these years and eventually joined it, abandoning at the same time his membership in the chapel, though not his religious faith.

The Bristol Socialist Society, which was inspired by a variety of socialist thinkers, including William Morris and Edward Carpenter, was an eclectic affair, providing a home, according to its historian, for 'all socialists, by whatever path they had arrived, Marxist, Fabian, Christian, Secularist'.[9] By the time Bevin joined, it had affiliated to the Social Democratic Federation (SDF), the most explicitly Marxist of the small socialist societies that had grown up in Britain in the last decades of the nineteenth century. Given his later views, Bevin's membership in the SDF had a number of ironies. The SDF distrusted trade unions as hopelessly compromised and unlikely to form the basis of a socialist revolution that it believed could be achieved only through political action. Although in practice the SDF worked with some success within the existing political system, and had a number of trade unionist members, it tended to preach a purist socialism that had no place for the new, still non-socialist Labour Party. Eventually its principal heir, the British Socialist Party, merged into the Communist Party. The mature Bevin completely disagreed with the SDF's idea of socialism and the best way to attain it. But the young Bevin, coming to socialism out of a nonconformist religious background, seems to have been attracted

5

by the idea of the 'co-operative commonwealth', the secular equivalent of the spiritual transformation promised by his nonconformist religion. The card inviting membership in the Society's Sunday school stated: 'Socialism is a religion teaching Morality and the Brotherhood of Man as taught by Christ and others. Its central principle (its God) is Love – Love of Humanity.' In his own Preface to the society's history, Bevin would later write that 'the outstanding feature [of the society's history] is not only of the work, but the record of those who found expression for their faith in the Socialist Movement'.[10]

Bevin's membership in the Bristol Socialist Society led him to his first public political activity. Through the initiative of the Society, a Bristol Right-to-Work Committee was formed in 1908 with Bevin as secretary. Responding to the worst unemployment of the entire decade, the Committee passed a resolution, introduced by Bevin, condemning the 'inaction of the Government with regard to the Unemployed', and demanding 'immediate legislation for the purpose of settling the question on national lines, which shall have justice as a basis, and not inadequate almsgiving'.[11] In part, the Committee wanted the government to utilise the Unemployed Workmen Act of 1905 that had created local distress committees with the power to provide work to the unemployed at wages below the existing market rate. But the Committee also made the broader demand that the government should recognise a right to work, a notion strongly supported by the young Labour Party in Parliament.

Bevin played an active role in the campaign of the Bristol Right-to-Work Committee, leading deputations, organising demonstrations and speaking in public. In his most memorable action, Bevin, as part of a drive to enlist the support of local clergy, organised a demonstration of the unemployed who marched into Bristol cathedral one Sunday in November 1908 to stand as silent examples of the consequences of unemployment. For Bevin, this whole campaign was an education. It made him familiar with methods of organising and strengthened his belief in the need for 'a complete social and economic revolution . . . to solve the problem [of capitalism]', as he told the annual meeting of the Bristol Committee in December 1908. 'We must feed the people in order that men may be strong enough physically and mentally to carry out that revolution which will come at no distant date.'[12] One of Bevin's most firmly held

6

EARLY YEARS

views – that the working class by virtue of its contribution to society had a right to a minimum standard of living – clearly arose out of these struggles. 'It was the right to live they wanted', he told the Committee. 'They had no right to starve the industrial army of the country because the capitalists had not enough work for them to do, any more than they had the right to starve the Army or Navy because there was no war at any particular time.'[13]

When the authorities failed to respond to these demands, Bevin ran for city council in 1909 as a socialist. He told the electors: 'Think! last winter in Bristol there were 5,000 heads of families out of work, 20,000 human beings suffering want and chaos, misery and degradation brought upon us by the private ownership of the means of life. I claim that Socialism, which is the common ownership of those means, is the ONLY SOLUTION OF SUCH EVILS.'[14] His slogan, 'Vote for Bevin – Down with poverty and slums', elicited some support but not enough to defeat the better financed Liberal candidate. His defeat and the consequent campaign of local business-men to have him fired by boycotting the mineral water he delivered produced a crisis in his life. He briefly contemplated becoming a missionary, an indication of the continued connection in his mind between his religious and political interests. But his employer stood by him, and his thoughts of retreating to the nonconformist ministry were displaced by other concerns. In 1910 he became involved in a Bristol dockers' strike through which he found the path to his life's work.

7

2 Trade union leader

Because of his public sympathies for the unemployed and his experience as an organiser, Bevin was asked in June 1910 to co-ordinate relief efforts for striking Avonmouth dockers. Shortly thereafter Harry Orbell, a leader of the Dock, Wharf, Riverside, and General Labourers' Union, asked him to organise the carters as a branch of the Dockers' Union, as it was known. In August 1910, Bevin, who still earned his living by delivering mineral water, called a meeting at which the Bristol carmen's branch of the Dockers' Union was formally established. Within a year, the branch had achieved remarkable success: over two thousand members, recognition from the employers, and an agreement that gave carters 26 shillings for a 67-hour week. Clearly, Bevin had flair as an organiser. Proud of his accomplishment, he kept his framed membership certificate, dated 27 August 1910, over his mantelpiece for the rest of his life.

Apprenticeship

In 1911, Bevin, now thirty, gave up his job delivering mineral water to work full-time as a regional organiser for the Dockers' Union at £2 per week. Doubtless he welcomed the chance his new job afforded him to expand his own horizons as well as to continue the work he had started three years earlier on behalf of the unemployed. But his job also provided the same spiritual satisfaction that he had found first in nonconformist religion and later in socialism, the vision of a transformed world. Bevin would always regard the trade union movement as something more than a practical instrument to improve workers' conditions.

> If I thought that the trade union movement existed [to get wages only], I would go out of it [he said in 1920]. I am in it because I believe, with

TRADE UNION LEADER

its great collective force and the fundamental principles on which it is based, it is destined to replace the old order and bring in a new, not merely political democracy, but economic democracy – a Promised Land of which we have already gained the Pisgah . . . A new life of liberty and love will take the place of the master-class oppression; men and women will walk in a newer and purer world.[1]

Bevin's outlook as a trade unionist was deeply influenced by his coming into the movement just as it was taking the shape it would retain for the next half century. In the mid nineteenth century, only a small part of the British working class had been organised into trade unions, mainly in those trades that required a craft skill – the engineers, the tailors, the stonemasons and so forth. These 'old' unions sought to restrict entry to their trade as a way of maintaining their bargaining position and ensuring that their wages and working conditions remained secure. Because they were able to function with some success, they tended to support certain aspects of Victorian capitalism. In particular, they rejected any state intervention in the economy, even on behalf of the working class, and urged co-operation with employers.

This situation began to change dramatically in the early 1870s. Responding to changes in industry itself – the increased use of machines and more concentrated forms of ownership – the trade union movement between 1870 and 1914 grew to exceed four million members; by 1920 it had reached over eight million, a majority of the adult male working class. This growth, however, was neither even nor smooth. Much of it occurred in three periods – 1871–73, 1888–92, 1910–14 – during each of which there was an explosion of working-class militancy. In particular, the emergence in 1889 of the 'new unionism', as it was known, marked what Eric Hobsbawm has called a 'qualitative change in the British labour movement and its industrial relations'.[2] In part, what was 'new' was the new unionism's attempt to organise workers like the dockers who had never been organised before. And although most growth in this period actually took place in the older unions, that was because they now extended their membership to include unskilled workers. Henceforth, trade unions tended to become national rather than regional, and more general in organisation, no longer restricted to a particular craft or trade. Some, moreover, were now led by socialists who wanted to use the state to aid their cause and who

9

ERNEST BEVIN

thought about organising not just a craft but the working class in general.

Bevin found his vocation just as this new unionist impulse surged through the trade union world again in 1910–14, a period highlighted by a series of massive strikes and the establishment and expansion of general unions. Bevin's optimistic sense over the next decade that trade unionism was an invincible force apparently derived from this expansive moment. Certainly, his view of trade unionism was a new unionist one, regarding almost all workers as potential recruits to his union. 'I went into a conference once', he later said, 'and an employer said to me: "You are a docker; what are you doing in our trade?" I said: "In one town I organise the midwives, and in another the gravediggers, and everything between is the Transport Workers."'[3] As an organiser for the Dockers' Union, Bevin recruited not only dockers and related trades – coal and grain porters, flour millers, bargemen, etc. – but also other trades. The dockers particularly relied on the Welsh tinplate workers, who, because they enjoyed relatively stable employment and higher wages, increased the size and financial resources of the entire union, providing much-needed support for the more vulnerable and erratically employed dockers.

Like a number of other socialist leaders of new unions, Bevin tended at this point to see the relationship between employers and workers as fundamentally antagonistic and to speak in terms of class conflict: 'The more wealth there is, the more bitter is the struggle of our class', he said. Or again: 'There is only one language the present governing class understand; there is only one method of reasoning they will bow to. It is only power they will yield to, and that is the power of organised labour in its economic capacity.'[4] In part, his socialism led him to see the particular struggles of the dockers or other groups that he organised as part of a wider struggle against a capitalist ruling class. But this view also grew out of his own experience with employers in these years. As he put it some years later, employers 'will beat us until we are too strong for them to beat us any longer'.[5] Many employers were willing to accept trade unions, but only on their own terms. In particular, they refused to accept the closed shop, the key to union power for the dockers, for without it and the job preference it brought, men had little reason to remain in the union. 'Take any dock in the country',

10

TRADE UNION LEADER

Bevin pointed out in 1914. 'What is the serious problem we have to face? It is that where the men have been organised the longest, and have been able to build up certain conditions, the employer is always doing his best to attract a big surplus of labour around him so as to intimidate the men who have got these better conditions.'[6]

Bevin's most formative experience of this sort of intransigence came from the London dock strike of 1912. The year before, the National Transport Workers' Federation (NTWF), a loose alliance of sixteen different unions, including the dockers, had come into being and immediately won a major victory over the shipowners that included wage increases and partial recognition of a union monopoly over hiring. This defeat infuriated the owners, who determined to regain what they had lost, while the union remained equally resolved to hold on to its new gains. The immediate cause of the 1912 dispute was therefore only an occasion for a conflict determined by the events of the previous year. In May 1912 the lightermen struck over wages and union recognition. The owners refused to make any concessions, while the NTWF, too confident of its own strength, and anticipating even greater struggles in the future, decided to support the lightermen. It was a miscalculation. The employers would not budge, in spite of government attempts to bring about a settlement. Faced with this intransigence, the NTWF tried to bring about a national strike, calling on its members throughout England to come out in sympathy. Although the head of the Dockers' Union, Ben Tillett, led the London dockers in a public prayer to 'strike [the employers' leader] Lord Devonport dead', neither God nor the other member unions came to the NTWF's support. In short, the lack of real unity within the NTWF led to its defeat. The results were disastrous. The employers took advantage of the occasion to undercut the union's attempt at securing a monopoly on the docks and to victimise men who had participated in the strike. The resulting bitterness lasted for generations; as late as the 1960s, some dockers refused to work with the sons of 1912 blacklegs.[7]

The strike made a lasting impression on Bevin, who had dutifully called out the dockers in Bristol, Newport and Cardiff in response to London. As he later recalled: 'The then Unions were beaten, many hundreds of men in the Port of London were victimised, deprived of their pensions and treated as hostages for no other crime than being

11

loyal to their fellow workers.' The employers would 'show no mercy; I could not awaken the slightest generous impulse'. Thus the strike confirmed his view that there was a fundamental conflict between the men and their employers and that only closer unity could check the employers' power. 'We were divided up into a large number of Unions', he said; 'our power was limited and the relentless attitude shown to us that day made me resolve to strive to establish unity among our people.' The 1912 strike marked, he later said, the origin of the Transport and General Workers' Union.[8]

In the short run, the most immediate consequence of the 1912 strike was the spur it gave to the creation of the Triple Industrial Alliance, which recognised the economic interdependence of transport workers, miners and railwaymen and attempted to co-ordinate their industrial strategies. To many observers at the time, the Triple Alliance seemed the strongest expression of the syndicalist ideal of broad class unity and ceaseless conflict with employers that was such a visible aspect of the period immediately before and after the First World War.[9] This was probably true for some members of the Alliance. But for Bevin and most other leaders the Alliance was more a way to prevent conflict than to seek it. Although deeply suspicious of employers and sympathetic to the syndicalist ideal of 'one big union', Bevin always preferred to avoid strikes. Nor did he ever entertain the syndicalist goal of a new industrial democracy to be brought about by a revolutionary general strike. Rather, like most Alliance leaders, he had a more modest idea in mind, namely, using the threat of joint action as a lever to move employers toward his goals. As he said in 1914:

> It is the consciousness on the part of the employer the whole time that he is negotiating with the coal trimmer, the docker, the carman, or the seaman that they have a central organisation behind them, representing the co-operation of their fellows in the same organisation, that gives the power to negotiate. It is not so much that it means a power to attack, as a power to negotiate, and that power to negotiate is the most valuable thing that we can have. Where there is practically one union covering all transport and the bulk of the general labourers' unions in one town, what is the first thing that the employers ask when you are organised on this basis? It is 'Will you strike together?' . . . I venture to suggest that if you can reply 'Yes,' that it strengthens your hands in winning concessions from those particular employers.[10]

TRADE UNION LEADER

Although historians now argue that there was little likelihood of the Triple Alliance engaging in a mass strike, and although Bevin clearly sought to avoid rather than to increase conflict, he expected the worst. He said in 1920 that Britain before the war had been on the verge of 'one of the greatest industrial revolts the world has ever seen'. This does not necessarily mean that Bevin expected the Triple Alliance to engage in a mass strike, but rather that the sheer weight of organisation it provided would be a means to 'produce' what he called 'a complete change in the conception of what . . . working class life ought to be'.[11] As he wrote during the war: 'We were carefully, but very deliberately, organising to put an end to this system.'[12] Such statements reflect the overly optimistic view of what trade union action might accomplish that Bevin entertained off and on until the defeat of the General Strike of 1926 decisively ended any such hopes.

By 1914, Bevin had been so successful as a regional organiser that he was appointed one of three national organisers for the Dockers' Union, a position with major responsibility. In these first three years as a trade union leader he had learned that employers would not voluntarily attend to the welfare of their employees or accept trade unions as their representatives, and, therefore, that the only way to achieve these goals was through increased organisation and co-operation. So far, these had been lessons learned mainly from defeat. The war would show that they also applied in victory.

The First World War

The outbreak of war in August 1914 brought the industrial unrest of the previous four years to an abrupt halt. International working-class solidarity, which socialists had celebrated as a bulwark against war, proved illusory, as socialist parties and trade union movements in every country rallied to the flag. Britain was no exception. Although a handful of British labour leaders, mainly members of the Independent Labour Party (ILP), held out against the general enthusiasm for war, the rest of the Labour Party and the trade union movement lined up behind the war effort. This was true of Dockers' Union head Ben Tillett, who before the war had expressed racist and jingoist sentiments. It was also true of Ernest Bevin.

Bevin, like Tillett, had, for the first week of the international

13

crisis, argued for neutrality. As a member of the National Transport Workers' Federation, he had supported the resolution it passed in 1913 to strike rather than accept the outbreak of war. But the emotion behind such resolutions, so strongly felt in peacetime, dissipated before the outpouring of nationalistic feeling that marked the start of the war. Bevin later said that he found himself 'left standing [by his own class] as a leader' when he initially opposed the war.[13] However, in contrast to Tillett, who fulminated against the 'Hun' while touring the country to drum up support for the war, Bevin was never carried away with patriotic fervour and did not share the popular enthusiasm for vengeance. In his maiden speech to the Trades Union Congress (TUC) in 1915, he called on the Labour Party 'not [to] indulge in mere rhetoric' but to 'give the actual facts' about their decision to support the war. The next year, he objected to the introduction of conscription 'while men were sacrificed through the bad strategy of the [General] Staff'. Given the widespread anti-German feeling at the time, it is to his credit that he also urged TUC members to meet with their German counterparts. 'You have got to take the Germans into consultation after the war', he said. 'You have got to reckon with the Germans as an economic factor. . . .'[14]

At the same time, Bevin rejected the views of the more radical socialists who saw the war as an internecine capitalist struggle. Further, as a trade unionist for whom loyalty to collective decisions was the highest virtue, he would have nothing to do with the ILP's opposition to the war. Instead, given the widespread support of the war by his followers – by April 1915 almost a quarter of the London dockers had enlisted – Bevin accepted 'passively the opinions of the majority of [the] men', as he put it in 1917, and devoted himself to protecting their interests. As he told the Triple Alliance in 1917: 'It is said I blow hot and cold on the war. I do not. What I am after all the time is that the only safe organisation, the only safe weapon for the workers – slow as it is at times – is that trade union form of organisation which at the extreme has stood the test every time.'[15]

This does not mean that Bevin simply spent the war concentrating on the mundane details of trade union work. The changes being wrought by the war on both the trade union movement and the working class itself had a profound effect on him, as on every other trade union leader. The war accelerated those trends which had already been making labour into a national force able to demand recognition by both business and government. The differences within the working class that had tended to undermine co-operation grew less important, as mechanisation increased and wartime regulations suspended, for the moment, divisive craft restrictions. Trade union membership expanded massively, particularly among general unions. In consequence, trade union leaders found themselves in a bargaining position of unprecedented strength. Bevin, now serving on the executive committees of both the Dockers' Union and the NTWF, was delighted to take advantage of the situation, as he made quite clear. At a conference with a group of employers early in 1917, for example, he said:

> What is capital prepared to concede? Will it concede, if labour-saving machinery is introduced, that it is to lighten the burden of the working classes? And then, after the War, will employers restore trade union conditions without question and not merely restore conditions so far as production is concerned, but accept the principle of real wages instead of mere money wages? If these points are not conceded, then peace can never be.[16]

In his most notable victory, Bevin, along with NTWF secretary Robert Williams, secured the first national wage agreement for transport workers. This was a major accomplishment because it prevented employers from playing off one group of workers against another and allowed the full strength of the men to be brought to bear on negotiations. It also created the conditions for trade union amalgamation by unifying the wage claims of a variety of hitherto distinct and localised transport unions. First raised in February 1918, the claim was presented to a conference of employers in March where Bevin made full use of the union's new position of strength: 'We don't want to have to start an agitation to get these or whatever proposals may be eventually expected', he told the employers. 'Agitation with this type of man is always difficult, and hard to know where it is going', whereas a wage increase with periodic review every four months would allow the men 'to settle down'. All of the employers agreed except for the head of the Port of London Authority, Lord Devonport, whose 'medieval attitude of mind', Robert Williams warned the government, would make the NTWF's endorsement of 'reason and a forbearing spirit . . .

15

unavailing'. Faced with the possibility of a stoppage in the ports, Lloyd George himself pressured Devonport, who denounced the transport workers' claims as 'a barefaced attempt to exploit the national situation' but nevertheless gave way. Bevin drew the appropriate conclusion. As he later recounted: 'I remember Lord Devonport stating that he would never submit, but we were successful. . . . That was a demonstration of national power.'[17]

Besides greatly increasing his bargaining power as a trade union leader, the war also drew Bevin and other trade union leaders into a new relationship to the state. The government's need for regularity in supplying the war effort forced it to take over or oversee key industries, including the docks. As part of this process, it became heavily involved in the direction and control of labour, drawing the established trade union leadership into a new role as administrators of official regulations. Bevin, whose growing power in the trade union movement came as much from his acknowledged ability and strength of character as from his official position, became in 1917 a member of the Port and Transit Executive Committee that oversaw both the docking facilities in all ports and the direction of dock labour. It must have been exhilarating for him just six years after delivering mineral water in Bristol to find himself sitting in Whitehall with some of the most powerful men in the country.

Bevin did criticise specific civil servants – he attacked William Beveridge and the 'sinister crowd' at the Ministry of Labour, for instance, for seeming to favour the introduction of 'coloured labour' from the colonies to overcome the labour shortage, and he found some government arbitrators 'far from satisfactory' in the awards they made. Nevertheless, the experience of working closely with employers and the state marked a key point in the evolution of his views. He said later, though with typical exaggeration: 'My experience during the war, when I was called upon to organise transport, taught me that if you have the confidence you have the capacity. The other class are not superior to us in brains; they are very often inferior. I also learned during the war that if an industry can be socialised for war it can be socialised for peace.'[18]

Bevin did not leap from this insight to a revolutionary conclusion. Rejecting any notion of violent change, he denounced as scheming 'professional politicians' those socialists who called on Britain to 'follow Russia' and work for complete peace on the basis of

16

working-class solidarity.[19] Bevin also seems to have been unaffected by the powerful shop stewards' movement of skilled manufacturing workers that at the height of its power in 1917 was putting forth demands for workers' control of industry. Instead, he was led by his wartime experience to the vision of a regulated capitalism.

This is evident from the plan for postwar economic reconstruction that Bevin set forth in 1917.[20] At its heart was the demand for union recognition that was always a driving force in his work. 'Before there can be any peace in industry', he wrote, the circumstances that allow 'one small class' to determine 'the conditions under which the large majority of the population work and live' had to change. But the change he envisioned was an extension of the wartime system:

(a) The right of Labour to control its conditions of employment. (b) The adjustment of payment on the basis of relative instead of subsistence wages. (c) The regulation of industry to prevent unemployment. (d) The recognition of the status of the employee as equal to that of the management. (e) The State must concede full opportunity for education.

This is a demand not for socialism as generally understood at the time, that is, for a change in ownership, but for a regulated capitalism that gave trade unions the right to control workplace conditions and granted a rising living standard to workers. As part of this new partnership, the 'greatest co-operation' was also 'needed between the State and the various forms of organisation which now are an integral part of our industrial system'. Together, this new tripartite grouping would regulate industry to end 'underconsumption' and provide full employment. 'It is not difficult to picture the possibility of the management and the organised producers in industry sitting around a table with all the commercial knowledge at their disposal . . . ', he wrote, 'taking into consideration the amount of available labour, together with the mechanical appliances; and produce the amount required to supply the communal needs. . . . ' What is particularly interesting in this scheme is Bevin's presentation of economic problems as soluble technical difficulties, not as inevitable conflicts arising from private ownership. Implicit in this scheme, too, was an ideal of planning, one that he would take up time and again during the next decades.

For all his talk of co-operation, Bevin never thought these

ERNEST BEVIN

changes would be accepted easily. 'There is nobody in the world', he told the Triple Alliance, 'who submits to anything but force. Force is the logic of reason after all and the only reason they will respond to is that which is backed up by power.' Bevin worried, particularly in the first years of the war, that employers might try to undo the gains which the war had brought both in wages and in organisational strength. Arguing for the complete amalgamation of the member unions of the Triple Alliance, for example, Bevin pointed out that 'it was after the war that had to be considered', and he judged 'that the present time to the termination of the war was likely to be the most serious time from the point of view of organised Labour'. He 'feared that unless the organisations were perfected they would be unable to grapple with the very serious problems which would arise later'.[21]

As these fears indicate, militant action for Bevin was always defensive, to protect living standards, not a deliberate means of working-class advance, which was instead to be achieved by organising and negotiating. Hence his recommendation to a suspicious TUC that they should consider the famous 1917 Whitley report, issued by a Ministry of Reconstruction committee charged with making 'suggestions for securing a permanent improvement in the relations between employers and workmen'. The committee proposed that there should be increased working-class representation in industry through the establishment of joint industrial councils of labour and management. Bevin found this appealing, doubtless because his own work with employers during the war had demonstrated to him what such co-operation could accomplish. 'If the Trade Union movement does not take the right step now', he told the TUC, 'the greatest opportunity of our history will be lost.' Nevertheless, he had no desire to substitute joint councils for collective bargaining. 'You cannot create Labour's right position in relation to industry by means of a joint committee of employers and workmen', he said.[22] The need for powerful trade unions remained the bedrock of all of his views, but the idea of industrial councils held out the possibility of institutional recognition for the trade unions and of national wage agreements. As he said in 1919: 'We cannot ever get a complete substitute for industrial or economic action; we can only hope to get the very largest percentage of benefit we possibly can by these Industrial Councils. . . . [They] can reduce economic strikes to a

18

TRADE UNION LEADER

minimum if the powers are used rightly.'[23]

The war showed Bevin that existing forms of capitalist economic organisation were not eternal. Working-class living standards could improve if irrational competition were replaced by co-operation and rational direction. But even if capitalism were not reconstructed, the trade unions seemed to be in a position to extract significant concessions from employers, since full employment gave them a strong bargaining position. In other words, whether the regulated wartime system continued or collective bargaining were restored, it seemed to Bevin that the trade unions would now be in the driver's seat.

Direct action

When the war ended in 1918 British society appeared to many people, not just to Bevin, to be on the verge of an historic transformation. After the December 1918 ('coupon') election, in which Bevin stood unsuccessfully for Parliament from Bristol, the Labour Party, with a new socialist programme, emerged as the major rival to the Conservatives, while the trade union movement, over 6.5 million members strong and growing, seemed to be in a position of unprecedented strength. Industrial unrest from an apparently radicalised working class was also widespread, fuelled by the wartime promises about the reconstruction of British society, by anger at wartime 'profiteering', and by the belief that the election result was somehow fraudulent, the product of euphoria from the military victory and a confused political situation. Six million days were lost to strikes in 1918; in 1919 the total was thirty-five million. French historian Elie Halévy wrote at the time that 'in the spring of 1919 it was difficult to resist the impression that England was on the edge of [a] social revolution . . . which was going to transform industrial organisation from the top to the bottom'.[24] Bevin saw the moment as a 'glorious opportunity' for the labour movement to achieve extensive social and economic changes, although he was deeply ambivalent about the way these changes should be brought about.

At times, Bevin was so optimistic that he seems to have thought that they would occur without struggle, as part of a general transformation of capitalism. He predicted in mid-1919 that 'inevi-

19

tably there must follow [from the coming trade depression produced by overproduction] a world revolution in methods, in conception of international exchange, from the point of view of hours of labour and standard of life. And I suggest that will come within five years from now'.[25] Usually, however, Bevin appreciated that the labour movement could not just sit back and wait to enjoy the fruits of this revolution but instead must harness its new strength to extract major concessions from employers and the government. But how was this to be done? Like many other trade union leaders, Bevin was affected by the postwar enthusiasm in the labour movement for direct action, the use of working-class industrial power to secure political changes. In 1919, he told the transport workers that 'the labour movement [was] justified in using any weapon' to secure its goals.[26] In that same year, he joined other Triple Alliance leaders in urging the Parliamentary Committee of the TUC to call a special conference 'to achieve certain political objects', including an end to conscription and to British intervention in Russia. Sometimes he even seemed willing to support violence: 'The whole of the capitalists were consolidated as one man and Labour must be equally united', he told a Bristol audience in January 1920. 'If class war broke into class battle, better that than perpetual penury and slave conditions.'[27]

In one famous instance, Bevin supported the London dockers' refusal in May 1920 to load the Jolly George, a ship bringing munitions to Poland for its war with the Soviet Union. At the triennial conference of the Dockers' Union meeting a few days later, he congratulated the men for refusing to have their labour 'prostituted'. 'I think the working people – I have not talked about direct action and general strikes – have a right to say where their labour and how their labour shall be used.'[28] But refusing to load munitions was, of course, a policy of direct action, as Bevin in effect indicated when he proceeded to argue that hindering support for Poland was justified because 'the present Government [do not have] the authority of the democracy of this country either to lend a single penny or to supply a single gun to carry on further war against Russia'. Hence the protest, Bevin implied, should be seen as an attempt to protect democracy from the surreptitious activities of the 'great financial houses' which had fomented the war to 'regain the grain belt of Southern Russia'.

TRADE UNION LEADER

Three months later, when it briefly seemed that Britain might become involved in the Soviet–Polish war, Bevin played an important role in the establishment by the TUC and the Labour Party of a Council of Action pledged to use 'the whole industrial power of the organised workers' to stop British involvement. Bevin acted as the Council's spokesman when it met with Lloyd George. 'We feel we cannot admit the right, in the event of a revolution in a country, of every other nation using . . . their armed forces to crush out or stem a change that is being made', Bevin told the Prime Minister.[29] This was his most famous endorsement of direct action in the immediate postwar period, one that he repeatedly held up in later years to make his opposition to the Soviet Union more palatable to the labour movement. But this was an exceptional moment. Like other members of the Council of Action, Bevin was willing to support direct action in this instance because of the massive public opposition to war. The Council could therefore present the threat of direct action not as support for the Russian revolution but as an attempt to prevent a war for which the government had no mandate. As Bevin and six other leading trade unionists said in an 'Appeal to the British Nation': 'We want peace – a real peace, a lasting peace, rather than endless war and threats of wars.'[30] When it became clear that the government had no intention of actually going to war, the Council refused to take any further steps, resisting in particular the calls of more radical local Councils of Action to take up the issues of Ireland and British troops overseas.

As Bevin's role in the Council of Action indicates, he was cautious about the use of direct action, in spite of his occasional inflammatory statement. Bevin, from the start of his career a trade union insider, feared that such actions would undermine the power of the official trade union leadership. He had supported the special conference in 1919 to achieve 'certain political objects' in part because he thought the alternative was 'sporadic action encouraged by persons without responsibility'. In addition, direct action as a means of working-class advance seemed to Bevin to be increasingly unworkable. As he said at the Labour Party conference in 1920, 'many strikes that had taken place in this country had been fiascos owing to orders and resolutions that could not be carried out when the time came'.[31] Instead, Bevin mainly focused during these first postwar years on increasing trade union organisation as the way to

21

ERNEST BEVIN

bring about social and economic change. 'Progress is slow', he told the dockers in 1921, 'but . . . constructive effort is the surest and safest.'[32]

This belief in the potential power of trade union combination underlay Bevin's support in 1919 and 1920 for the reorganisation of the Trades Union Congress, which at the time lacked virtually any centralised direction. Its directing body, the Parliamentary Committee, was, as Bevin charged in the *Daily Herald*, 'merely a deputation to wait upon Ministers'.[33] For Bevin, as for others, the growth of large-scale corporations and centralised employers' organisations – the Federation of British Industries was created in 1916, the National Confederation of Employers' Organisations in 1919 – made clear the need for an equivalent national form of trade union organisation, while the war, as we have seen, had demonstrated the capacity of trade unions to expand beyond mere collective bargaining for better wages and shorter hours. But although the example of government control during the war had brought such things as the nationalisation of the mines and the railways 'within the realm of actual politics', Bevin argued, what 'troubled' him was 'the unreadiness of the great Labour Organisations to step in and take control'. Labour, 'a great shapeless mass . . . without a head to direct', was unable to act because 'no National Body representing the whole of the Trades Unions of the Country with any real directive authority' was able to exert pressure and overcome the sectional rivalries that made protest ineffective.

Bevin was clearly not alone in this view, for shortly after he presented his ideas in the *Daily Herald* steps were taken to reorganise the Trades Union Congress. Out of this eventually came the modern form of the TUC, the basic plan for which, adopted in 1920, was devised by Bevin. It replaced the Parliamentary Committee with a General Council able to co-ordinate industrial action, mediate internal disputes, co-ordinate demands applicable to all workers and provide propaganda, but not to interfere in the internal affairs of individual unions. The Council was to consist of representatives from different industries – the final scheme provided for thirty members representing seventeen industrial groups – along with specialist departments. For Bevin, this new 'general staff', as it was often called at the time, would 'create a greatly improved equipment and efficiency, so that strikes will be less because of the power

22

TRADE UNION LEADER

of our organisation'.[34] Clearly Bevin, although attracted to direct action, particularly in 1919, looked mainly to organisation as the lever with which to move British society.

Bevin in these years was certainly not a radical trade unionist like Robert Williams, who wrote in 1921 that 'before the General Strike the General Election pales into insignificance'; nor was he simply a right-wing moderate. What he called himself, a 'revolutionary conservative', was an apt description, capturing both his basic caution and his desire for extensive social change.[35] On the one hand, Bevin eschewed violence and for all his socialism was, as we have seen, willing to accept the existing capitalist system if it provided the working class with an adequate standard of living. Believing that rapid change could be counterproductive, and that a direct confrontation with business and the state was likely to fail, he also stressed that gradual improvement brought about by increasing organisation was the royal road to working-class advance. On the other hand, Bevin did advocate extensive changes in the structure of British society, including nationalisation of key industries and a permanent place for the trade union movement in the management of both business and the state, changes that had they been put in place at the time would have seemed revolutionary.

Bevin also continued to speak in terms of class conflict and of the need to force concessions from a hostile ruling class. He remained deeply suspicious of employers and willing under certain circumstances to endorse militancy. For one brief moment in 1919, for example, he rejected the establishment of a joint industrial council for the docks because it would 'diffuse' the NTWF's 'energies', which aimed to 'strengthen their position by attacking one Port at a time'.[36] Similarly, like other Triple Alliance leaders, he denounced the National Industrial Conference, a group of employers and labour leaders summoned by Lloyd George early in 1919 to consider the relationship between capital and labour. Bevin said the Conference's aim was to 'side-track the efforts of the men and women who are struggling for better conditions at this moment'. 'The leopard had not changed his spots', he belligerently told the Conference. 'It is as big an effort now to get a bob or two for your workpeople as ever it was. . . . I have never yet convinced an employer. I will tell you what has convinced him – the economic power of the Unions we represent and no other weapon.' A year later, he was still saying the

23

ERNEST BEVIN

same thing: 'It can truly be said that labour views every action of the employing classes with suspicion.'[37]

The Triple Alliance and Black Friday

As the immediate postwar years demonstrated, Bevin had every reason to believe that only economic power, not an appeal to justice, would bring change. The government's initial response to working-class militancy was a successful strategy of concession and delay, in particular by stymieing the miners' demand for the nationalisation of the mines. Then, as the economy began to weaken, employers' organisations and the government took a more traditionally confrontational stance against the working-class insurgency. 'We must show Labour that the Government mean to be masters', Lloyd George wrote to Conservative Party leader Bonar Law in late 1920.[38] By the end of 1921, Bevin's 'glorious opportunity' of 1919 had been missed: the government abandoned its promises of reconstruction in favour of fiscal retrenchment, a policy that increased unemployment and undermined the strong bargaining position of the trade unions.

The lost opportunity of the immediate postwar years was bound up above all with the inability of the Triple Alliance to overcome its internal differences and fashion an instrument able to compel change. Bevin thought the Alliance would certainly fail without more centralised leadership. If it were not made into a 'real organisation', he warned his fellow Alliance members in 1920, it would be shown up as a 'paper alliance', a prediction that came true all too soon.[39] During these years, however, Bevin's own commitment to the Alliance remained cautious; in 1919, for example, when the railwaymen struck without consulting their allies, Bevin played a key role in the formation of a mediation committee, fearing that confrontation would lead to a 'civil war' for which labour was not prepared.[40] By 1920 his caution was reinforced by the growth of unemployment, which made transport workers particularly susceptible to blacklegging. 'We have in London a combined membership of nearly 20,000 men out of work', he explained to the miners in 1920. 'That has created a very different situation. . . . I do not want to fight but I do want to have my army behind me if I am in for it, and I want to have a decent chance of winning.'[41]

24

TRADE UNION LEADER

All of the problems of the Alliance – the differing needs of the members, mutual suspicions, and the failure to create machinery for real united action – were revealed in the failure of the railwaymen and transport workers to support the miners on 'Black Friday'. In late 1920, the British economy entered into what turned out to be a long-term depression. Employers, faced with increased competition, falling prices and disrupted trade, attempted to cut wages, that is, to impose the burden of the depression on the working class. This was particularly true in the mining industry where the price of coal fell from 83 shillings to 43 shillings per ton between the end of 1920 and mid-1921. The government, which still retained control over the mines, responded to these developments by returning them to private hands even sooner than originally planned. In turn, the owners announced a return to district (i.e., local) wage bargaining and drastic cuts in wages. When the miners refused to accept these terms, insisting particularly on the importance of national negotiations, the owners began a lockout on 1 April 1921. The Triple Alliance initially resolved to strike unless the government agreed to continue discussions. But then, in complicated negotiations, the miners' executive decided by only one vote not to accept a government offer to continue talks, after Miners' Federation Secretary Frank Hodges had made ambiguous comments on 14 April about what was negotiable. At that point, their partners in the Alliance, not eager for a showdown and feeling weakened by the growth of unemployment, called off the strike. The day of this betrayal, as it was seen by much of the labour movement, April 15, became known as Black Friday.

Bevin's initial reaction to the plight of the miners was, as he put it, 'diffident', because the Triple Alliance 'had not made adequate preparations for such a move'. But this reluctance faded as he became convinced that 'if the miners should lose their fight, the consequences will be an attack from all sides and in the whole world on the workers' standard of living'.[42] Nevertheless, in spite of his correct conviction that the attack on the miners was part of a general attack on the working class, Bevin joined other NTWF leaders in refusing to support the miners on 15 April. In part, Bevin was angered by the miners' stiff-necked insistence that their partners should have nothing to do with planning for a strike until they had actually joined it. 'Get on t'field', the miners' leader Herbert Smith

25

ERNEST BEVIN

told them. Bevin's position was that 'if there is going to be unity in action there must be unity in counsel'. As he explained after the event: 'When I saw no chance of making the Triple Alliance the real Executive [of the] movement – this independent action of the groups going on and these changes taking place without consultation with one another – I felt it was leading the men to absolute disaster, and, honestly, I voted at that stage for calling off the strike. . . . I do not apologise for it.'[43]

Underlying his irritation with the miners' leaders was a concern that unemployment had so weakened the transport workers that they could not have sustained a strike, particularly given the emergency preparations the government had made to keep supplies moving. The miners *had* been high-handed, and Bevin was certainly correct to fear that the government's emergency preparations might defeat a strike, but Beatrice Webb's conclusion at the time was also correct: 'The leaders clearly funked it; Thomas, Bevin and even Williams. . . . '[44] By failing to support the miners they weakened the entire trade union movement and opened the door to a more general attack on the working class. Even if a strike had been defeated, the situation could not have been much worse, and it might well have given employers and the government pause before they pursued their attack on wages and working conditions.

The Shaw Committee

While the trade union movement was suffering serious defeats in the first three years after the war, Bevin himself, ironically, was having his greatest personal triumphs. At the start of this period he was still relatively unknown outside the trade union world, except to a small number of employers and government officials. Even the staff of Labour's major newspaper, the *Daily Herald*, got his name wrong. 'By-the-way', he wrote to George Lansbury in 1919, 'will you please make a note of my correct name; your staff has a keen desire to designate me "Frank" which although a very nice name is really not mine by right.'[45] By mid-1920, however, Bevin was famous throughout England as the 'Dockers' K.C.' because of his role in presenting the dockers' case for a wage increase to an arbitration tribunal, the Shaw Committee.

Attempting to take advantage of their new strength and the

26

TRADE UNION LEADER

economic boom that briefly followed the war, the dockers in 1919 asked for an increased wage of 16 shillings per day. The shipowners, availing themselves of recent legislation, proposed that the dockers should submit their claim to a court of arbitration. After some debate, the executive of the NTWF, encouraged by Bevin, agreed. The government then appointed a seven-man court under the chairmanship of Lord Shaw that met between 3 February and 11 March 1920. In only a few months Bevin mobilised the small staff of the London office of the union, as well as numerous regional officials, to help him prepare the dockers' case, which he now expanded to include a reform of the hiring system on the docks and a system of guaranteed maintenance. Bevin's performance before this committee fully deserves the praise that it has been given; it is no surprise that it made his reputation. He eloquently argued the dockers' case in long opening and closing statements, skilfully led a number of expert witnesses through testimony to buttress the dockers' claims while cross-examining, sometimes with devastating effect, the witnesses testifying on behalf of the employers. His defence of the dockers is worth considering at length because it reveals the basis of many of the policies and positions that he would defend for the next three decades.

Bevin began with a simple proposition: dockers' wages and conditions were inadequate to maintain a decent standard of life. By this he meant not merely that wages were too low for subsistence, but also that they were inadequate to provide for leisure or intellectual opportunities. He denounced the notion that wages should be determined in relation to the minimum that a worker could get by on. '[I] resent with all the best that is in me having my life calculated the whole time on the basis of what I can just subsist upon in the way of food in a miserable three or four-roomed house', he said.[46] Throughout the inquiry, Bevin strove to stake a claim for the dockers based not on the prewar notion of a poverty line but on the demand for a 'higher standard of life', one that provided both 'status' and the possibility of 'culture and opportunity'. Labour, he argued, had 'growing aspirations', including a desire for cultural development that had been created by the expansion of the educational system after 1870. It was therefore cruel 'to refuse us the wherewithal to give expression to those aspirations which have been created'. Ultimately, Bevin was arguing that the working class

27

had a right to full membership in British society. 'I object', he said, 'to the working class being segregated from the rest of the commmunity and placed on a food basis', meaning subsistence level. Workers 'do not want the gramophone, or the common record and the grinding tune any more than the other classes. Why should they be condemned to it?'[47]

In the most famous moment of the inquiry, Bevin demolished the Cambridge statistician A. L. Bowley by forcing him to defend each item of a subsistence budget for a docker's family that he had calculated. The ludicrously inadequate amount of food Bowley had allowed drew Bevin's scorn: 'I do hope before you draw up another budget that you will spend some time in the docks and see how they have to live', he said. 'I do make this suggestion, that if people are going to be experts there is nothing like a test of the actual work to find out exactly what is necessary.' At one particularly dramatic point, Bevin produced in court the amount of bacon that Bowley had allowed for a docker and his wife and asked the statistician to explain how it was 'sufficient for a breakfast for a man to go and discharge ships and carry heavy grain and the rest of it. . . . I want to ask any employer, or you, or the Court, whether a Cambridge professor is a competent judge of a docker's breakfast. . . . The point is this, that we have to examine it in the light of a man, and not of a gentleman who sits down to see how little we can live on.'[48]

Bevin's claim for the dockers rested, on the one hand, on the labour theory of value, a notion with a long heritage in the labour movement. 'The docker who is distributing goods is contributing as much to the national well-being as the capitalist who is manipulating money or handling shares', Bevin insisted. As such, he had 'the right . . . to a piece of bacon as well as the rich. . . . The working classes who really do the work of the world should have the best. . . .'[49] He asked Sir Alfred Booth, chairman of the Cunard Steamship Company, if he thought he was 'any more to the community than the docker who handles your ship? . . . Do you think it right to ask a man to live and maintain himself on what you would not dream of asking your own family to live upon?' Ultimately, this was a matter of equity. 'In view of the wealth of the country', he asked, 'is there any reason why our class should be singled out to go without?' On the other hand, Bevin based his argument for a higher living standard on a new and expanded idea of citizenship. The dockers' claim, he

TRADE UNION LEADER

told the court, was 'justified on our rights as citizens'. Citizenship, Bevin now argued, included not just political and legal rights but economic ones. As he said at the end of the inquiry, a docker should be 'clothed decently as a citizen has a right to be clothed'.[50]

Underlying Bevin's demands for inclusion of the dockers in society and for an expanded definition of citizenship was the experience of the First World War, which seemed to many people to have given the working class a new moral claim on society. A 1919 editorial in the *Manchester Guardian* gives a sense of this mood:

> Below [contemporary unrest] is a very genuine and far-reaching demand, which was growing in volume before 1914 and has merely been made articulate by the war, and in particular by the general sense that it is the plain man and not the high and mighty who has bled for the country and saved it. The demand is that industrially and socially we shall become a community in the future in a far truer and fuller sense than we have been in the past.[51]

In both his opening and concluding statements, Bevin stressed that the dockers had earned the right to a better standard of living because they had 'played their part . . . in the hour of crisis in this country', as had their union, 'every officer of [which] had been more or less a State servant during the war'.[52] Citizenship in this part of Bevin's argument was thus based on nationalism, on a shared acceptance of the British state. Implicitly, Bevin was arguing that the state had failed to recognise a corresponding obligation to the men who had accepted its claim over their lives. As he observed, 'The most bitterly resentful and the most bitterly disappointed man that we have in our ranks is the man who has been over the top and who comes back now to find things even worse than when he left them . . .'[53]

Bevin's desire to have the dockers included within British society can be seen as well from his insistence that what he wanted to accomplish by making the dockers more responsible was to stabilise relations between employers and men and to strengthen the shipping industry. 'The greatest object we have in view is to get greater discipline and better citizenship', he said.[54] Thus Bevin agreed with the employers that the dockers were too indisciplined, too irregular in their habits. The difference was that he attributed this fault to the conditions in which the men found themselves. 'I think the men are

29

ERNEST BEVIN

what they have been made by the conditions of employment, and I do not think it is good.'[55] As much as any employer, he argued, he wanted the dockers to accept their obligations. 'We have got to have service and we have got to have discipline', he said. 'Whatever my politics may be, I am not prepared at any time to suggest to the men that there should be looseness in their method of life, whatever class they may belong to.'[56] But for Bevin the key to this discipline lay in higher living standards. 'We believe in developing self-discipline as against maintaining control by economic poverty and fear.'[57] Or as he testified to another committee investigating conditions in the port of London, 'It is necessary, if we are to develop the right kind of citizenship and good discipline for all those engaged in this trade, for us to have something to lose.'[58] There may well have been an element of calculation in this argument, but Bevin also genuinely believed that, if treated decently, the working class would prove to be as loyal in peace as it had been during the war. As he pointed out: 'I have been a driver of horses, and I have learned . . . that there are two ways of getting a horse to go: one is to feed him, stable him, harness him well and comfortably, and you do not need a whip; the other is to starve him and use a whip. I am pleading for the first method as the best method for carrying on the industry of this country.'[59] Bevin the socialist could also be a benevolent paternalist.

Bitterly resentful about the general assumption that only those with the appropriate birth and education were capable of contributing to society, Bevin insisted to the Shaw Committee that workers were as able as employers. Were working-class representatives in government departments 'inferior in brain power, and unable to understand these problems about capitalisation', he asked Sir Leo Chiozza Money? In what was surely his hardest moment during the inquiry, Bevin failed to budge Lord Devonport, his nemesis on the Port of London Authority, about this issue. Devonport simply insisted that 'man for man I would pick three better men [from the 'capital class'] than your labour representatives'. In this instance, Bevin was left to fall back on sarcastic references to his own 'dull mind'. But his pain and continued sensitivity about society's lack of recognition of him is evident from these interchanges. The failure to make use of working-class talents was also, he thought, inefficient. 'On the organisation and manipulation side of industry the genius

TRADE UNION LEADER

that is going to waste, that is latent there in Labour, is appalling from the point of view of the well-being of the State.'[60]

Bevin complemented his argument about the working class with a similar insistence that if trade union leaders were treated as equals, they would help make the existing capitalist system work more efficiently: 'If you want Labour to accept responsibility it must carry with it corresponding power, and unless we are given power of determining it is unfair to ask us to accept responsibility for effecting administrative matters. . . . But give us the power to have the making of the orders, and we will not shrink the responsibility of carrying them out.'[61] This was a plea for just the sort of corporatist partnership between the trade unions and business that Bevin increasingly saw as the most effective path of working-class advancement. 'If there was a closer co-operation', he said at one point to indicate why business might want to accept this arrangement, 'or at least an understanding between the managerial staff – I emphasise the managerial staff – and the paid delegates of the Union, who operate on the dock to watch the men's interest as well as to try and see that agreements are kept,' they would be able to stop 'chiselling off part of a day'.[62] Bevin would often return to such offers of co-operation in succeeding years, but only the unusual circumstances of the Second World War would allow them to become a reality.

Willing as he was to co-operate with employers, Bevin still remained belligerent when he thought that working-class living standards might be threatened. Thus, to the employers' argument that increasing dockers' wages was impossible because of the subsequent effect on other workers' wages, he replied:

> If that is to be the policy of the employers, that there is consolidated capital which prevents consideration of this on its merits, I can only say that, much as everybody would regret it, it must bring its inevitable consequences to this country, of the working classes lining up in exactly the same way to deal with all their questions in mass form by exactly the same method. . . . [It] is going to lead to a position in this country which means the lining up of labour against the lining up of capital and a fight to the finish.[63]

Such rhetoric demonstrates once again both Bevin's willingness to live with British capitalism, as long as it provided a fair day's wage, and his acceptance of militancy when that wage was threatened. As he said to another court of inquiry: 'We would rather use brains than force, but when brains are met by bullying there is only one answer.'[64]

The Shaw Committee awarded the dockers their wage claim and accepted Bevin's argument about the need to establish a system of regular employment, to 'decasualise' dock work. Although employers' resistance ultimately prevented decasualisation, the inquiry did lead to the establishment of a joint industrial council. Hailed in both the labour and the national press, Bevin's brilliant defence of the dockers permanently established his reputation as a trade union leader. In May, the Dockers' Union recognised his importance by creating a new position, Assistant General Secretary, to which he was then appointed at a salary of £650 per year. The Shaw Committee's decision confirmed Bevin's belief that it was not necessary to strike to obtain advances for his members. By showing the value of unified action and enhancing Bevin's prestige, it also created the conditions for Bevin's most famous and lasting accomplishment, the foundation of the Transport and General Workers' Union.

The Transport and General Workers' Union

For Bevin, the ideal way to run industry would be through a partnership between trade unions and employers. Until then, as he constantly argued, the relationship between the two sides of industry would be determined by their relative strengths. As we have seen, Bevin always maintained that the key to working-class advance lay in organisation. Only by overcoming their differences and uniting as broadly as possible would workers gain 'the power to negotiate . . . the most valuable thing that we can have'. As he said in 1914: 'The whole curse of our class is that they have been jealous of each other.'[65]

For the transport workers, unity had indeed been difficult to achieve, even after the creation of the National Transport Workers' Federation. Hampered by rivalries among its constituent members and by its federal structure, the NTWF was unable to act effectively to defend transport workers' interests. This was most clearly demonstrated in the 1912 strike when the various organisations failed to hold together and the union went down to disastrous

TRADE UNION LEADER

defeat. As we have seen, Bevin later said that the strike had determined him to 'strive to establish unity among our people'. During the war he steadily supported a policy of closer union. As he explained in 1919: 'One of the reasons for adopting the policy for dealing with masses of men instead of small sections, or groups, or districts, was the fact that experience of the past has taught us how easy it is for the employing classes to use not only one port against another, for instance, but even one country against another. . . .'[66]

Taking advantage of his recently acquired prestige, Bevin immediately pushed for the creation of a new transport workers' organisation. In March 1920, the Executive Committee of the Dockers' Union agreed and consultations began with the shipping staffs and the Liverpool dockers. In July, a committee representing the Liverpool and London dockers then invited fourteen unions to join in creating a new organisation to 'secure the greatest possible solidarity' and 'meet the new combinations of capital in the shipping world'. As Bevin told other transport workers: 'All the aim that I have . . . is to try to find the best way to have the most powerful bargaining power with the man on the other side of the table.' Representing a wide variety of trades, the thirteen unions that attended the August conference passed a resolution in favour of 'one big union' and appointed a drafting committee, with Bevin as secretary, to create a scheme.[67]

In December, a delegate conference, now including road transport workers as well, approved the new scheme. Bevin defended it on the grounds that 'all success of recent years had been by co-ordinating and acting as if [they were] amalgamated'. The conference sent out ballots to the differing unions with a covering letter signed by Bevin and NTWF president Harry Gosling urging approval on the grounds that 'the great industries on the employers' side stand together! Labour must do likewise.'[68] The ballot was victorious, in large part because of Bevin's tireless negotiations with other unions and extensive efforts to drum up support. In May 1921, a delegate conference approved the creation of the new Transport and General Workers' Union as of 1 January 1922. That same conference elected Gosling as President and Bevin as the new General Secretary, lifetime appointments.

The structure of the new union was largely Bevin's creation and reflected his sense of the need to create strong centralised direction

33

while respecting traditional forms. By adopting this approach, Bevin overcame the great stumbling block of previous amalgamation attempts, the demand that all unions should submerge their identities in a new organisation. Bevin always insisted that the 'conservatism' of the British worker must be respected, that it was impracticable to ride roughshod over existing prejudices. 'You cannot with a sort of magic wand wipe [prejudices] all out or ignore them and transfer the whole thing into an absolutely new state of organisation', he said. 'There must be a period of evolution in order to arrive at that complete unanimity which we desire. . . . I do believe in the line of least resistance in these things. I do not believe in trying to attempt the impossible. . . . '[69] To this end, the new union was divided into six differing trade groups (general workers, docks, waterways, passenger service, commercial road services, and administrative, clerical and supervisory) that represented the various trades amalgamated in the new organisation. These groups were responsible for wage negotiations and the daily interactions of each group and preserved, in altered form, the structures of the fourteen unions uniting to form the TGWU. In addition, the staffs of the old unions were kept on by the TGWU, although this made it overly bureaucratised for the first years. The different trade groups were linked in turn by area (thirteen in all), in order to overcome parochialism and compel their co-operation. Strikes of the combined membership had to be approved by a Special Delegate Conference. 'I do not want to be in a position to sacrifice the men or to victimise them before I am sure of their strength', Bevin said.[70] However, finances, decisions about all other strikes and all matters of general policy were to be decided only at the centre, by the elected Executive Council composed of one representative from each area and one from each trade group and presided over by the General Secretary. Thus, although general policy was determined by an elected Biennial Delegate Conference, real power lay with the General Secretary and the union staff.

Ten years after he had given up delivering mineral water, Bevin had risen to the top of the trade union world and achieved a position able to command the attention of even the most recalcitrant employer. It was an accomplishment of which he was understandably proud and which he sustained with much hard work. He often spent seven days a week on TGWU business, with few breaks: an evening at the music hall, listening to records or, later, to Chelsea football matches on the radio, a drive in the country in his yellow touring car, or an occasional trip to the seashore. But his role in the founding of the TGWU also fed his growing egotism. Jack Jones, a later General Secretary of the TGWU, has remarked how Bevin 'let everybody know' that he 'had been the driving force in building the union'.[71] Bevin always referred to the TGWU as 'my' union and rarely credited the contributions of others to its creation, a characteristic that reflected a more general self-centredness. Bevin 'talked about himself non-stop', Lord Moran later recorded.[72] Hugh Dalton later noted in his diary how Bevin was 'as usual, very full of himself'.[73] Walter Citrine wrote bitterly of 'Bevin's habit of arrogating to himself the credit for proposals that rightly belonged to others' and his failure to acknowledge 'the work of members of the T.U.C. or his own staff'.[74] Although his ability and accomplishments were widely praised, Bevin remained unable to acknowledge others and deeply suspicious of rivals.

The organisational form of the TGWU, which gave great power to the General Secretary, reflected Bevin's belief that the more organised and united trade unions were, the more gains they would be able to secure from the existing system. For all his belief in working-class potential, Bevin had a decidedly mixed view of the working class and he feared what would happen without a disciplined organisation. 'The rank and file is very often a handicap rather than the urging force that you want', he said, 'Self-preservation is in us all, and it is in our members very often.' In consequence, as Jack Jones noted, Bevin believed in a 'hierarchical view of union organisation in which full-time officials should be very much in charge of shop stewards and members. A union was an army with a general at the top.'[75] It is perhaps not coincidental that by the early 1920s Bevin was known as 'Napoleon Bevin'.[76] Certainly, he was neither shy of power nor afraid to use it. As he said once, 'You know you are most often right when your people are most against [you] than when you are most popular.'[77]

Because of his belief in the need for disciplined organisation, Bevin always placed prime importance on loyalty. That, combined with his own personal sensitivity to attack, meant that he did not tolerate critics well. 'He was a man who could not brook opposition', Walter Citrine later said. Citrine's judgement might be

ERNEST BEVIN

considered suspect since he and Bevin did not get along, but others who knew Bevin also testify to this. 'Ernie always used to say that he didn't like yes men around him', one TGWU official recalled, 'but as soon as you got the man who had ideas, my God it was a different story.'[78] When particularly angered, Bevin often saw disagreement as treachery; hence his frequent claim that he had been 'stabbed in the back' and his harshness to opponents inside the TGWU. Jack Jones tells this story about Bevin's response to three dockers who had instigated a ban on overtime to protest against the unions' acceptance of wage reductions in 1931: 'At Bevin's instigation, the three leaders of the ban were expelled from the union and lost their employment. It was an example of his ruthlessness. He brooked no opposition. I, and others, got our branches to send in resolutions asking for the reinstatement of the men, but without avail. Bevin was not prepared to show mercy even to men whose crime was opposing wage reductions.'[79]

Bevin's belief in the need for discipline and loyalty was immediately tested by the collapse of the postwar economic boom at the end of 1920, when he found himself unable to secure new advances for TGWU members and was forced to preside over a retreat from the gains of the war years. Starting in March 1921, employers made a series of demands for wage reductions and changes in working conditions. With unemployment rising rapidly, the union could only fight a delaying game. Negotiations, Bevin explained to his members, 'came at a time when the whole of the economic circumstances were against the possibility of a successful national strike'. His strategy under these circumstances was to give way over wages but fight to maintain working conditions. As he explained in 1922: 'To get the 8-hour day established it took thirty years of effort. You can recover wages – the money side is not so difficult. When trade revives, then is the chance to recover wages. But it is the conditions. Conditions take years to recover . . . and you must fight to keep them.'[80]

Under these circumstances, it is not surprising to find rank and file discontent developing, particularly among the dockers, whose wages had been reduced by 4 shillings per hour by early 1922. In July 1923, Hull dockers began an unofficial strike to protest against the application of a further 1 shilling per hour reduction as negotiated by the union. TGWU officials who advised them to

36

TRADE UNION LEADER

return to work were 'shouted down'. The strike then spread to other ports, everywhere fuelled by economic hardship. 'One of the strikers [in Liverpool] said that if they got six days work a week they would not mind a shilling a day being taken off their wages, but his own case was that he had only had three half day's and one whole day's work in close on three months.' In London, the *Manchester Guardian* reported, 'men have come out because they regard the shilling reduction as the last straw'. If the press reports are credible, it seems clear that the protest was 'a remarkably spontaneous movement among the poorest paid of the dock workers. . . . ' As the *Guardian* reported: 'A good deal of criticism of the union officials is heard at the strikers' meetings and there is talk of the strike being the start of a new movement in which the rank and file will rule and not "well-paid officials".'[81]

Regarding the unofficial strike as an act of treachery, Bevin accused its leaders of 'stabbing this union in the back'.[82] While recognising discontent over the wage reduction, he insisted that the main aim of the strike was to 'smash' the TGWU. Although the Communist-led Unemployed Workers' Movement had encouraged the strike, Bevin's charge was patently untrue. But there was an unbridgeable difference here between Bevin and the unofficial movement. For Bevin, maintaining the integrity of the TGWU was paramount. The key to the union's strength was its ability to 'demonstrate that [it] represented what it claimed', as he explained to a delegate conference. 'There are between 200 and 300 agreements held by this union. If the policy is now to be that an agreement may be made one day and broken the next, adopt that policy, but do so with your eyes open. If you do, trade unionism will be finished as an organised means of dealing with wages and conditions.'[83]

The strike reveals both Bevin's tendency to personalise opposition to his policies and tensions, inherent in the union, between its commitment to collective bargaining and traditions of rank and file autonomy. What the men experienced was a loss of power to a seemingly distant trade union bureaucracy. But what Bevin saw was the weakening of the union's institutional strength, a strength based on its ability to deliver workplace discipline, and a concomitant return to localistic struggles that had historically proved inadequate to defend the men. 'I cannot view with equanimity the prospect of

37

ERNEST BEVIN

reverting to the old bad methods of spasmodic sectional bargaining', he said, 'leading only to throat-cutting and bad blood between men who, under the aegis of the Transport and General Workers' Union, have opportunities for friendly and mutually advantageous relationship which cannot fail to be of the utmost ultimate benefit of all concerned.'[84] It is also clear that Bevin understood that the unofficial strike was not just the work of Communists or those opposed to the union, since shortly afterwards he led an official strike that won a 2 shilling per day wage increase and removed the main source of rank and file discontent. As one Ministry of Labour official observed, 'The events during the last unofficial strike compel the Union to take a firm stand on this occasion.'[85]

A believer, in his own way, in the Fabian view of the 'inevitability of gradualness', Bevin saw the development of the TGWU as part of a broader 'evolutionary process' that would make it possible initially for the dockers to obtain guaranteed maintenance and a decent standard of living, a goal that was not in fact realised until the Second World War, and eventually to gain the 'control of industry'.[86] Believing that working-class subordination was rooted in economic weakness, Bevin saw trade unions as providing the material basis to challenge ruling-class domination. 'Before our movement developed, you responded to the whip of the master', Bevin told the dockers in 1920. 'You obeyed him in your work because you feared him. You were afraid of the sack, and you swallowed your convictions. . . . I want you to respond to the call – the call of liberty. I want self-discipline, self-sacrifice, self-control, to take the place of the whip of the past.' Concretely, the union made this possible by removing 'forever from the weapons of the employer his ability to starve us into submission'.[87] Instead, the union established the basis for a gradual but steady improvement. It 'represented', Bevin said, 'the new scientific development in organisation.'[88]

The General Strike

Bevin's rapid rise from anonymous membership in the working class to leadership of one of the largest trade unions in Britain is perhaps sufficient to account for his continuing belief that the condition of the working class might still be dramatically and rapidly changed.

38

TRADE UNION LEADER

That hope was ended by the General Strike of May 1926, which, for the British trade union movement, marked the definitive end of the period of direct action that had begun in 1910. The General Strike, along with the Mond–Turner talks that began a year and a half later, marked a boundary for Bevin, too. In these years, his views of trade union action took their final form, remaining substantially unchanged thereafter.

The miners' struggle that climaxed in 1926 was part of the broader postwar crisis of British capitalism. The staple industries, the basis of Victorian economic success – mining, shipbuilding, textiles – had entered into permanent decline, while newer industries – automobiles, electrical, chemicals, aircraft – had not expanded to the point where they could provide the basis of a new prosperity. The question was how this transition from older industries to newer ones was to be effected. The staple industries needed to be modernised if they were to compete with new industrial rivals. But what incentive did owners have to modernise in a period of declining sales? Ultimately, the key question was whether the burden of change in a period of economic depression should fall on employers, the state or the working class, through lower wages, longer hours and a speeding-up of production.

The British coal mining industry presented many of these problems in microcosm. Dependent on exports for its prosperity, mining was particularly hard hit by increased competition from more efficient national producers, as well as by the development of alternative fuels, particularly oil. Its problems were made worse by inefficient management. It was, Kenneth Morgan has observed, 'perhaps the worst-run segment of British capitalism'.[89] Half of all mines had been in production before 1875 and fewer than a quarter were mechanised. The whole industry was badly divided among 1400 firms, about 300 of which produced over 80 per cent of all coal. After the war, the miners' attempts to force the state to assume responsibility for modernising and rationalising the industry had failed, and the burden of the postwar economic crisis had been imposed on them in the form of reduced wages, a burden that served mainly to maintain owners' profits, not to provide capital for modernisation. The miners' situation had improved somewhat in 1924 because the French occupation of the Ruhr had briefly ended competition from Germany and increased profits. But the restora-

39

tion of the German mining industry, combined with the Baldwin government's 1925 decision to restore the gold standard and the prewar value of the pound sterling – a decision that aided British financial institutions but damaged the export trade by overvaluing the pound – sent the mining industry into further decline.

The owners were determined to impose the cost of this crisis on the miners, proposing in June 1925 a further cut in wages of between 10 and 25 per cent – it varied from district to district – and a longer work day. Equally important, they insisted that wages should no longer be negotiated nationally, with a fixed minimum wage rate that allowed miners at profitable pits to earn more, but locally, at the district level. This undercut the most important gain the miners' union had achieved, that the industry should be treated as a whole, as well as the viability of the union itself.

The owners' demands left the miners little room to manoeuvre and virtually assured a test of strength. Anticipating this development, the miners had already begun to turn to potential allies in the trade union movement. In March 1925, they invited the transport and railway workers and several other unions to discuss the creation of an industrial alliance. When the crisis came to a head before the new alliance could be established, the miners turned for support to the TUC General Council, which responded favourably because it became convinced that the coal owners' attack was the prelude to a general attack on the working class. As Walter Citrine put it: 'If the industries fought singly they would be broken singly. Only if they could get Trade Unions to rally to the support of the miners now had they any chance of settlement in other industries threatened by attack.'[90] Eventually, it was agreed with the transport unions to support an embargo on coal, a plan approved on 30 July by a special conference of trade union executives, including Ernest Bevin. 'I am not one of those who goes looking for troubles', he said. 'No one does – but when vital principles are raised, then you have got to choose whether it is even not better to go down altogether than submit to them, and re-build afterwards.'[91] Faced with the united opposition of the trade union movement, the Baldwin government backed off its original insistence that it could do nothing to solve the crisis and agreed to provide a subsidy to the industry for nine months while a Royal Commission under Sir Herbert Samuel investigated possible solutions to the impasse.

TRADE UNION LEADER

Bevin saw the victory of 31 July 1925, hailed as Red Friday by the *Daily Herald*, as securing the position of power that he had wanted since the end of the war. It marked, he told the TGWU Executive Council, 'a very definite milestone in the history of Trade Union progress'.

> What has occurred, is that the Unions have demonstrated in collective capacity that the financiers and capitalists cannot look to reductions of wages as a solution of their problem, and so, if they are to save themselves they must turn to other means. On the other hand, the State has learnt that that great section of the community, the producing class, has called a halt to the encroachment of the parasitic interests, and the State will be driven to save itself from the internal pressure of the workers, just as much as it was driven by the war to save itself from external pressure. That will mean . . . that sheer economic interest will drive the State to indulge in collective efforts, stage by stage, to preserve its own existence.[92]

Bevin's optimism was a reflection of the euphoria in the labour movement in mid-1925 rather than a realistic assessment of the course of events. He underestimated the opposition of both employers and the state to economic reconstruction in the interest of the working class, and, even more important, failed to consider how the labour movement would deploy this new power if its demands were not granted. 'Really it is a glorious period to be living in!' he wrote. 'The events that followed the Napoleonic wars determined the basis of living for a hundred years that followed. What an opportunity presents itself to us now that, *realising the world is still in a fluid state*, it is OUR chance to mould it in the way that will determine the condition of millions yet unborn!'[93]

To be sure, Bevin did not think that this opportunity allowed the labour movement to create socialism. 'Not for one moment do I believe that you will pull down the citadel of capitalism about your ears', he said. And he rejected all talk of force as 'playing their game . . . the excuse they want to use arms against the people in civil strife'.[94] Rather, 'the demonstration of power will usher in an era of constructional effort . . . which will lay a sound basis for generations to come'.[95] By this Bevin meant that business and the government would now be forced to work with the trade union movement to devise a solution to the economic crisis that addressed the need both to modernise industry and to preserve working-class living stand-

41

ards. Bevin strongly sympathised with the Samuel Committee's Report, which recommended extensive reorganisation of the mining industry in exchange for immediate wage cuts, because it seemed to provide the prospect of such a remedy. As he wrote shortly after the General Strike: 'I felt that if minds were applied with the right determination to give effect to it, what with re-construction, re-grouping and introduction of a new element of management of the industry, there would, in the end, be produced a *Higher* wage.'[96] In short, Bevin did not see any fundamental conflict between the owners and the miners that could not be resolved with good will. On the eve of the General Strike, he told the special conference of trade union executives: 'We are told "you are up against stern economic facts," but the whole process of the mind of man has been to conquer the forces that have been against him, either forces in nature or elsewhere, and it is not beyond the wit of man, if the best brains of the country are brought together . . . to find the way out without depressing the standard of living of the men engaged in the industry.'[97]

Such an approach had no chance of success either with the bitter and suspicious miners or with the stubborn and selfish coalowners, nor with the government itself. Believing that it was not the business of the state to solve economic problems, the Cabinet determined not to back down again and spent the months after Red Friday preparing for a possible strike. The owners, encouraged by other business leaders who wanted lower coal prices and the freedom of manoeuvre that they believed a victory would bring, remained adamant. The miners, although willing to offer some concessions – trading reductions in the number of jobs for wage stability – refused to budge until they could be assured that changes would be made in the industry and that their basic demands would be met. Neither they nor the owners were willing to accept the Samuel Report.

In contrast to the government, the more moderate TUC General Council, which Bevin joined for the first time in October 1925, did little to prepare for a renewed conflict beyond hoping that the crisis would be resolved by negotiation. When no face-saving compromise developed, however, it had no choice but to support the miners, lest it be accused of treachery. Once again, then, the General Council called a special conference of trade union executives that met from 29 April to 1 May while last minute negotiations took place. When

TRADE UNION LEADER

these broke down, the General Strike began on 3 May.

Although Bevin worked very hard until the last minute to achieve a compromise solution, he strongly supported the General Strike on the grounds that working-class interests were under attack. As he told the special conference: 'This habit of certain sections of the employers meeting us with a big stick has got to put out of the way once and for all. . . . No one section of the community should deliberately attempt to enforce its will because of its economic position upon millions of workers. . . . That forever must be taken out of the hands of any one class of the community.'[98] Bevin now thought that an embargo on coal, the tactic threatened in 1925, would fail and that the labour movement therefore had to engage in a 'much wider dispute than anything attempted before'.[99] The conference agreed and eventually accepted his proposal for a strike that gradually extended as different unions joined it. 'We look upon your yes', he told the conference, 'as meaning that you have placed your all upon the altar for this great movement, and having placed it there, even if every penny goes, if every asset goes, history will ultimately write up that it was a magnificent generation that was prepared to do it rather than see the miners driven down like slaves.'[100]

From Bevin's perspective a fight had been imposed upon the unions. 'We are not declaring war on the people', he said. 'War has been declared by the Government, pushed on by sordid capitalism . . . . The Challenge HAD to be accepted.' Retreat would have opened the leadership to charges of cowardice or treason. 'If at the eleventh hour there had been such a debacle as Black Friday', he later said, 'my opinion is the movement would have been demoralized for at least a decade if not longer.' Inaction also opened the prospect that official leaders would lose control of the movement. 'Unofficial strikes would inevitably [have] develop[ed]', he explained later. 'That would have produced anarchy [in the trade union movement], and, more than like[ly], bloodshed. It would have been uncontrollable and disaster would have followed in its train.'[101]

During the next nine days, Bevin played a central role in the running of the strike. When the initial working-class response to the strike overwhelmed the General Council, Bevin, according to Walter Citrine, 'made a suggestion that he, personally, should be put in general charge of the Strike Organization. There was a storm

43

ERNEST BEVIN

as a consequence, and a good deal of straight speaking.' Bevin insisted to Citrine, however, that 'We must not have too many generals in this business'.[102] Although Bevin eventually emerged as a dominant figure on the Strike Organisation Committee that was created on 4 May to run the strike and that successfully imposed order on the initial chaos, his offer to oversee negotiations was rejected. These remained in other hands.

In spite of the continuing support of most of those called out, the strike failed to have a crippling effect because the government was able to keep supplies moving and to dominate the public presentation of the strike, insisting throughout that it was unconstitutional. In these circumstances, the General Council, fearful that the strike would either collapse when strike pay ran out or come under the control of unofficial leaders, backed down after nine days, seizing on an unofficial memorandum put forth by Sir Herbert Samuel as sufficient grounds for calling off the strike. Bevin thought that the Samuel Memorandum, which provided for reorganisation of the mining industry in the long run in return for immediate wage cuts, offered the best possible 'solution of the mining trouble'. Much to his annoyance, however, the miners disagreed. 'Bevin thought the miners were doing just what they did in 1921', Citrine observed. 'Once they had got the General Council to serve their requirements then they would hold us down ruthlessly.'[103] In the event, the General Council brushed aside the miners' objections and called off the strike on 12 May. The Council, Bevin later said, 'were responsible for four times as many people as they [the miners] had in the field. . . . The question of whether the Miners accepted [the Samuel Memorandum] or not was discarded altogether.'[104] Afterwards, Bevin put it more harshly: 'For the Miners to leave us at that moment was an act of selfish treachery.' And he criticised them for refusing to compromise. 'I must say that leaders who only fight on the bellies of their people are not fit to be leaders.'[105]

When they called off the strike the General Council assumed that the government would not only accept the Samuel Memorandum but also oversee an end to the lockout of the miners and the reinstatement of all those who had been on strike. Whether this was an act of collective self-delusion, misunderstanding or deception is difficult to say, but certainly Bevin shared in it: 'The assurance was definitely given by [the negotiating committee] that SAMUEL

44

TRADE UNION LEADER

COULD DELIVER THE GOODS.' At a heated General Council meeting he later insisted that he 'would have voted against calling the strike off' if he had understood that no assurance had been given.[106] At the time, he was particularly disconcerted to discover, when he and other representatives of the General Council went to Downing Street to call off the strike, that nothing had been promised. At that meeting, Bevin urged Baldwin to make a statement about victimisation, but the Prime Minister refused. Bevin, at least according to his own account, was horrified. Returning from the meeting he told his companions: 'Something has happened and the best way to describe to-day if we are not jolly quick is that we have committed suicide. Thousands of members will be victimised as the result of this day's work.' He immediately turned all his efforts to prevent that from happening, beginning with a brief continuation of the strike. 'We have called off the strike against the constitution, as you put it', he told Baldwin later that day, 'and we have called a constitutional strike to defend our wages and agreements.'[107] Bevin had his hands full in the coming days travelling around the country to secure the reinstatement of the TGWU's members but was able to announce proudly at the end of the month that only 1500 had not been taken back.

In the succeeding months, Bevin insisted that the only debatable issue in the General Council's decision to end the strike was whether they had the power to do so. As he told the TGWU's area secretaries: 'We took the line that the Miners were no more in it than anyone else. I want you to take that line all the way round. If you don't, you can never again have a united movement in this country.'[108] Although the miners disagreed, Bevin certainly believed the General Council had the right to call off the strike. In fact, Bevin also thought that the General Council had acted correctly, insisting that they could have won a victory if the miners had not been so stubborn. Had they accepted the Samuel Memorandum, he said, 'the country would have pinned the Government to it. . . . If the Miners had been with us the country would have been so electrified, the Samuel Memorandum would have been adopted and there would have been no counter-attack.'[109] That was at best a debatable conclusion. So, too, was Bevin's final verdict that the strike had been a success. Although admitting that the strike was 'the biggest sacrifice the movement has ever made', Bevin argued that such 'a

45

ERNEST BEVIN

wonderful exhibition of solidarity' would have effect. 'Even the governing class of this country, who, in the end, *know when to retreat* for their own safety, will be compelled by this demonstration of unity to pay greater regard to the consequence of their own policies than hitherto. It has produced a *New Alignment of Forces.*'[110] In reality, the only new alignment of forces that was produced was inside the trade union movement, where left-wing advocates of direct action lost all influence. In other respects, the General Strike represented a tremendous defeat. The miners were eventually starved back to work; the miners' union was crippled for over a decade; the mines remained archaic; the government continued to take a hands-off position on industrial modernisation; the trade union movement lost more members; and Bevin's 1925 vision of an 'era of constructive effort' was buried.

The Mond—Turner talks

Bevin was, however, right in one respect. In the aftermath of the General Strike, some employers and government members did seek to work out a more co-operative relationship with the trade union movement. Initially, this attempt failed. In 1927 a vengeful Conservative government passed the Trade Disputes Act prohibiting sympathetic strikes and restricting union contributions to the Labour Party. Few things aroused Bevin's class anger more than this piece of legislation, which seemed to him both vindictive and hypocritical, since employers had 'for ages' used Parliament 'to defend the right of the propertied and moneyed classes'. He wrote to Lord Weir, head of the National Confederation of Employers' Organisations, that he was 'more than ever convinced that the Big Interests represented in your confederation must be behind this thing, or it never would be pushed by the Government with the zest that it is . . . . It is intended to try and cripple us for the future.'[111]

Given the bitterness created by this legislation, it is not surprising to find that Bevin initially declined employers' invitations in late 1926 and early 1927 to enter into discussions about improving industrial relations. It was, he wrote, impossible to 'do anything with the threat of a political dagger in our backs'; talks would only cause 'suspicion and destroy the confidence our members have in us'.[112] In addition to fears of splitting the trade union movement,

46

TRADE UNION LEADER

Bevin was determined to use such talks to restore the much weakened authority of the TUC. As he explained to the Executive Council of the TGWU:

> I was also actuated in my mind [in rejecting such individual overtures] by the fact that the General Council is the organised expression of the Labour Movement on the industrial side. For good or ill, it has been created the central pivot, and therefore, if the employers desire to meet anyone on the organic side of Labour, it is necessary that they should recognise that body as the spokesman of Labour – the body which the Government were seeking to dismember, weaken or destroy.[113]

Eventually, a group of 'big businessmen of a "progressive outlook," independent of cautious employers' organisations', and led by Lord Mond, the chairman of Imperial Chemicals, issued an invitation to the TUC that granted the recognition Bevin wanted.[114] 'We realize that industrial reconstruction can be undertaken only in conjunction with and with the co-operation of those entitled and empowered to speak for organised labour', Mond wrote to Walter Citrine in November 1927.[115] After some debate, the General Council, which was chaired by Ben Turner, agreed to meet with them. Although very little came of the Mond–Turner talks, as they came to be called, they nevertheless represent a decisive moment in the evolution of the British trade union movement. Bevin constantly referred to them in the next decade as having pointed the TUC in a new direction – towards corporatism, that is, a formalised partnership with employers and the state, and entirely away from direct action.

Bevin, as we have seen, had long desired closer co-operation with employers. Like a number of other labour leaders, he distinguished between owners of industry or managers, whom he often regarded as practical men of affairs like himself, and financiers, whom he blamed for causing the problems of industry. He told the TGWU's Biennial Delegate Conference just before Red Friday, for example, that it was the banks that had forced the coalowners to act as they did. 'In this fight . . . you are up against the real people. Not the mere industrialists, but the financiers behind the whole business. If the industrialists had any sense they would be on our side. . . .' Similarly, he told the TUC in 1927 that he 'agreed with many of our leading industrialists, not on the capitalist side but on the manage-

47

ment side of industry, which is somewhat distinct from the owning side, the management side of industry has a good deal in common with ourselves. They are exploited by capital just as we are exploited. . . .'[116] Implicit here was the idea that there had now been a divorce of ownership from control in industry that made labour–management co-operation possible.

Despite this belief, however, Bevin had until the General Strike continued to entertain the notion that trade unions, if sufficiently organised, could *force* concessions from capital and impose their agenda for economic and social change. This idea was destroyed by the General Strike, from which Bevin and like-minded trade union leaders, most notably Walter Citrine, drew two major conclusions. First, the strike had ended any lingering hopes that capitalism was going to give way to socialism. 'I believe the present system is going to last longer than me', Bevin told the General Council in January 1928.[117] Second, it now seemed clear that the government commanded the resources to defeat any national strike of the sort once envisioned by the Triple Alliance. In February 1927, when Bevin met with the officers of his union, Harold Clay, one of his main assistants, began the conference by pointing out that the General Strike had demonstrated that the 'resources and powers of resistance' of the employers and the state in 'a widespread and sustained fight are greater than those on our side'. Hence success is 'extremely unlikely' because 'you get to a point where the strike either fails or it changes into a definitely revolutionary movement, a movement for the overthrow of the government'.[118]

Thus, the move by Bevin and others toward closer and more formal co-operation with business reflected what they saw as their available options. Revolution was not on the horizon. 'It is all very well for people to talk as if the working-class of Great Britain are cracking their skins for a fight and a revolution and we are holding them back', Bevin said to the TUC. 'Are they? There are not many of them as fast as we ourselves. . . .' The General Strike also seemed to have demonstrated that direct action led nowhere. 'Is the strike the only way to fight? Cannot we fight by discussion as well as by starvation? Cannot we fight by intelligence?' he pleaded with his critics at the 1928 TUC.[119] Even the routine trade union defence of workers' interests was difficult because of the weakened state of the movement. Recovering pre-strike conditions and the huge loss of funds 'virtually meant re-building the organisation', Bevin pointed out.[120] Nor was there any use simply waiting for socialism to make its gradual appearance. In the meantime, workers' interests had to be defended.

> As a Trade Union official let me say this [he told the TUC], that I have never lost my Socialist philosophy, . . . but I do know as a representative of men, that whatever my Socialist philosophy is, I have got to argue dirty money on the docks to-morrow, and I have got to state the problem that is arising for my members every day. . . . If I have to get the raising of the school age and acknowledgement of the right of workers to a pension at 65, I cannot wait for the demise of the capitalist system.[121]

For taking such a line, Bevin, like other members of the General Council, was accused at the time of class collaboration, a charge that, while in many respects correct, was also too broad. The dominant capitalist class in Britain was not a monolith. It was divided between those with financial interests – bankers, insurance brokers, commercial traders, investors, stockbrokers, etc. – centred in the City of London, and industrialists, who, in turn, were divided between those with large firms, often connected to expansive newer industries – Mond is a perfect example – and smaller capitalists. What Bevin now tried to do was forge an alliance with the large industrialists, that is, with the more progressive wing of British capitalism. As he told the TUC in defending against attacks from the left on the Mond–Turner talks:

> Everybody knew that there are two types of employers in this country . . . the type that seeks to weaken, to pulverise, and make the unions spend money – anti-union at heart. But there is another type of employer, I think, who is more advanced – the type who says, 'Break up the unions if you will and destroy their power, but when you have destroyed it you still cannot deal with the Labour problem.' There are employers with sufficient vision in this country who know that for stability, for progress, for dealing rationally with Labour problems it is better for everybody there should be a thoroughly well-organised Trade Union Movement.[122]

The Mond–Turner talks were thus premised on the potential shared interest of trade unions and employers, including their joint stake in preventing damaging industrial disputes. The TUC aimed to gain recognition of the unions and to protect workers from victimisation for union membership, both of which goals seemed particularly important at a point when unions were weaker than they had been since before the war. The TUC also hoped to protect itself and its affiliates from company unions, a particular problem after the General Strike. 'I am going to claim for the Mond Conference', Bevin told the TUC, 'that it acted as the greatest check on company union growth that has taken place in this country.'[123] From the employers' point of view, recognition of the TUC and its members protected against possible Communist influence and helped to contain rank and file militancy. As the TUC pointed out, recognition provided 'stability, as regards labour conditions, which is of great advantage to the employer'.[124]

Both sides also agreed that rationalisation of industry, as it was called at the time, was in their mutual interest. The employers realised that new machinery and new methods would be useless if the workers refused to accept them, while the unions saw rationalisation as the key to increased productivity and therefore higher wages. 'We do not believe that we can get a decent standard of living without Rationalisation', Bevin said.[125] Shortly after the General Strike, Bevin had travelled to the United States as part of an investigating commission. What he found there, he thought, was the future: large-scale industrial organisation and mechanised assembly-line production. This process was already occurring in Britain, but slowly and haphazardly, and without regard for its effect on the working class. For Bevin, the choice seemed clear: 'Rationalisation is coming in spite of us', he told the TUC, 'and the question is, are we going to be inside the movement, taking part in what is going on and taking our place in it?' What was central here for Bevin and most TUC leaders was not the wage relationship itself, but wage rates, job security and trade union representation. 'If they took away from their people the fear of hunger and privation during the period of reconstruction, they would wipe out nine-tenths of the opposition to reconstruction and the introduction of new processes', Bevin told the General Council.[126] The question of workplace democracy was never raised as an issue.

Ultimately, both the trade unions and the employers wanted state support for industrial modernisation and for the welfare of workers it displaced, since only the state could determine credit policy,

50

TRADE UNION LEADER

support investment and provide adequately for workers put out of their jobs by industrial modernisation. Bevin was easily enlisted in this cause, not least because he assumed that the state was a neutral institution that could be steered in any direction. He told the General Council that he thought the state should 'take this entire matter [of rationalisation] up through one of their departments and deal with it scientifically'. There should be 'a national recognition of the revolution which is going on in industry' and the 'problem of displacement' should at least be reduced to a science'.[127]

The progressive industrialists who participated in the Mond–Turner talks also hoped to enlist the General Council in pressuring the state to change those policies that benefited financial interests at the expense of industry. Bevin, as we have seen, was already convinced of the invidious power of finance. He told the employers' side of the talks that industry 'was suffering from . . . the financial manipulators' actions following the war', and that he was appalled at the way 'combines were [currently] buying out other concerns, which meant workers . . . had to work to get them interest on the added capital'. Eventually, the Mond–Turner conference issued a memorandum identifying the return to the gold standard in 1925 as a major cause of British industrial problems and calling for a change in national credit policy. 'Currency and banking policy pursued by the Treasury and the Bank of England ought in future to be framed in such a way that the special interests of industry are safeguarded and furthered', the conference concluded.[128]

Unfortunately for Bevin and other TUC leaders, neither the state nor the majority of employers were willing at this point to participate in this plan for a corporatist world. The progressive businessmen of the Mond-Turner conference were unable to secure the assent of their respective business associations – the Federation of British Industries and the more reactionary National Confederation of Employers' Organisations – to the conclusions issued by the conference. Some employers were still unwilling even to recognise trade unions; most of those who did refused to admit a right to consultation over anything other than wages and working conditions. Similarly, the state, although willing to sanction amalgamation and arrangements that protected British industry during the depression, remained wedded to a restrictive financial policy and to a hands-off attitude towards industry.

51

ERNEST BEVIN

In his attack on the General Council for participating in the Mond–Turner talks, the miners' leader A. J. Cook argued that they were 'asking for [the] stabilisation of capitalism, which means the servile state. You want to strengthen it instead of fighting it. . . . You cannot be a Socialist and at the same time help the employers rebuild capitalism. . . . We must either decide to stand by capitalism and abandon Socialism, or to work for the destruction of capitalism. There is no middle ground.'[129] To pose the issue in such blunt either-or terms was typical of Cook. Yet the miners' leader had a point, as the 1929 Labour government would soon demonstrate. Nevertheless, creating a 'middle ground' was more possible than Cook realised. It was precisely this ground that Bevin would attempt to establish during the next decade.

3 Social democrat

As a trade union leader, Bevin did not change substantially after the Mond–Turner talks of 1928–9. He never wavered from his conviction that trade unions were *the* crucial institutional protection for workers in a capitalist society: 'Whatever our defeats or gains on the Political side may be, the immovable defence of the workman is always the Trade Unions.' He also adhered to the corporatist position he had first entertained during the First World War and embraced after the General Strike, an event which he now characterised as having brought about 'a complete change in the economic outlook in this and other countries, and a new and better approach to the problems arising in industry'. With the exception of the London busmen, there was little opposition inside the TGWU to the course that he was steering during these years. Bevin himself regarded it as a great success. 'Our industrial policy has been justified to the full', he told his Executive Council in 1935.[1]

Although Bevin maintained a very busy schedule as General Secretary of the TGWU, an increasing amount of his time and energy was now devoted to wider concerns. He became an active member of the TUC's new Economic Committee, established in 1929 to consider broader questions of public policy. Most importantly, as a dominant member of the General Council, he began to exert more influence inside the Labour Party, which he had always supported but had viewed until now as having its own 'role to play'. Bevin had not had any part in the reorganisation of the Labour Party in 1918, when it adopted a new constitution and committed itself for the first time to create a socialist Britain. And in the 1920s, his interventions in Labour Party affairs had been confined mainly to speeches at the annual conference, although he had fully committed the TGWU's resources to elect Labour candidates. But now, through his membership on two government committees, Bevin tried, and failed, to influence the economic policy of the 1929

53

ERNEST BEVIN

Labour government. After the disastrous electoral defeat of 1931, however, when Labour began to rethink both its domestic and its international policies, Bevin was in a position to help reshape British social democracy, which in the course of the decade took on a new form in response to the two great issues of the era – mass unemployment and the rise of fascism.[2]

The Labour government of 1929 and the Macmillan Committee

The 1929 election brought Labour to power for the second time as a minority government with Ramsay MacDonald as Prime Minister, just in time for the start of the Great Depression. Unemployment, which had hovered around one million in the 1920s, began to grow rapidly. The MacDonald government proved unable to cope with this crisis. The key figure, Chancellor of the Exchequer Philip Snowden, was rigid and arrogant, a former clerk in the Inland Revenue Department who embodied the government's belief that until Labour won a majority and was able to create socialism it had to accept capitalist economic orthodoxy, which decreed that balanced budgets, retrenchment, and the maintenance of the gold standard were the key to prosperity. In this view, government spending to relieve unemployment was not only futile but also dangerous.

At the Labour Party conference of 1929 Bevin had appealed to the MacDonald government to 'listen to some of us as well as the commercial people in order to solve this problem'.[3] The government responded to the extent of appointing a new Economic Advisory Council, which included Bevin as well as G. D. H. Cole and John Maynard Keynes. Here and elsewhere Bevin urged a stronger government response to unemployment, including more spending on public works. He said at the Labour Party conference of 1930 that he was 'concerned about . . . whether the Government had . . . really made up their minds that [unemployment] must be faced; that the State must accept responsibility for unemployment'.[4] Above all, Bevin wanted Labour to support the policy he had endorsed at the Mond–Turner talks of aiding progressive industry, rather than finance. On the Economic Advisory Council he even argued, in opposition to Keynes, for the heresy of devaluation, on the grounds that 'the deterioration of the conditions of millions of

54

SOCIAL DEMOCRAT

workers was too high a price to pay for the maintenance of a single industry [the City of London]'.[5] Such advice was firmly rejected by Snowden, who remained wedded to Treasury orthodoxy, thereby confirming Bevin's growing suspicion that Labour's leadership was intellectually bankrupt.

The government also paid no heed to its own Committee on Finance and Industry, known as the Macmillan Committee, appointed in 1929. The story of this committee has been related in some detail elsewhere, particularly the ways it served as a platform for John Maynard Keynes to present his criticism of existing economic orthodoxies.[6] Although ultimately unheeded, the committee provided a seminal forum for what would emerge in the 1930s as Keynesian economics. For Bevin, membership on the committee over nearly two years expanded his grasp of economics and his confidence in rejecting the dominant views so inflexibly adhered to by Snowden. Above all, his experience on this committee would set him firmly on the path towards which he had been instinctively groping for over ten years.

Bevin's role on the Macmillan Committee was unique: he alone consistently denounced the official economic orthodoxy – 'this barbaric method of attacking the people's standard of living', he called it – that wages must be cut in order to restore the competitiveness of British industry.[7] Instead, he insisted that the main reference point from which to judge policy should be the living standard of the working class. This view enabled Bevin to challenge the 'experts' called by the committee, many of whom had either no understanding of or no concern with the human consequences of their recommendations. When the economist Josiah Stamp, for example, testified that real wages needed to be cut, Bevin responded: 'I am always interested to ascertain what economists mean by real wages. On what basis do you found it? . . . How do you measure the commodities that make up a man's life? That is what puzzles me. . . . We hear that railwaymen's wages are high. Well, it takes a jolly good chancellor of the exchequer of a wife to make them reach from Saturday to Saturday.'[8] In a heated exchange with another committee member, the economist T. E. Gregory, Bevin insisted that 'wages have nothing to do with unemployment at all'. Gregory sarcastically remarked that 'we may have a revolution in economic theory in which everything we used to say will be found

55

ERNEST BEVIN

to be entirely wrong', to which Bevin shot back, 'well, I think that is so.'[9]

Bevin's experience on the committee provided him with more sophisticated economic arguments to support his already firmly-held view that British financial interests – the Bank of England and the City, both represented in the government by the Treasury – were largely responsible for the plight of the British economy. By insisting that a stable pound sterling was the *sine qua non* of economic policy, the financial community, according to Bevin's view, imposed a crushing burden on industry in the form of high interest rates and lowered prices. The 'economic system', Bevin concluded, 'must necessarily ruthlessly bankrupt the [entrepreneur] and impoverish the [workman] . . . but . . . maintain in practical security, the rentier.' But why, Bevin now asked, should the rentier be sacred? 'We are all prepared', he observed, 'apparently with a kind of fatalistic feeling, to allow two or three millions of our people to go on suffering like this, but we must not do anything at all to shake or shock the confidence assumed to be associated with money.'[10] Others on the committee were, of course, disturbed at the degree of unemployment, but Bevin alone was willing to consider whether the privileged position of British financial interests should be the main focus of government policy. In one rough note Bevin made for himself he asked 'whether from the point of view of the community who have to live by their hands, policy should be directed toward retaining London as the centre in relation to foreign exchanges?'[11] This was indeed economic heresy, as was his conclusion that, if the depression were to be overcome, the gold standard could not be sustained. 'The more I examine the evidence and the more I look at the problem', he said, 'I really cannot see how it is possible to maintain the gold standard and abolish unemployment at the same time.'[12]

Bevin argued to the committee that 'industrialists', a category in which he included himself, had struggled with some success after the war to arrive at a new economic equilibrium in the face of declining prices when 'suddenly the whole thing [was] upset by the steps taken in 1925 [i. e., the restoration of the gold standard at the pre-war parity] which thr[ew] every bit of work that the two parties in industry had done out of gear. We [were] faced with rising unemployment, bitter disputes, and a new level of wages to be

56

SOCIAL DEMOCRAT

fixed, without notice, without consideration, without guide, without any indication as to what its object is.' This analysis led Bevin to the conclusion that some control had to be established over the financial decisions that affected both industry and the working class. 'Can you see any reason why a position could not be created where the monetary difficulties might be discussed with the same frankness as wages and conditions and these other factors are discussed; so that the rest of the community engaged in our industrial advancement might be equally informed of the monetary situation?' he asked one Treasury official.[13] The implicit notion here of managing financial policy to insure industrial expansion would later become central to the welfare state.

Besides the power of finance capital and of the Treasury, however, there was an additional problem: the incompetence of the bourgeoisie. Factory owners, Bevin argued, were failing to respond to economic developments by modernising their methods, just as bankers remained too focused on their own narrow ends. 'With regard to rationalisation', he asked Josiah Stamp, 'what consideration have you given to the mental capacity of the people who are called upon comparatively suddenly to run these big units?' He asked Montagu Norman, the governor of the Bank of England, whether he thought 'the time has arrived when some kind of training for the purpose of taking a broader view of banking is not also necessary?'[14] Such moments represent Bevin at his best: challenging established authority, defending working-class talents and knowledge, insisting on a worker's right to a decent standard of living. They also indicate how his experience on the Macmillan Committee showed him, as he would put it a few years later, that 'many of the things which the workers were led to believe were too profound for them were not really mysterious'.[15] The revelation that the established authorities had no idea how to overcome the economic crisis reinforced his confidence in his own judgement. At one committee meeting, Reginald McKenna, the chairman of the Midland Bank and former Chancellor of the Exchequer, turned to Bevin and said: 'I should very much like to tell you a story', to which Bevin replied, 'Is it that experts can never see the light?'[16]

It is not surprising that Bevin the socialist would tell the Macmillan Committee: 'industry is not the property of the proprietors . . . it is a national matter, . . . the people's livelihood depends

57

on it. . . .' He mainly argued in the committee, however, not for socialism but for the use of the state to create a more efficient capitalism. He asked the chairman of the National Provincial Bank:

> Can you suggest to the Committee anything that can be created in this country which can be watching and which can act as a bridge between Parliamentary compulsion and the compulsion that the bankers can exercise – some institution that is not quite Parliament and is not quite banking, but which at the same time is watching industry and can prevent this sort of inherent conservatism of industrial managers ruining our industry before they take action?[17]

Bevin, who had long been familiar with J. A. Hobson's idea of underconsumption, saw here not only a sign of bourgeois incompetence but also a systemic problem that might need permanent repair. Pointing out that just before and during the war there had been nearly full employment because of arms spending, he questioned 'whether it is not an abnormal position but a normal position, with which you are bound to be faced under the present system; whether, unless you are diverting large sums of State money to something or other which employs labour which private enterprise cannot and never will employ, there is any solution'. Doubtless, Bevin had arrived at such conclusions in part after listening to John Maynard Keynes's brilliant discourses to the committee, but his solution to the economic problem was also consonant with his own corporatist views, that is, his belief in the need for a regulated capitalism. That Bevin thought such a solution would be possible if it were seen as non-political is a measure of his own politics. 'If you want to get freedom of mind in the country to approach the problem', he told the committee, 'you must talk about removing it into the non-party sphere.'[18]

Eventually, the Macmillan Committee concluded, guardedly, that the traditional policy of *laissez-faire* had to give way to 'an era of conscious and deliberate management'. But the members disagreed about what kind of action should be taken. Keynes, Bevin and four other committee members stood strongly against reducing wages, at least without a corresponding reduction in the income of other classes. They urged some form of import tariff and the support of exports, along with capital development schemes, including a National Investment Board. While agreeing particularly with the

SOCIAL DEMOCRAT

need for development schemes, Bevin, along with the Co-operative leader Thomas Allen, also favoured devaluation and 'a large measure of State planning and reorganisation, particularly in the basic industries, with the provision of Transport and Power as State services'.[19]

In private, Bevin drew even stronger conclusions from his experience on the Macmillan Committee. The existing economic system, he wrote in a rough note to himself, was 'incompatible with modern civilisation, education, and the advancement of knowledge'. If persisted in, it would 'produce physical revolution'. Like the rest of the committee, Bevin saw that the classical economic ideal of free trade could no longer be sustained. 'To leave our industries languishing and our people to the tender mercies of a worn-out 19th century system is an insane policy', he wrote. His private musing shows that he arrived at this conclusion because of the example of the 'Russian 5-year-plan' that to his mind had established the value of economic planning. With planning, 'cheap finance', and 'large contributions to research, organised marketing and distribution . . . there is no need for reduction of wages or for the old methods at all'.[20] Thus, Bevin's experience on the Macmillan Committee led him to the vision of a middle way, neither *laissez-faire* capitalism nor complete state ownership. It was this vision that Labour would establish as reality when it came to power in 1945.

The crisis of 1931

By early 1931, unemployment was approaching three million. Business interests, irritated at the previous year's 5 per cent tax increase, loudly insisted that only reduced taxes and lowered government spending could revive the economy. MacDonald and Snowden agreed. They were particularly dismayed by the increase in spending on the unemployed and by the prospect that the next budget would be seriously unbalanced. In these circumstances, they appointed a committee in February 1931 under Sir George May to consider national expenditure. Packed with representatives of the business community, the committee was designed by Snowden to produce a report that he could use to overcome the resistance of his own colleagues to reduced government spending.

The May Committee's report — 'the most foolish document I

59

ERNEST BEVIN

ever had the misfortune to read', Keynes said – which recommended cuts of almost £100 million to balance an estimated deficit of £120 million, appeared on 31 July just at the start of a European banking crisis that led to a run on the pound sterling. The crisis became the occasion for a bitter political struggle over government financial policy. As the sterling crisis mounted in August, increasing pressure was put on the government to cut expenditures, particularly on services. The pressure came above all from Treasury and Bank of England officials, in collusion with Conservative politicians, who used the opportunity to insist that 'confidence' could be restored and the crisis ended only if government spending were curbed. As Sir Montagu Norman said in private, the country would pull through 'if we can get [the government] frightened enough'.[21]

Accepting the premise that the crisis came from 'the complete want of confidence in [the government] existing among foreigners', as the Bank of England had put it, MacDonald and Snowden pushed their own colleagues to accede to a programme of drastic economies, including cuts in unemployment benefits, in order to balance the budget. In this they were largely successful, securing general agreement between 13 and 18 August 1931 to reductions of £56 million. Final agreement, however, could not be reached. The key moment came on 20 August. That morning, the leaders of the opposition parties, whose support had been solicited as a way of increasing pressure on Labour, rejected the proposed spending cuts as inadequate. Later that day, MacDonald and Snowden held a series of meetings with representatives of the National Executive of the Labour Party and the Parliamentary Labour Party, both of whom were willing to co-operate, and with representatives of the TUC General Council, who were not. In a speech that Bevin later characterised as 'not worthy of an ordinary shop steward reporting the settlement of a local wage problem', MacDonald told them that they could 'trust' the government, which was only 'bowing to necessities'.[22] That same evening, MacDonald and Snowden met again with representatives of the General Council, who refused to accept that the burden of the crisis should be imposed on the unemployed, the most vulnerable section of the working class. Snowden, whom Bevin detested, tried to impress this group with the gravity of the situation. 'If sterling went', he said, 'the whole international financial structure would collapse, and there would be

60

SOCIAL DEMOCRAT

no comparison between the present depression and the chaos and ruin that would face us in that event.' Bevin, the minutes of the meeting record drily, 'disputed this statement, but Mr. Snowden insisted that his own view was correct'.[23]

Although Bevin accused MacDonald of 'dramatising' the situation, he and the General Council acknowledged the need to balance the budget. But they wanted to impose the necessary cost on the propertied, particularly rentiers, instead of on the unemployed and state employees. As Bevin told his Executive Council on 17 August, 'We must stand firm for the equitable distribution of the new burdens over the community as a whole, based upon the capacity to pay.' MacDonald, who objected to trade union officials attempting to limit the autonomy of politicians, rejected their advice. He saw the 20 August meetings as 'practically a declaration of war', as he put it, and proof that the General Council 'are rigid and think of superficial appearances . . .'.[24] In fact, the Council, thanks in part to Bevin's work on the Macmillan Committee, had arrived at a more correct understanding of the economic crisis and of potential solutions to it.

While the General Council's opposition to cuts in services and pay failed to move MacDonald and Snowden, it did stiffen waverers in the Cabinet, most significantly Arthur Henderson. With the Cabinet now unable to agree on a financial programme, MacDonald on 23 August went to the king to resign. Instead, however, he allowed himself to be convinced by George V and others that the seriousness of the crisis required him to carry on as Prime Minister. The next day he formed a National Government made up of leaders of the opposition parties and the few Labour ministers, including Snowden, who remained loyal to him.

In the course of the next few days, Bevin was deeply involved in the deliberations to determine what the attitude of the labour movement should be to the new government. Hugh Dalton reported that Bevin and other trade union leaders were 'full of fight'. 'This is like the General Strike', Bevin said. 'I'm prepared to put everything in.' Bevin had actually been in a belligerent mood since the spring, when he told his Executive Council that 'as each day passes I regret more than ever the fact that the centralised movement of 1926 was broken up. If loyalty had been exhibited then – and when I use the term loyalty I mean discipline, not only in coming out but in coming

61

back – there could be no question as to our withstanding the present attack.'[25] In spite of these statements, Bevin never contemplated employing industrial action to influence government policy. However, in the next few days he and other TUC officials did urge Labour Party leaders to take a completely oppositional stance to the new government and to adopt the General Council's programme rejecting cuts in services in favour of higher taxes on the wealthy.

The new National Government proceeded to cut the salaries of teachers, the armed forces and policemen, as well as the benefits of the unemployed, who now had to pass a family means test after their insurance was used up in order to receive relief. In spite of these measures, international pressure on the pound continued unabated and within a month the government was forced to abandon the gold standard and accept devaluation. 'Some of us had recommended that we should go off the Gold Standard in an ordered and honest way, but we were not listened to', Bevin ruefully observed.[26] All of Snowden's dire warnings were proved false. Unemployment did not rise, while the economy benefited slightly from the lower value of the pound.

When first formed, the National Government was to be temporary, until the crisis had been overcome, but once the pound had been devalued, the question arose whether to keep the government in existence. MacDonald had been expelled from the Labour Party in September, so he had nowhere else to go. The Conservatives, although initially reluctant, became genuinely alarmed at a now seemingly radicalised Labour Party that promised to soak the rich. They therefore agreed to participate in a broad anti-Labour front. Accordingly, it was decided to call an election in October. MacDonald and Snowden, raising the fictitious spectre that Labour would confiscate the savings of ordinary people, denounced their former colleagues, in one instance even calling the Labour programme 'Bolshevism run mad'. It was a successful strategy. The National Government won an overwhelming victory, reducing Labour to a rump of forty-six seats and ushering in a decade of Conservative ascendancy.

For Bevin, the crisis of 1931 further strengthened his views about the pernicious power of international finance. 'This is all part of a plan to break down the standard of living in this country', he said afterwards. 'All this is primarily to save the great merchant bankers of the City.'[27] Pressed into service in the 1931 election, Bevin unsuccessfully stood for Parliament from Gateshead, taking as his major plank the need to socialise credit and impose control over the 'one man who is exercising greater power than any autocratic king ever exercised in the history of Great Britain', that is, the governor of the Bank of England. His placards read: 'Vote for Bevin and public control of banking in the interest of trade, commerce and the people.'[28]

The only bright light for Bevin was the trade unions' refusal to accept cuts. Had they done that, he insisted, there would have been a more extended attack on wages. 'We can at least say we have maintained our trade union position', he told his Executive Council in November 1931.[29] This was a narrow view that left open the question of protecting the unemployed. How that was to be done effectively became the focus of crucial debates in the labour movement for the rest of the decade.

The Society for Socialist Information and Propaganda

In the aftermath of the 1931 crisis, Bevin and other moderate leaders of the labour movement attempted to devise a programme that could both address the economic crisis and win electoral support. Most immediately, however, the crisis led Bevin to a short-lived alliance with left-wing intellectuals, whom he customarily shunned. In the 1920s, the strongest representative of the Labour Left had been the Independent Labour Party (ILP). After the failures of the 1924 Labour government, the ILP had worked out what one historian calls 'the most constructive response to British economic problems by any political group in the inter-war period'.[30] The ILP had proposed that Labour when it next took office should create what it called a 'living wage', an agreed-upon standard for all citizens to be achieved through a variety of measures: family allowances, a redistribution of income through taxation, legislative creation of a minimum wage, national control of the banking system, including control of currency and credit, the nationalisation of transport and utilities and state direction of inefficient industries, as well as important measures of workers' control. Although, as we have seen, Bevin shared a strong dislike of MacDonald, and had himself supported a number of the ILP's suggestions, he opposed

ERNEST BEVIN

their campaign for the living wage on the grounds that it might limit collective bargaining. 'I stand four-square against political interference with wages', he told H. N. Brailsford, the editor of the *New Leader* and a leading advocate of the ILP's programme. But since Bevin soon afterwards publicly supported a 'definite weekly minimum' wage, it would appear that what he really resented, as he put it to Fenner Brockway, was the ILP's 'dabbling in the wages question', that is, treading on his turf.[31] And after Brailsford criticised the General Council's actions in the General Strike, Bevin's opposition to the ILP turned nasty. Brailsford, said Bevin, cast 'doubt and suspicion' instead of displaying 'loyalty'. 'That is and always has been my whole complaint against the so-called "intelligencia" [sic] and their "superior" attitude of mind. . . . The "superior class" attitude is always there in relation to the trade union leader who comes from the rank and file and we feel it.'[32]

By 1930, however, the inadequacy of another MacDonald-led government induced Bevin to co-operate with the very 'intelligencia' of whom he was so suspicious. In that year, Margaret Cole, G. D. H. Cole, and several other Labour intellectuals 'reached the conclusion that something drastic and public ought to be done to recall to Ministers the programme and the policies on which they had fought the election'. The outcome was a series of weekend discussions held at Lady Warwick's Easton Lodge, where, Margaret Cole later wrote:

> The highlight (or the prize exhibit!) of the whole conference was Bevin, who took full part in all discussions, formal or informal, and enjoyed himself immensely, holding a kind of court in which he told anecdotes of the past of THE MOVEMENT – he always put it in capitals – to an admiring ring of questioners, and also displaying a grasp of economic and financial essentials which some of the younger intellectuals had scarcely thought to find in a trade union official.[33]

Out of these meetings came the Society for Socialist Information and Propaganda (SSIP), founded at the TGWU's headquarters on 15 June 1931. Bevin was elected chairman.

Bevin, who was initially an enthusiastic supporter, saw the SSIP as 'an attempt to work out problems and to give the new generation something to grip . . . to fill the niche for the next decade, like the Fabians and early Socialists did for us'.[34] As the official SSIP

64

SOCIAL DEMOCRAT

statement of purpose posed its aim: 'Twenty years ago, it was the basic ideals of Socialism which neeeded to be stated in the simplest possible terms; to-day it is the practical problem of its introduction that is becoming increasingly important.'[35] In their meetings, SSIP members discussed how to achieve a socialist Britain: nationalisation – which industries to be taken over and when – the reform of parliament, planning, government reform, and plans for controlling banking and credit. They issued a series of pamphlets and study guides on different topics, all aimed to create a 'really practical Socialist Policy', and held a series of ten lectures on 'problems of socialist reconstruction'.

These discussions radicalised Bevin, if temporarily, as evidenced by his endorsement of the SSIP's analysis of the economic crisis during the 1931 general election: 'The capitalist system stands condemned by its own failure. . . . In these circumstances, the policy of achieving Socialism by slow and gradual stages goes by the board; for it rested on the assumption that capitalism would remain in working order during the period of transition. Now that Capitalism is fast breaking down, we have to make haste with the construction of the new Socialist order that is to replace it.' To create that socialist order, the SSIP called for socialisation of the Bank of England and the joint stock banks, reorganisation of the basic industries as public services, a national plan of production that included the direction of investment and an expansive credit policy, and public control of foreign trade. 'If capitalists obstruct, we must take full emergency powers to depose them from their positions, and replace them by nominees of our own. If the Lords stand in our way, we must demand authority to create enough peers to make an end of them and their veto once and for all.'[36] Ironically, Bevin would soon become a staunch opponent of exactly the sort of emergency measures that he now promoted, although he never acknowledged his rapid change of position.

Bevin's temporary radicalisation is also evident from the proposals that he, along with the economist Colin Clark, made in January 1932 for a drastic reorganisation of the state designed to make possible its intervention in the economy. Bevin and Clark proposed to increase the power of the Prime Minister's office in order to give it more control over social and economic policy. In particular, they proposed transferring many of the Treasury's functions to the office

65

ERNEST BEVIN

of the Prime Minister in order to 'surmount the strong and inevitable bias of the Treasury against any considerable legislative commitments of the sort a Labour Government would wish to make.'[37] The Treasury, now reduced in power, would create a National Investment Board to provide loans to public authorities and state enterprises as well as capital for projects approved by a new Industrial Development Board. New Ministries of Planning and Industry would oversee economic development and coordinate a 'general plan' for the entire country. A new Ministry of Social Service would co-ordinate and extend existing programmes, while a new Ministry of Power and Transport would supervise the publicly run utilities as well as the mines and the railways. What was most significant about this plan was Bevin's temporary rejection of the belief that the state was a neutral institution and his acceptance of the left-wing view, which he would soon come to oppose, that the very structure of the state needed to be fundamentally reshaped.

It did not take long for Bevin's relationship with the SSIP to turn sour. The occasion was the division of the Independent Labour Party in July 1932, when a special conference voted to break with the Labour Party. The remainder of the ILP then suggested to the SSIP that they should combine to form a new socialist group that would continue to work within the Labour Party. Bevin was not enthusiastic. In the subsequent negotiations, the affiliationist minority of the ILP insisted that one of its members, Frank Wise, should head the new organisation, the Socialist League. Bevin was deeply hurt that he was offered only membership on the executive committee. 'So far as personalities are involved in the matter, I dismiss them from my mind', he wrote to Cole. 'At the same time, I shall always watch, as long as I am in the Movement, the antics of careerists who seem to think we have created the Movement as a sort of ladder for individuals.' What is most striking here is Bevin's sense of ownership of the 'Movement'. He declined to participate in the new Socialist League or the New Fabian Research Bureau. 'I think it better I should stick to my last', he wrote to G. D. H. Cole.[38]

Margaret Cole has written that Bevin concluded from his experience with the SSIP 'that intellectuals of the left were people who stabbed honest working-class leaders in the back'. Alan Bullock has added that Bevin disliked intellectuals because of what he saw as their 'unreliability and irresponsibility . . . [their] haring off after

SOCIAL DEMOCRAT

new ideas and enthusiasms'.[39] Both Bullock and Cole imply that Bevin's attitude was a response to the way intellectuals actually behaved. But it would be more accurate to say that Bevin's attitude towards intellectuals – a term he used to describe a whole variety of people with whom he disagreed, including Ramsay MacDonald, G. D. H. Cole, Aneurin Bevan, George Lansbury and Harold Laski – is another instance of his own egotism and his intolerance of critics. On the one hand, Bevin expected his power as the leader of one of the largest unions in Britain to be acknowledged by socialist intellectuals who themselves lacked any equivalent power. He could be generous when treated with appropriate deference, but was otherwise unforgiving. He was also simply contemptuous of intellectuals who didn't appreciate power. Kingsley Martin relates one illustrative story:

> I recall his [Bevin's] characteristic retort to Sir Charles Trevelyan, who was Minister of Education in the Labour Government, a baronet, a landowner, and Lord Lieutenant for Northumberland. Sir Charles, an admirer of Russia and a Left-Wing Socialist, suggested that the workers should strike in protest against the foreign policy of Chamberlain. 'You want a strike?' said Bevin. 'O.K. I am to call out 600,000 dockers; will you call out the Lord Lieutenants?'[40]

On the other hand, Bevin had an unwavering faith in his own judgement, which was, indeed, at times, brilliant, as his contribution to the Macmillan Committee shows. But as A. J. P. Taylor has correctly pointed out, Bevin's 'mind [also] ran over with cock-eyed ideas; and his rambling talk, if taken down, could have gone alongside Hitler's *Table Talk*'.[41] Many of these 'cock-eyed ideas' simply reflected his lack of education, such as his view that the 'old Austrian-Hungarian Empire was economically the soundest thing that existed in Europe'.[42] But he was also capable of making totally wrong-headed political judgements. During the Second World War, for example, he thought that 'politically-minded' Indians could be 'sidetracked . . . by just paying no heed to them', while with rising living standards 'the Indian peoples as a whole . . . [would] not trouble their heads about political development'.[43] Similarly, he had complete faith in his own understanding of the 'psychology' of the British working class. 'You have got to study human psychology, and the most conservative man in this world is the British Trade

67

ERNEST BEVIN

Unionist when you want to change him', he said in a claim that he would make repeatedly. 'You can make a great speech to him on unity, but when you have finished he will say: "What about funeral benefits."'[44] In short, Bevin displayed many of the characteristics he imputed to the intellectuals he denounced, including an ability to change positions rapidly without admitting it, as demonstrated by his changes after the General Strike and the 1931 crisis. Thus, what the disparate group that Bevin called 'intellectuals' shared was a lack of deference towards his own positions, and a judgement about the political sensibilities of the British working class that differed from his. By denouncing even other working-class leaders like Aneurin Bevan as intellectuals, Bevin portrayed as a form of class antagonism his own discomfort with disagreement.

Corporate socialism

The debacle of 1931 showed that Labour's policy, a vague commitment to socialism in the future combined with a rigid adherence to capitalist economic orthodoxy in the present, had reached a dead end. Understandably, then, the 1931 crisis had led to, and would continue to produce, attempts to work out more precise ways to implement Labour's long-term socialist goals as well as to address the most pressing needs of the moment. As Bevin told the TUC, they should 'never allow a Labour Minister to go in again without having all his plans prepared'.[45] MacDonald's and Snowden's desertion and the decisive electoral defeat of 1931 also opened the way for the rise to power of a new generation of Labour Party leaders during the course of the decade, men who sought to redefine the party's socialism. The exact content of that redefinition, however, was a subject of often intense debate between the Labour Left, who wanted a more extensive and complete commitment to control of the state and of the economy, and the Labour Right, seeking to work out a way to create what would today be called a mixed economy. Bevin as a member of the Labour Right played a key role in this process and in the eventual development of what Geoffrey Foote has called 'corporate socialism'.[46]

There was always a blurring in Bevin's political views between his desire to create what he called 'a great co-operative commonwealth' and his desire to reform the existing capitalist system. On the one

68

SOCIAL DEMOCRAT

hand, he was committed to the idea of public ownership as necessary to overcome the indignities and hardships that workers had to endure in a capitalist society, and as the main path to overcoming the 'hateful . . . middle class mentality' of superiority.[47] Standing for Parliament in Bristol in 1918, he had advocated 'public ownership of the Banks, Railways, Mines, Minerals, Land and all other forms of monopoly', as well as the continued public control of factories built for war production. Although his list of industries to be nationalised would change over the years, his commitment to the goal of public ownership did not waver. As he said in 1936, 'under the capitalist system of ownership, there is a definite limit to our progress'.[48]

On the other hand, there was a marked tendency in Bevin's thought to come to terms with capitalism if it could be purged of its worst aspects, particularly unemployment. This tendency derived above all from his work as a trade union leader, which pushed him towards a concern, as he put it, 'with facts as they are'. Bevin maintained a strong positivist faith that economic and social problems were open to rational solution, that 'scientific effort' and the 'best brains', as he said, could overcome poverty. In other words, Bevin's labourism, his belief that capitalism could be reformed, led him to view economic problems not as rooted in private ownership but as technical difficulties that could be solved by intelligence and good will. He had argued to the Shaw Committee, for example, that the dockers' problems 'can easily be worked out if there is a disposition. It is not a conflict between capital and labour at all, as far as I can see. It is the application of common sense to industry, with both sides willing to utilise common sense.'[49] He told the Rowntree conference of managers and foremen in 1924 that he 'wanted to see the State itself set up an economic council of impartial men and women who would examine the factors that composed industry, take into account the new psychology of the workers, and investigate how far industry to-day was thwarted by the dead hand of the past'.[50] In this labourist ideal, trade unions had a definite role to play in making capitalism more efficient as well as more equitable. As Bevin put it, the 'combined Labour in the industry', meaning management and workers, shared an interest in increased production. His own 'job, the large scale organisation of labour', was 'akin' to that of the 'real director of industry', who had to 'have imagination, technical ability; [and] be a master of

69

ERNEST BEVIN

psychology'.[51]

The primacy of Bevin's reformist concerns led him to view the Labour Party primarily as an instrument to further the goals of the trade unions. 'Every trade unionist knows the best investments we have made have been in political effort', he told his Executive Council.[52] The notion that the Labour Party was an 'investment' inevitably created a tension between Bevin and the party, which did not always do what he wanted. Bevin had been so disappointed with the 1924 Labour government, which had threatened to use emergency powers against a TGWU strike, that he had tried, without success, to get the Labour Party to pledge never to take office again without a firm majority. Two years later, when Ramsay MacDonald criticised the General Strike, Bevin accused him of 'stabbing us in the back' and told Arthur Henderson that he would no longer support the Labour Party as long as MacDonald was its leader.[53] The rift was patched up eventually, but Bevin's belief that the Labour Party existed to defend the interest of the trade union movement remained a source of continuing tension.

In the aftermath of the electoral defeat of 1931, the Labour Party came much closer to fulfilling Bevin's ideal of it as an instrument of the trade union movement because the General Council asserted increased control over the greatly weakened party. The almost defunct National Joint Council (called the National Council of Labour after 1934), which had been established after 1918 to coordinate relations between the Labour Party and the TUC, was reconstituted with a trade union majority. Bevin became its most powerful trade union member. It may be somewhat of an exaggeration to say, as Henry Pelling does, that Labour in the 1930s was the 'General Council's party', but certainly Bevin thought it was. 'I want to say to our friends who have joined us in the political Movement', he lectured the Labour Party, 'that our predecessors formed this Party. It was not Keir Hardie who formed it, it grew out of the bowels of the Trades Union Congress.'[54]

The contradictions in Bevin's political views are demonstrated by his role in reshaping British social democracy after 1931. At the 1931 TUC conference, held shortly after the political crisis, Bevin seconded a resolution calling on the General Council to advance a policy of planning for a regulated economy. 'I think', he said, 'we are just at the parting of the ways.' By this he meant that the crisis

70

had now forced Labour to work out real alternatives to the existing economic system. 'The Labour Movement cannot be content to fight just blindly against going back [to the old economic forms]; it is absolutely essential that some new approach to economic order should be made.' But both here and at the Labour Party conference that year Bevin did not have that much new to offer beyond a plea for more study and better use of 'the brains we possess'. He denounced 'usury' and the gold standard, argued for the nationalisation of industries that were 'ripe' for public control, and the capital levy, but aside from a favourable reference to Soviet planning as having 'introduced a new motive for industry', he failed to spell out what exactly Labour should do.[55]

In the previous decade, Bevin had worked to convince the trade union movement to support an expansionist credit policy and government control of the Bank of England. After 1931 he added support for the state and planning to this agenda. 'Any system that relies on sheer pressure instead of plan is an anachronism', he told the Labour Party in 1931. In *The Crisis*, written in 1931 with G. D. H. Cole, he argued for an expansionist monetary policy to be achieved by cancellation of war debts and reparations, public control of the Bank of England and the joint stock banks, and the creation of a National Investment Board. If agreement could not be reached on reform of the international financial system, Bevin and Cole suggested creating an empire trading bloc that would 'make [Britain] the centre of a new system which will challenge the predominance of gold as a basis for currency and credit, and provide at least the nucleus of a new world order in finance'. In endorsing an expansive monetary policy, Bevin and Cole correctly identified one key way that the economic crisis might have been overcome, but their major proposal, to revive international trade, was impractical, not least because Britain's colonial trading partners had no desire to be the saviours of the British economy.

Two years later, Bevin published *My Plan for 2,000,000 Workless* in which he put forward a series of suggestions, most of which had long been common in the labour movement, on how to redistribute the burden of unemployment. Raising the school leaving age to sixteen and providing adequate pensions for those over sixty-five would reduce, he argued, the number of workers at either end of the age spectrum. Echoing a standard TUC position, Bevin also suggested

ERNEST BEVIN

shortening the work week in order to spread the available work around, although realising that this went against 'the prejudice of many of our own people', who counted on regular overtime to increase their total wages.[56] It is debatable how much good these measures would have done. It would have been virtually impossible in fact to provide a pension sufficient to encourage early retirement, and working-class parents would have objected to the loss of their children's incomes. At best, the measures Bevin proposed would have made only a marginal difference to the unemployment problem since they did nothing to stimulate demand, that is, to increase the total number of available jobs.[57]

Bevin in these years was also taken with the idea of imperial development. As early as 1927, after a trip to the United States, he had proposed the creation of a united European trading bloc that could rival the market available in the United States. But his thinking had doubtless been influenced above all by his membership after 1929 of the newly created government Advisory Committee on Colonial Development. By 1930 he had come to accept the idea of a revenue tariff, although he continued to have mixed feelings about outright protection, rejecting, for example, the Macmillan Committee's endorsement of it. 'I do not believe that tariffs can solve our problem of unemployment', he told the TUC in 1930, in part because, given British industry's current management, tariffs would only encourage 'inefficient and out-of-date methods'. On the other hand, he had 'never accepted, as a Socialist, that an inflexible Free Trade attitude is synonomous with Socialism'. At that meeting, he defended the General Council's proposal for developing closer economic ties with the empire in a somewhat confusing set of speeches. 'I am no imperialist, but an Empire exists', he argued, with a 'tremendous fund of raw materials' that could be further developed. Ultimately, there should be a 'world federation' to create 'an easy access to the raw materials of this planet', but in the meantime he 'believe[d] in organising ourselves'. Such organisation would unite business, the trade unions, and the state, and exclude the financier, 'utilising the great resources under our command not merely for our own benefit but for the advancement of humanity as a whole', exactly the claim, of course, that British imperialists had always made. At the same time, he made clear that British working-class interests were to be paramount:

72

SOCIAL DEMOCRAT

I sit on a Colonial Development Committee under an Act passed by the Labour Government and I see the expenditure of millions of pounds going for the development of areas where native races have not yet begun to be industrialised. You talk about the coal trade. Ought there not to be some control against the possible development of coal in Tanganyika and in East Africa, which might come into competition with your coal here at a time when the world does not want it?[58]

Bevin's thinking in the early 1930s shows how difficult it was to develop a practical reformist programme. His general emphasis on the need for increased state intervention, for planning and municipal development, pointed to ways in which the economic crisis could be overcome. He was also prescient in grasping the need for a new financial and monetary policy and the significance of Keynesian economics as it emerged during the 1930s; he helped as much as any trade union leader to win the labour movement's support for monetary management and an 'aggressive Keynesian expansionism'.[59] But most of the specific proposals Bevin himself advocated, although commendable for 'putting humanity first', as he put it, would have made little difference to unemployment.

Bevin wanted to create a more efficient capitalism in order to improve the living standards of the working class, but his reformist belief was also tied to a larger political strategy. Labour, his chosen instrument of reform, remained a minority party, in part because of the 'Toryism of our own people'.[60] Bevin thought that these 'remnants of a dying serfdom', as he put it, could be overcome by a programme of immediate social reforms. If a minimum standard could be created, he had argued in 1919, 'you can begin to develop a very much higher standard of intelligence among the people and produce the necessary capacity to assimilate ideas leading them on the road to advancement'.[61] Simply waiting for a crisis only created 'despondency, apathy, and a hopelessness' that 'sapped the vitality of the people', while raising the standard of living by incremental steps actually created the basis for socialist education because it broke 'down the barrier caused by fear. . . . The lower the standard of life and the nearer to abject poverty the people are', Bevin argued, 'the more difficult is it to induce them to fight to bring about a change; so desperate is their condition that they fear losing the little they have.'[62] Thus, in contrast to most others in the labour movement, Bevin thought that to secure socialism it was necessary

73

ERNEST BEVIN

not for capitalism to fail but for it to prosper.

For all his reformism, then, Bevin did not abandon a belief in socialism, however attenuated his view of it had become. Through his membership in the 1930s on the TUC's Economic Committee and on the National Council of Labour, he helped to draft Labour's plans for controlling what came to be called the 'commanding heights' of the economy, although the actual details of these plans were largely the work of Herbert Morrison, a gradualist, deeply concerned with administrative efficiency, who said later that his supreme purpose in public life was the 'achievement of tidiness'. Morrison insisted that industries should be reconstituted as public corporations, run by committees of experts, including former owners. The touchstone of these industries was to be not justice but efficiency; 'socialism must be successful', he said.[63]

Morrison's first version of the public corporation, his 1931 bill for the creation of a London transport authority, earned him bitter criticism from Bevin, who objected to the fact that trade unions were not automatically represented on the governing body. It was, he wrote, 'the worst form of public control'.[64] (Bevin never forgave Morrison for this lack of respect for the trade unions and opposed him thereafter so vindictively that it is hard not to suspect some degree of personal jealousy as well.) Bevin and the TGWU persisted in their criticism, which Morrison rejected on the grounds that statutory representation of the unions would open the door to representation of other 'interests'. 'If Socialism is to be successful, the test of appointment to the management bodies of public corporations has got to be the test of business ability and nothing else.'[65] Aside from his objection to the lack of statutory trade union representation, a battle which he eventually lost by default after 1945, Bevin in the 1930s accepted Morrison's plan to create public corporations on the model of the BBC and London Transport, that is, for a form of corporate socialism. It was a plan that provided no scope for direct workplace democracy.

Bevin's acceptance of a corporate socialism was based in part on his perception of British capitalism. Bevin saw early that capitalism in Britain was heading towards increased concentration and rationalisation. As a member of the Committee on Trusts in 1918, along with J. A. Hobson and Sidney Webb, he had signed an 'addendum' to its report, pointing out that 'Free Competition no longer governs

74

SOCIAL DEMOCRAT

the business world' and welcoming 'association and combination in production and distribution . . . as both desirable and inevitable'.[66] Such perceptions had shaped the trade union strategy he followed after the First World War. Nevertheless, the young Bevin lacked a clear sense that society was indeed organised according to a system; he tended to present social problems as the fault of some particular group. Although of course he eventually acquired a more sophisticated economic understanding, throughout his career Bevin would continue to indict specific groups, not capitalism itself, for poverty, unemployment and the shortcomings of the British economy. At the 1917 TUC, for example, he blamed 'middle men' and their 'parasitic influence in the manipulation of commodities' for the high price of food, and called on the Parliamentary Committee to 'work for the removal of every middle man who comes between the producer and the consumer'. Usually, however, it was financial interests that he blamed for causing the shortcomings of the British economy. 'The present system of banking . . . [is] a kind of Hidden Black Hand on the whole industrial system', he said in 1919. Similarly, he told the TUC in 1921 that 'the real fundamental cause of the present disorder is finance'.[67]

At times, his view of the nefarious power of finance took on overtones of a conspiracy theory, implying that the real villains were Jews. 'It is the game of Shylock versus the people', he told the Labour Party in 1931, 'with Shylock getting the pound of flesh every time.' Even more pointedly, he told the TUC in that same year: 'It is a terrible burden is this usury. You will remember that in the Old Book the prophet of Nineveh lectured the Jews about quarrelling over money-lending, and he told them they must not lend money to each other in future but only lend it to the gentiles. The prophet's direction appears to have been carried out.'[68] The point here is not that Bevin held a fully fledged anti-Semitic view of the world; he did not. But his emphasis on the power of financial interests meant that he saw socialism mainly as a way to control them. The primary problem, in his view, was thus not a question of public versus private ownership. He had no quarrel with those industries where management seemed to do its job efficiently, but only with monopolies and those industries where remote financial interests prevented industry from competing successfully and thereby providing adequate rewards for its workers.

75

ERNEST BEVIN

The various plans for Labour's new programme that Bevin helped to draw up in the 1930s were opposed by the party's left wing, which wanted what it believed to be a firmer commitment to socialist change. Although he had briefly supported many of the proposals that the Left championed throughout the 1930s, Bevin became one of their major opponents, both in the inner policy-making circles of the TUC and the Labour Party and in public. In fact, Bevin's greatest strength as a speaker, at least in this period, was not presenting reasoned defences of Labour Party policy but making emotional attacks on the left wing. Although some of his speeches read poorly now – they can be illogical or bombastic – Bevin could be inspiring, and he was always forceful, with a deliberate style of plain, bluff speaking. Sometimes this style, which succeeded by force rather than finesse, could break down completely, as in 1925 when his attack on Ramsay MacDonald was almost shouted down by the Labour Party conference. But often it was effective. Francis Williams, the editor of the *Daily Herald*, described Bevin as having 'a raw strength which compelled conviction. The very clumsiness of his sentences, his contempt for syntax and the niceties of pronunciation, the harshness of his voice and powerful emphasis of his gestures seemed when he was speaking to a mass audience to make him the embodiment of all natural and unlettered men drawing upon wells of experience unknown to the more literate.'[69]

But Bevin's speeches were not simply the unconscious expression of a man of the people; there was also considerable art to them. In many of them, Bevin skilfully deployed his own credentials with the trade union movement in order to secure assent for his position. In speaking against left-wing resolutions for greater trade union unity, for example, he would invariably refer to his credentials as a proponent of unity, thereby presenting his position as essentially disinterested. Similarly, he always insisted on his sympathy for the Soviet Union when attacking it before a labour audience, frequently referring to 'his' founding of the 1920 Council of Action. To an extent that was considerable though impossible to gauge precisely, Bevin's persona as the quintessential working man was carefully cultivated.

The fight within the Labour Party over domestic policy centred on two issues, the extent of Labour's programme of socialist

76

SOCIAL DEMOCRAT

controls and the degree to which it should accept constitutional rules. The experience of 1931 had made the Labour Left, and even for a while moderates like Clement Attlee, suspicious of parliamentary institutions. They feared that a victorious Labour government would be sabotaged by capital flight, bureaucratic opposition, and (bourgeois) civil disobedience. To guard against this they urged that when it came into office Labour should commit itself to the use of emergency powers, including the power to govern by decree. Although Bevin had favoured this position in 1931, by 1933 he was arguing strongly against it on the grounds that it was both electorally weak and dangerous. Free speech, he said, 'is a matter of consequence to the Trade Unionist – a very vital thing. . . . We are going to jump out of the frying pan into the fire. We cannot forget the psychology and attitude of our own people. The British race is very peculiar; it will not go about threatening to "thug" people, but it will defend itself when it is hit. And who is going to fire the first shot in this battle?'[70] This was vintage Bevin, defending democracy with a mixture of, on the one hand, valid civil libertarian and practical arguments – emergency powers were dangerous and unpopular and wouldn't 'deliver the goods' to trade union members – and, on the other, quasi-chauvinistic invocations of national character.

In addition to seeking emergency powers, the Labour Left also tried to get the party's commitment to government control of the entire banking system, as opposed to the moderate Hugh Dalton's idea that only the Bank of England should be nationalised. In the belief that the 1931 crisis had been a 'banker's ramp', majority sentiment in the Labour Party insisted that the party should commit itself to nationalisation of the joint stock banks as well. In this case, too, Bevin presented a powerful voice on behalf of the more limited programme. At the 1932 Labour Party conference Bevin opposed extended nationalisation on the grounds, first of all, that it was impractical: 'I am not going to tell the electors that I am going to do something I cannot do. . . . ' Second, he insisted, there was no need to nationalise the banks, which were outmoded anyway. 'When I get the source I can create an entirely new machine of my own making to give effect to my own policy', one that does 'its own merchant banking direct from the producer and getting rid of the middleman's usury'.[71] This was both inconsistent, since Bevin had

77

ERNEST BEVIN

himself advocated complete control of the banking system, and far more impractical than the notion of nationalising the joint stock banks. He was effectively ridiculed by Cripps, who thereby joined the ranks of those intellectuals to be denounced by Bevin. The motion to nationalise the joint stock banks was made official party policy, although it was eventually dropped quietly by the leadership.

By the end of the 1930s the Left's demands for a more radical domestic programme were defeated and a 'middle way' was worked out. Labour's *Immediate Programme* of 1937 called for 'some measures of socialism and some other measures of social improvement', as Hugh Dalton put it.[72] It was, in short, the first recipe for a mixed economy. The *Immediate Programme* provided for the nationalisation of major utilities and a limited number of industries, to be converted into public corporations on the Morrisonian model. Although the *Programme* rejected a full-scale Keynesian fiscal and monetary policy, it did provide for the use of the state to make capitalism more efficient (in order to increase the size of the economic pie available to workers) as well as various measures to improve social welfare and more controls over the economy. Although limited as a vision of socialism, it was a practical programme, much of which Labour would be able to effect when it eventually came to power. But it did not suggest what Labour might do to defend the interests of its working-class supporters before it won an electoral majority. It was that question – how to act now – that during the 1930s produced some of the most bitter disputes in both the Labour Party and the TUC.

Communists and direct action

Even in his most radical moment during the period immediately following MacDonald's desertion, Bevin never seriously contemplated a return to the militancy of the pre-1926 period. Although deeply dismayed by the government's callous treatment of the unemployed and its apparent accommodation to fascism abroad, he rejected any attempt at using popular pressure to force a change in its policies. Throughout the 1930s he insisted that the TUC had to persist in slowly building up its strength and winning increased recognition – 'It is from organisation that . . . power must be derived' – while Labour had to demonstrate moderation and

78

SOCIAL DEMOCRAT

reliability if it were to secure middle-class support and electoral success. 'We must win the people over first, however long it takes', he said.[73]

Bevin believed in the use of education and propaganda to create responsible socialists; hence his strong support for Labour's newspaper, the *Daily Herald*. 'Unless we can develop an intelligent democracy', he wrote, 'although Labour may get votes, it will not have power. . . . To develop an electorate from whom real power to change the existing order of things can be derived, we must so write and present our case as to produce all the enlightenment necessary.'[74] When the *Herald* ran into overwhelming financial difficulties at the end of the 1920s, he was instrumental in arranging a deal with a publisher that relaunched the paper on a more commercial basis and insured its success throughout the 1930s. Typically, he always referred to it as 'my paper'.

Bevin never voiced doubts about this moderate strategy; indeed, he celebrated it. 'It is curious', he ruminated, 'how the British Movement develops. It has no theory, but by constant pressure and the submitting of new ideas and proposals in the various trades, it is assuming a place in industry and playing a part to a greater extent than most people realise.'[75] By the end of the decade, he was contending that the trade union movement had won unprecedented influence, having 'virtually become an integral part of the State and its views and voice upon every subject, international and domestic, heard and heeded'. With that influence came a 'responsibility on the Movement never dreamed of by our predecessors. . . . Those were the days of advocacy. Ours is the day of administration.'[76]

It is certainly true that the 'unions turned toward government from the beginning of the 1930s', as one historian has observed, and that the TUC gained increased status and recognition, as evidenced by its membership on over a dozen official committees and the knighting in 1935 of Walter Citrine and Arthur Pugh, the head of the Iron and Steel Trades Confederation.[77] It is also the case that the TGWU, after a long period of stagnation, resumed its earlier growth, reaching almost 700,000 members by 1939. Overall, the wages and conditions of its members improved during the decade. In certain instances, too, patient negotiation produced notable successes. In the flour milling industry, for example, Bevin negotiated agreements that provided for a guaranteed week and compensa-

79

ERNEST BEVIN

tion to workers whose jobs were lost to rationalisation. The TGWU lobbied with some success on behalf of the 1930 and 1933 Road Traffic Act and the 1937 Road Haulage Wages Act that improved the wages and conditions of lorry drivers. And Bevin helped to instigate the TUC's campaign, highly successful by the end of the decade, for holidays with pay.[78]

Overall, though, as Noel Whiteside observes, 'the hallmark of the politics of Citrine and Bevin during the 1930s was its spectacular lack of success'.[79] While the condition of individual unions improved from the mid-1930s onward, the overall strength of the TUC remained low (it achieved its 1926 level only in 1936) in part because it failed to organise actively. Writing at the time, G. D. H. Cole attributed this lethargy to the TUC's suspicions that 'every sign of trade union militancy' represented the 'machinations of a handful of Communists'.[80] Nor had the TUC become an 'integral part of the State'. Bevin's claim to this effect greatly exaggerated the success of the TUC's corporatist policies. As he himself pointed out in 1936, 'since 1931 Labour had been treated like a caste apart'.[81] Had it not been for the Second World War the TUC might never have achieved institutionalised representation in the state. Above all, with respect to the two major issues of the decade, unemployment and the rise of fascism, the TUC had no effect on government policy.

Whether a more militant TUC stance would have proved more effective must remain a matter of conjecture, but it is easy to see why the cautiousness of the TUC's policies frustrated and angered many in the labour movement. Unemployment in the worst-hit communities was over 50 per cent. Poverty remained widespread and visible. According to Seebohm Rowntree, 31 per cent of the working class in York lived below the poverty line. John Boyd Orr found that 10 per cent of the population and 20 per cent of all children were chronically ill-nourished, while almost half the population had some deficiencies in their diet. When Mosley's fascist movement staged militant demonstrations in the mid-1930s, the TUC (and the Labour Party) insisted that the only way to prevent its growth was through education, leaving the Communists to organise a series of effective mass counter-demonstrations. In spite of the indifference to unemployment of the government's policies and the danger of fascism, Bevin and other labour leaders rejected any hint of returning to a policy of direct action. This was

80

SOCIAL DEMOCRAT

both a matter of deliberate strategy – moderation seemed essential to win both recognition from the state and the support of the middle class for the Labour Party – and simultaneously a way of distancing themselves from the Communist Party, which became in the 1930s the leading advocate of militant opposition to government policy.

Relations between the Communist Party and the labour movement had begun badly and grew quickly worse. In the period after its formation in 1920, the British Communist Party, increasingly tied to Soviet direction by its membership in the Third International, tried to follow a 'united front' policy of co-operation with socialist parties and reformist trade unions. Although its attempts to join the Labour Party were rebuffed, it briefly had some success with the TUC. But it soon became clear that there was no meeting point between the reformist TUC and the revolutionary Communists. 'The Communists could not conscientiously reconcile the Communist basis with the basis of evolutionary democracy that the Labour Party represented', Bevin said.[82] Although this characterisation does not fully express the differences in goals and tactics between the two movements, it clearly shows the extent of the mutual antagonism, which only grew stronger after the Communist International in 1928 adopted a policy that declared total opposition to reformist socialists, whom they now labelled counter-revolutionaries with 'social fascist' tendencies.

After Hitler's triumph in Germany in 1933, facilitated in part by the ferocious enmity between German Communists and Social Democrats, international Communist policy reverted to the endorsement of co-operation in a united front with other socialist parties. In Britain, in fact, Harry Pollitt and J. R. Campbell had been working since 1930 to move the CPGB toward such co-operation, which had considerable appeal to the Labour Left. Co-operation implied a more active response to the government's treatment of the unemployed and its appeasement of fascism. However, the success of the corporatist strategy that Bevin and other TUC leaders had endorsed depended on their being able to 'secure the trade union movement's assimilation into the power structure of the state'.[83] They therefore opposed movements favouring a united front – whether of union rank and file or the unemployed – that had any Communist affiliation and that threatened this strategy or the increasingly centralised power of the TUC.

81

ERNEST BEVIN

As John Saville has noted, 'all the major political initiatives and campaigns for which the 1930s are remembered were conducted either against the expressed wishes of the Labour [Party and TUC] leadership or without their approval'.[84] At times, Bevin and other labour leaders seemed so concerned with their own anti-Communism that larger issues became lost, as is clearly shown by their attitudes to the National Unemployed Workers' Movement (NUWM) and the London Busmen's Rank and File Movement.[85]

The NUWM arose in response to the economic collapse of 1920–1 and was mainly led by Communists, although it was 'not simply a subsidiary' of the British Communist Party.[86] At any one time it never reached more than 10 per cent of those out of work, but it became a major protector of the unemployed in the interwar period. On a daily basis, it acted as a service organisation, defending the unemployed before government bodies. Nationally, it organised and led a series of demonstrations and hunger marches that dramatised their plight. Encouraging progress came in 1934, when demonstrations were followed by the restoration of the 10 per cent cut in benefit made in 1931. Early the following year there were massive protests against new legislation that changed the system of benefit payment and reduced the income of many of the unemployed. Faced by such popular opposition, the government retreated.

Although TUC leaders briefly co-operated with the NUWM, they soon objected to its Communist leadership and its demands for militant action.[87] After 1926, they refused to have anything to do with it, repeatedly declining its requests to address the annual conference. The NUWM, said Citrine, 'was not out so much for the purpose of organising the unemployed as for finding a propaganda means to beat the Trades Union Congress and the Trade Union Movement'.[88] Such a response might have been justifiable if the TUC had defended the unemployed, but its own response throughout the interwar period remained tepid. To be sure, it had opposed cuts in unemployment benefit in 1931, but it was only after 1932 that it established associations for the unemployed, and these were limited in scope. Although the TUC objected to the means test, it nevertheless participated in the administration of the 1934 Unemployment Relief Act, so eager was it for recognition. When massive protests erupted in 1935 in response to government cuts in benefits, the 'instinctive reaction' of the TUC was 'to increase its vigilance

82

SOCIAL DEMOCRAT

against the popular front', that is, to any co-operation with Communists. The National Council of Labour, including Bevin, issued a statement appealing 'in no partisan spirit' to the 'national conscience', joining the public protests only 'after the crisis had been resolved'.[89]

Bevin's attitude was completely consistent with that of the TUC. He denounced unemployment and the low scale of relief, but his objections were limited to phrases. 'The main purpose of the means test', he said, ' . . . is to emphasise the difference between the workers and the masters.' It 'should be fought with vigour'. But the key to change was continuous education, not militant demonstrations. 'Simply denouncing the means test will not get us anywhere', he said.[90] So little would Bevin acknowledge the effectiveness of NUWM activities that he even claimed credit for the restoration of benefits in 1935, attributing the 'complete reversal of Government policy', to the labour movement's 'efforts'. This was a very partial truth, and, in fact, he had insisted the year before that the TUC had 'gone as far as it dare with [its own] unemployed associations'.[91] Michael Foot's judgement remains correct: 'Official labour was sluggish, wary and bureaucratically pedantic in providing leadership for the great protest against poverty and industrial decay.'[92] What the story of the NUWM shows is that a more militant posture could produce political results.

A similar conclusion can be drawn from the story of the London bus workers, who had a long tradition of industrial militancy and maintained a syndicalist belief in direct control of the workplace and a corresponding distrust of leaders. Organised around garages that provided points of contact and solidarity, bus work required a lot of local negotiation, particularly around endlessly changing schedules, that encouraged a militant stance. Proud of their relatively well paid position and jealous of their own independence, the London bus workers had originally threatened to secede from their union, the United Vehicle Workers, when it was amalgamating with the TGWU. Although Bevin denounced such opposition as led by men who 'were often on the side of, or inspired by, employers', he agreed that the busmen should have their own directly elected sub-section, which became the Central Bus Committee.[93]

Tensions between the London busmen and the TGWU built up during the 1920s. There was widespread discontent with Bevin for

83

ERNEST BEVIN

refusing to allow the bus section to pursue on its own an increase in wages, particularly after he had supported such demands by the dockers and the tramwaymen. The union's acceptance of intensified working conditions – larger buses that had to be driven at higher speeds – further alienated the busmen. Tensions came to a head in 1932 when the London General Omnibus Company moved to cut wages, speed schedules and dismiss six hundred workers. In response to the union's failure to stop the bus company's demands, the London Busmen's Rank and File Movement (RFM) was created in August, with its own organisation and journal, *The Busmen's Punch*. Communists who were active in the union played a key role in founding and maintaining the RFM, but the leadership included a number of non-Communists and the movement attracted widespread support because it responded to the men's increasing frustrations over deteriorating conditions.

The Rank and File Movement established itself by leading a series of large demonstrations against the company's proposed changes, forcing Bevin to reopen negotiations in order, as Alan Bullock points out, 'to cut the ground from under the unofficial committee's feet'.[94] As a result, the company withdrew its demands, with the signal exception of faster schedules, in exchange for which it agreed to a shorter day. Throughout the 1930s, the question of speed was central to the RFM's agitation. For Bevin the issue was something that 'had to be faced', an unavoidable rationalisation of the industry that might be used to obtain concessions on wages or the length of the working day.[95] The men, however, insisted that the speed-up affected their health. By 1933, the unofficial leaders had won control of the Central Bus Committee and thus representation at the Biennial Delegate Conference. Since they were now constitutionally elected leaders, there was little Bevin could do to curb their power, particularly since for the next few years they observed established union procedures and themselves contained spontaneous rank and file action.

Because of their new position and their widespread support among the busmen, Bevin decided not to move against them, although he continued to call for 'absolute discipline' and to denounce supporters of unofficial actions as 'very often agents provocateurs for somebody'.[96] It was only a matter of time, therefore, until the conflict re-emerged. The 1932 agreement that

84

SOCIAL DEMOCRAT

Bevin had negotiated 'required a surrender of lightning strikes, walk-outs and go-slows', the very tactics that 'militant lay officials and activists' saw as the basis of their power on the shopfloor. Bevin was not opposed to militancy per se, because his bargaining power increased if owners thought the men were really willing to strike. But his corporatist ideal of the union as a disciplined army required unity and control from the top and had no place for an autonomous Rank and File Movement that could undermine the union's ability to fulfil its agreements.[97]

The decisive struggle between Bevin and the busmen came in 1937 over the issue of a seven-hour day. In April 1936, the Central Bus Committee, responding to pressure from below and eager to prevent a split in the Rank and File Movement, requested Bevin to begin negotiations for a seven-hour day. He and the TGWU Executive consented on the condition that the busmen agreed not to involve the tramwaymen, which they did, although eventually this agreement undermined their own bargaining position. Bevin doubted that the busmen's demand could be won but had no choice, given the decision of the men. Although the demand was diluted to seven and a half hours, the London Passenger Transport Board (LPTB), which since 1933 had controlled all public transport in the capital, refused the claim. In response, the union gave the Transport Board notice on 31 March 1937 that it was going to terminate its agreement. The Central Bus Committee was then given plenary power to conduct the strike that began on 1 May, just as London was getting ready for the coronation of George VI. Before the London strike began, the provincial busmen also came out; but the TGWU Executive Council refused to sanction their action, which prevented them from linking up with their London counterparts.

Although the official inquiry that was immediately called issued an interim report recommending an easement of scheduling and an investigation of the busmen's claim that they needed a shorter day to protect their health, a judgement that Bevin supported, the busmen voted overwhelmingly to stay out on strike. Their position was undermined, however, by the failure of the other London transport workers, tramwaymen and trolleymen, to join them. In part, this failure reflected old rivalries between the two groups, including the busmen's own insistence that they should be more highly paid. But it also indicated the way in which Bevin and his Executive Council

85

ERNEST BEVIN

had doomed the busmen's strike by refusing to call out the trolleymen and tramwaymen on the grounds that this would violate their contractual obligations to the Transport Board.

With the strike going nowhere, Bevin now revoked the powers that had been given to the Central Bus Committee to conduct the strike and arranged a settlement directly with the LPTB on the basis of the interim report of the conciliation committee. Taking advantage of the situation, he then broke up the RFM. After an inquiry in June 1937, its leaders were expelled from the TGWU and it ceased to be an organised force in the union. A small breakaway union, the National Passenger Workers' Union, enjoyed some brief success but was contained after Bevin allowed those RFM leaders who remained loyal to the TGWU to be readmitted. Thus, Bevin's vision of a hierarchical trade union structure recognised by management had triumphed over the busmen's ideals of rank and file autonomy and militancy, ideals which had only a small place in the corporatist world he wanted to create.

Foreign policy

The development of social democracy in the 1930s involved an attempt to work out a new socialist programme that could offer a realistic agenda of reforms and thus the possibility of electoral popularity. To Bevin and other labour leaders, winning majority support increasingly seemed to require a new foreign policy as well, one that came to terms with power politics and the need to defend British national interests. Their call for a more realistic foreign policy to cope with the growth of fascism in Germany, Italy and Japan evoked passionate debate within the labour movement, but by the end of the decade British social democracy had acquired a new international outlook. In this redefinition of Labour's foreign policy, Ernest Bevin played an even more important role than he did in the creation of Labour's new domestic programme.

There was a general agreement within the labour movement that socialist principles were indivisible. As Arthur Henderson told the Labour Party in 1934, 'Labour's policy at home and abroad forms one organic whole.' In both places, Henderson went on to say, Labour's policy recognised the 'brotherhood of man' and applied the 'principle of co-operation' to break down 'national and racial, as

86

SOCIAL DEMOCRAT

well as class, barriers' and to secure 'social justice and freedom'. Everything that Labour did, therefore, should be made 'with reference' to its 'grand objective', the creation of a 'Co-operative World Commonwealth'.[97]

The difficulty lay in translating these ideals into a practical programme. Traditional diplomacy, with its emphasis on the balance of power, seemed to offer no solutions, since it produced only national competition and war. Instead, Labour turned in the 1920s to the League of Nations to provide a way to overcome 'international anarchy'. If all nations adhered to its principles, Labour believed, disputes could be settled peacefully. In the event that a nation refused to see reason, the application of sanctions would bring them to their senses. Most of the labour movement believed that this acceptance of 'collective security', as it was called, did not require the use of force. Sanctions, it was assumed, would be moral or economic, not military, and would work because no nation would dare to defy the League.

This belief in the efficacy of peaceful sanctions was consistent with Labour's strong commitment in these years to disarmament. Few in the labour movement were absolute pacifists, that is, opposed to the use of force under any circumstance. But majority sentiment held that warfare was an unacceptable instrument of policy, a sentiment made all the stronger by the revulsion most felt at the carnage of the First World War. At several annual conferences, Labour passed resolutions opposing all war, even agreeing at Hastings in 1933 to use industrial action to resist war no matter what the circumstances. 'The rulers must know that if war comes they will fight with a divided nation', Charles Trevelyan said at this conference. 'They can make their bourgeois war themselves, but they will make it without the workers.'[98] But the rise of fascism in Italy, Germany and Japan increasingly called this position into question. Labour was thus faced with the dilemma of coping with the unprecedented international environment created by the rise of fascism while maintaining the movement's opposition to war and armaments.

The conflicts over the Labour Party's international policy were more complex than can be related here in detail. But we can focus on those aspects of the story in which Bevin played a prominent role and which indicate how he helped reshape British social democracy's international outlook. The first is the struggle to convince the Labour Party to abandon its total renunciation of war and acknowledge that support for collective security might necessitate the use of force. The second is the question of whether rearmament should be supported even with government in the hands of Tories. The third is the issue, raised by the Labour Left, of how to fashion a socialist foreign policy and mobilise popular support for it.

Like other TUC leaders, Bevin thought the Labour Party's 1933 commitment to strike in the event of war was unrealistic. A strike, he told his Executive Committee, would be 'a very puny and ineffective instrument' since so few countries other than Britain had effective trade union movements, while independent trade unions had been 'destroyed' in the fascist countries, a fact which made a deep impression on him. 'Ought we, in the light of these facts to go on talking glibly, misleading the people and ourselves as to what we could do with the General Strike weapon in the event of world war?' he asked.[99] At the 1934 Labour Party conference, Bevin and other leaders succeeded in overturning the previous year's decision to strike in the event of war and in recommitting the party to support for collective security through the League of Nations 'until a new type of civilisation' had been created. That this commitment involved the possible use of armed force, however, would only be explicitly acknowledged at the 1935 party conference where Bevin carried out his most famous intervention in the ongoing debate about foreign affairs.

By the time the party met in 1935, Italy was openly preparing to conquer Abyssinia. While the National Government vacillated in its response, Labour Party leaders called for the use of all necessary measures under the League to stop 'Italy's unjust and rapacious attack'. Presenting this policy to the 1935 Labour Party conference as an endorsement of 'collective action in defence of peace', Hugh Dalton argued that Labour had to accept that Britain was a 'Great Power in the world'. The question, he argued, was this: 'Are we going to play the part of Great Power to-day, a Great Power for peace, a Great Power for righteousness, a Great Power for Socialism, a Great Power for social justice among the nations?' By posing the question in this way, Dalton appealed to the delegates' desire to see Britain as a benevolent power and evaded the more problematic issue: Did acceptance of Britain's role as a great power

SOCIAL DEMOCRAT

require an acceptance of Britain's traditional imperial interests?

In opposition to Dalton and the official party position of support for the League and collective security, Stafford Cripps presented the left-wing alternative. The issue was not, he said, what Britain should do, but 'who is in control of our actions'. The League, he charged, had 'become nothing but the tool of the satiated imperialist powers', while the Conservative Party, 'backed by the great industrialists and capitalists', could not be trusted 'with the lives of British workers'. Thus the war that would likely result from supporting collective security to stop Mussolini would simply further the interests of capitalism and imperialism; Labour should not be implicated in it. Although Cripps correctly predicted that the government would make a deal with Mussolini, he had no real alternative to offer until a socialist government was elected. 'It is unfortunate, tragic, but inescapably true, that the British workers cannot at the moment be effective in the international political field.' And what was Labour to do if it could not win the next election or mobilise enough popular support to change government policy? To that question Cripps had no answer.

Cripps was joined in his opposition, though from a different viewpoint, by the widely revered George Lansbury, the leader of the Labour Party. A devout Christian, Lansbury supported total pacifism, a position that put him in conflict with his own party, although he had faithfully represented its policy in public. Having been prevented by Citrine a few weeks earlier from telling the TUC his objections to the party's policy, Lansbury now determined to speak out. 'I have never been more convinced that I am right, and that the Movement is making a terrible mistake, than I am to-day', he told the conference, urging it to reject all use of force. 'I believe that the first nation that will put into practice practical Christianity, doing to others as you would be done unto, that that nation would lead the world away from war and absolutely to peace.' It was a moving peroration, however remote it might have been from the realities of Hitler's Germany, and temporarily, at least, it appeared as if he might carry the conference, which gave him a standing ovation.

As Lansbury sat down, however, Bevin rose from his seat and advanced to the podium with what Francis Williams called 'his customary rolling walk'. After slowly surveying his audience, he

89

ERNEST BEVIN

launched a fierce attack on both Lansbury and Cripps. Arguing that Lansbury had had the opportunity at the National Council of Labour and at previous conferences to voice objections and that he should have resigned if he found the party's policy unacceptable, Bevin accused him of 'betraying' the movement with his 'disloyalty' to its decisions. This was unfair. Lansbury had tried to resign but had been prevailed upon by the National Executive to stay. Bevin then attacked Lansbury for telling the conference that he might resign but without definitely committing himself to do so. 'It is placing the Executive and the Movement in an absolutely wrong position to be taking your conscience round from body to body asking to be told what you ought to do with it', he said.

After savaging Lansbury, Bevin turned on Cripps, accusing him of 'cowardly . . . stab[bing] us in the back' by resigning from the National Executive of the Labour Party in opposition to its support for the League, which was, of course, exactly what he had just said Lansbury should have done. 'The middle classes are not doing too badly as a whole under Capitalism and Fascism. Lawyers and members of other profession have not done too badly', he lashed out, vaguely linking Cripps to the rise of fascism. 'The thing that is being wiped out is the trade union movement.' Bevin's attack, Hugh Dalton later said, was 'one of the most brutal and at the same time effective performances' he had ever seen at a party conference.[100] Although Bevin told the conference on the last day that he regretted having to participate in this debate, in fact, he revelled in his own performance. When reproached for the violence of his attack on the gentle Lansbury, he replied: 'Lansbury has been going about dressed in saint's clothes for years waiting for martyrdom. I set fire to the faggots.'[101] Lansbury resigned the leadership of the Labour Party a few days after the conference ended.

Bevin's famous speech to the Labour Party conference was rambling and incoherent in places: it included a defence of the British empire and the Monroe Doctrine, as well as absurd claims that 'the coloured races . . . have been pacifist' and that China was 'the greatest pacifist nation in the world'. But it was not designed to persuade the delegates to the conference to endorse collective security through the League of Nations. The speech barely mentioned the larger issue of policy, the conference's endorsement of which was predetermined by the bloc vote of the larger trade

90

SOCIAL DEMOCRAT

unions. Why then did Bevin think it necessary to attack Lansbury and Cripps with such ferocity? Ostensibly, he wanted to make Labour more electable by having it demonstrate that it was capable of governing. To him, this meant that public division in the party, yet alone criticism from the party leader, had to be ended. Decisions, once arrived at, had to be accepted and applied. 'If the movement is going to win the country, when it is faced with a crisis, it has got to give confidence it is capable of coming to a decision', he told the conference.[102] Or as he told his Executive Council in May 1936, 'the Movement having decided to back collective security and the League policy, it must be prepared to face the consequences of its own act'. Unless the habit of running away from a decision is 'dropped in the Labour Movement there is no chance of it ever attaining office in this country'.[103]

In fact, by forcing Lansbury to resign, Bevin badly damaged Labour's public position, as the politically astute Stanley Baldwin quickly appreciated. Less than a month later, Baldwin called an election in which Labour, now led by the unknown and uninspiring Clement Attlee, improved its parliamentary position but still won only 154 seats. Thus if electoral calculation was the object, Bevin's speech badly misfired. It seems more likely that Bevin's main goal was precisely to push Lansbury into resigning in order to make sure that everything Lansbury stood for — pacifism, total opposition to imperialism and a foreign policy guided by Christian morality — would be replaced by greater 'realism'.[104] As he told his Executive Council: 'If we are to win the votes of the people they must be told quite frankly where we stand. They want to know whether they can rely on us doing all we can to give them security and whether we will, in any crisis that develops, do the job and face the consequences.'[105]

Although the 1935 party conference ended opposition to collective security, it failed to end the party's suspicion of armaments, particularly in the hands of the existing government. The Hoare–Laval pact of late 1935, by accepting Mussolini's conquests, only confirmed these suspicions. As a result, in 1936 the Labour Party conference voted to oppose rearmament, though Bevin argued against its decision. In that year, too, the Parliamentary Labour Party, as a way of showing its disapproval of the government, voted once again against the service estimates. To Bevin, refusing to

91

ERNEST BEVIN

support rearmament while insisting on the need to contain fascism seemed the height of inconsistency. He told the TGWU Executive Council that he could see no 'way of stopping Hitler and the other dictators except by force'. The Party needed to 'frankly and honestly face the situation and remove all ambiguity' about its policy.[106] Bevin became so exasperated that in August 1936 he even told the National Council of Labour that he thought the trade unions and the Labour Party had come to a 'parting of the ways. . . . The Trade Unions would have to strike out on their own. They were the first people to be destroyed if Fascism came.'[107] This attitude, however, was short-lived, because he soon came into a position that enabled him to influence the Labour Party to accept his point of view.

In the autumn of 1936 Bevin became chairman of the General Council while Hugh Dalton became chairman of the Labour Party National Executive Committee. 'Bevin and I co-operated closely during this year of our simultaneous chairmanships, both on international and home affairs', Dalton later wrote.[108] Capitalising on their institutional positions, Bevin and Dalton succeeded in convincing the National Council of Labour, over which they presided, to change its position on rearmament. In consequence, in 1937 the Parliamentary Labour Party only abstained from the vote on the service estimates, maintaining its symbolic protest against the government's policy, but not opposing rearmament. By the next year, Labour was actively encouraging increased military preparations.

As their position on rearmament indicates, Bevin and Dalton were attempting to reverse Labour's international outlook and have it come to terms with traditional diplomacy and armaments. In this attempt, they were bitterly opposed by the Labour Left, who argued that Labour had to develop a socialist foreign policy and not lend any support to the Tories whose opposition to fascism could not be trusted. Instead, the Left sought to co-operate with other socialist parties, particularly the Communists, with the aim of mobilising popular resistance to the government's policies. Bevin and other official leaders rejected such a course of action as dangerous to the position of the Labour Party and as an electoral liability. They also distrusted the Communist Party, which had viciously attacked them only a few years earlier. Whether the Left's strategy could have

92

SOCIAL DEMOCRAT

proved effective is open to debate, but given the bloc vote of the large trade unions it had no possibility of securing support from the Labour Party, which grew less and less tolerant of dissenters in these years – Cripps and Aneurin Bevan were briefly expelled – as it created a 'new managerial orthodoxy', what has been aptly called 'social-democratic centralism'.[109]

At the Labour Party conference in 1934, for example, Aneurin Bevan made a strong plea for working with Communist and related groups, arguing that the reason the party was forbidding any association with such groups was because they brought 'into bold relief the incapacity of the Party leadership in the face of the situation'. Responding for the Executive, Bevin was both unfair and vicious. He began by reminding his listeners that 'the Trade Unions in this conference when they formed this Party took a step that entitles the Party itself to recognise their responsibility to these great organised bodies'. He then insisted that 'if you do not keep down the Communists, you cannot keep down the Fascists', a view that echoed the party's official policy of defending democracy against all forms of dictatorship. He ended by attacking Bevan for trying 'to let the Fascists in' by voting in the House of Commons for a measure to 'the detriment of the trade union movement'. In fact, the measure proposed to give non-union workers the same status as unionised workers in appeals against the decision of the Unemployed Assistance Board. When Bevan understandably protested, Bevin taunted him with being too thin-skinned. 'No, in this conference, Aneurin Bevan, you are not going to get the flattery of the gossip columns that you get in London. . . . You are going to get the facts.'[110]

The Labour Left probably most resented Bevin's opposition to them in these years over the issue of Spain, where a popular front government elected in 1936 faced armed revolt by the Right under the leadership of General Francisco Franco. In the resulting civil war, fascist Italy and Nazi Germany provided extensive financial and military aid to Franco, while democratic England and France observed the policy of non-intervention that all powers had ostensibly accepted but that they alone maintained. Only the Soviet Union gave aid to the Spanish republic.

The National Council of Labour initially supported the government's policy as a 'very bad second best', as Arthur Greenwood

ERNEST BEVIN

explained to the 1936 Labour Party conference, the best available policy for the Spanish republic, and the only one the British public would accept.[111] Although sympathetic to the republican cause and soon willing to abandon the policy of non-intervention, the labour movement's official leadership was never willing to mount an active campaign for 'arms for Spain' or do more than support humanitarian aid. They tended to see Spain as a 'backward and feudal country' whose civil war had 'little relevance to Britain' and 'distracted attention from the real threat of a resurgent Germany'.[112] At one point, Bevin described the conflict as a clash between 'two great powers . . . Russia on the one side with her policy, and who could deny that the temporal power of the Vatican is the driving force behind this business. . . . One works through the red International and the other through the Pope.'[113]

For the Left, in contrast, Spain was the great political and moral cause of the decade. The Left saw republican Spain as the embodiment of all of their own hopes for social change. Its defence seemed the last chance to stop a triumphant European fascism. Above all, the Left wanted a more activist policy, one that would somehow provide arms to the republic and pressure the Conservative government into allowing support for it. 'The Committee of Inquiry [to determine the effectiveness of non-intervention] will take weeks and weeks', William Dobbie told the Labour Party in 1936, 'and in the interval the democracy of Spain is being murdered and we are assisting in the assassination.'[114]

Like other trade union leaders, Bevin sympathised with the Spanish republic but defended the official policy of non-intervention. At the 1936 meeting of the TUC, he denounced the Labour Party's critics as inspired by Moscow. 'We have tried to come to a British decision', he said.[115] Even when that policy was abandoned in 1937, he remained reluctant to take a strong stand over Spain. In part, Bevin wanted nothing to do with the Communist Party, which had strongly endorsed the Spanish cause, or with any sort of united front. He also feared that strong support for the republic might divide the labour movement, since a number of Catholic workers opposed the republican cause. Even worse, if support included armed intervention, it might lead to a war with Germany for which Britain and the British public were not prepared. Like other leaders of the TUC, Bevin's stance reflected as well a concern to prevent

94

SOCIAL DEMOCRAT

the power of the General Council from being disrupted by any autonomous rank and file movements in defence of Spain. It was a cautious policy that gave precedence to the 'defence of labour movement institutions . . . over broader political objectives'.[116] Nevertheless, Bevin was certainly right to connect the Spanish cause to the labour movement's general approach to foreign affairs and to insist that 'some of [our] cherished beliefs . . . may have to be revised and the whole situation reviewed'.[117]

As Hitler's Germany continued to expand, the Left's position became increasingly difficult to sustain. Denouncing fascism while opposing a rearmament programme that was ostensibly aimed at curbing fascism was an irreconcilable contradiction. Nevertheless, the Left continued to argue that the government could not be trusted to use these new armaments to oppose fascism and would more likely turn them against the Soviet Union. Given that even after the conquest of Czechoslovakia Chamberlain still hoped for a reconciliation with Hitler, the Left had at least some basis for its suspicions. At the 1937 Labour Party conference, Aneurin Bevan ridiculed Bevin for saying that the Chamberlain government's stance had 'revived hopes that Britain may yet stand beside the liberty-loving nations of the world'. Did Bevin 'really mean that the Government's rearmament policy has re-assured Czechoslovakia in the light of the Government's betrayal of Abyssinia, of China, of Spain?' Bevan asked. He went on to argue with some cogency that support for rearmament would lead the party to support the foreign policy of the Conservative government: 'You cannot collaborate, you cannot accept the logic of collaboration on a first class issue like rearmament, and at the same time evade the implication of collaboration all along the line when the occasion demands it. Therefore, the Conference is not merely discussing foreign policy; it is discussing the spiritual and physical independence of the Working-class Movement in this country.'[118] Nevertheless, despite this reasoning, the refusal to support rearmament under Conservative auspices could hardly be sustained, no matter how ambiguous the government's policy might be, while Hitler continued to advance from strength to strength.

Bevin and other labour leaders argued successfully that the labour movement had no choice but to support the government's rearmament programme. 'The first Movement that will be wrecked with

95

the coming of Fascism is ours', Bevin told the Labour Party in 1937. 'We have had thousands of resolutions, but we cannot stop Fascism by resolutions.'[119] Bevin, along with Citrine and Dalton, deserves full credit for moving the party into complete opposition to appeasement by 1938 and support for rearmament, thereby establishing Labour's claim to be a 'national' party that would eventually pay electoral dividends. They were certainly right that there was no choice in the face of fascist aggression. But the Left also had a point. Labour had obtained no concessions for its support of rearmament. More important, there was a slippage in Labour's policy during these years, a move away from internationalism towards endorsement of traditional British nationalism and imperialism. The belief of leaders like Henderson and Lansbury that a socialist foreign policy was possible now gave way to support – however much this was denied – for traditional British interests. The crushing of Lansbury marked one step in this direction, as did, in part, the support for rearmament. We see this, for example, in the debate at the 1937 party conference, when James Walker, responding for the Labour Party National Executive to Bevan and other critics, argued that 'under the British flag there is more democracy than there is under the flag of any other country in the world. And that does not mean I am backing up the National Government'.[120] To accept the traditional view that the mission of British imperialism was benevolent, while denying that such acceptance constituted support for the Conservative government upholding Britain's traditional world role, was to draw a very fine line indeed. Compare, in contrast, George Orwell, who in 1939 said that it was nonsense to call the British empire democratic when it was 'in essence nothing but [a] mechanism for exploiting cheap labour'.[121]

This shift in Labour's international policy is also evident in Bevin's thought, which had long been marked by a utopian belief that world peace would be created by the unlimited expansion of trade, a belief that perhaps indicates the influence of his years in Bristol, a centre of trade and a gateway to the empire. Bevin had always believed that rivalry over raw materials was the 'fundamental cause of war'. He told the TUC in 1935 that 'the thing that has been poisoning the sources of international relationship has been the speculation associated with the development of mining and the production of raw materials in the various parts of the world'. If

SOCIAL DEMOCRAT

twenty-five key materials were internationally owned and open to purchase, he went on, '90 per cent of the world causes of war would be entirely removed'. His remedy for this was a vague notion to 'carry [the empire] a stage further' and move towards 'world organisation'.[122] By this he seems to have meant that there should be some form of international organisation to control raw materials and allow access to them to all countries 'on due payment'.[123]

In the course of the 1930s, Bevin's vague ideas about the international ownership of minerals, which were common in the labour movement, became more directly imperialist. In 1938 he proposed a sort of consortium of imperial powers which would 'pool their colonial territories and link them up with a European Commonwealth'.[124] After his trip that summer to a commonwealth conference in Australia, he adopted a variety of neo-imperialist positions. Bevin urged that other countries, including the United States, should be invited to 'come within our preference system', producing 'a real pooling of the whole of the Colonial Empires in the world and their resources'. The 'Colonial Powers would then be in a position to offer to "have not" nations free entry into such a system if they would renounce the way of war'. British policy would give 'them all a chance for a "place in the sun" and a right to develop their standard of living. Open up all these great God-given things for the benefit of humanity.'[125] Bevin the benevolent paternalist had now expanded his reach to global proportions. 'We must return to the position as trustee for our Colonial territories', he said. That his goals were paternalist does not make them less imperialist even when expressed in terms of the 'commonwealth idea'. And his attempt to enlist the empire in a plan 'to offer appeasement to a very wide area of the world', as he put it, had no more chance of success with the fascist countries than did Lansbury's Christian pacifism.[126]

By 1938, British social democracy had taken on a new shape. It had developed a viable reformist programme and a new international policy. With its new emphasis on the need to defend aggressively the national interest and to develop Britain as the centre of a world empire, Labour was even challenging the Conservatives' claim to be the 'national party'. Labour's leaders, in turn, displayed a new confidence, evidenced in part by the more critical tone they adopted to the Chamberlain government and denunciation of the Munich

97

ERNEST BEVIN

agreement of late September 1938. At the Labour Party conference of 1939, Bevin, typically, attacked appeasement as the policy of the City of London. 'Behind Chamberlain are the bankers', he said; 'they are the principal supporters of appeasement for Germany'.[127] The radical distrust embodied in such statements led Bevin and other trade union leaders to oppose all forms of conscription in preparation for the war. 'If we agree to a series of military organisations to be used in connection with industry we are simply forging a weapon that may be used against us during peace time'.[128] Until government promised to endorse the 'conscription of wealth' and stopped 'truckling to dictators' the trade unions would have no confidence in it, Bevin insisted.[129]

Bevin and other TUC leaders now tried to use the government's need for their co-operation with the rearmament programme to win concessions for the trade union movement. In February 1939, the TUC tried to obtain a promise to repeal the 'vindictive' Trade Disputes Act of 1927. Although Bevin assured the government that the act was unnecessary because another general strike 'might be ruled out', it failed to respond. In April, the TUC urged the government to support more public works to offset an anticipated growth in unemployment. This, too, failed, as the Treasury advised Chamberlain to reply that only 'sound monetary policy' could restore prosperity.[130] In June, the National Council of Labour met Chamberlain to demand that negotiations with the Soviet Union for an alliance be conducted with more dispatch.[131] Such demands also had no effect. Nothing shows the hollowness of Bevin's claim about the TUC's new position in the state than this total inability to budge the Chamberlain government on issues of both domestic and foreign policy, even at a point when their bargaining position was relatively strong.

Bevin's mistrust of the Chamberlain government was also based on a belief that the traditional ruling class was unable to run the war. 'The tremendous capacity of the so-called upper and middle classes', he said in 1938, 'is nothing but a myth. The working class ought to gain confidence that it has been demonstrated that these "great people" are not competent to run anything.'[132] This assertion would be confirmed during the first year of the war. So would his belief that the working class would have to rescue England. 'I cannot help feeling', he told his Executive Council, 'that the Trade Union

98

SOCIAL DEMOCRAT

Movement will be called upon to bear the greatest burden in connection with this awful difficulty. The other classes seem to be effete and inefficient, while others are screaming about short-term policies, ill-considered trifles and fictitious unity.'[133] The war would soon prove the prescience of this prediction.

4 Minister of Labour

On 3 September 1939, two days after German troops invaded Poland, Britain declared war on Germany and the Second World War began. The start of the war should have immediately brought an end to a 'low, dishonest decade', as W. H. Auden called it, but in fact things continued with remarkably little change for another eight months. Chamberlain added a few Conservative critics to his administration, most prominently Winston Churchill, but no Labour or Liberal Party member would serve under him. Fearing the long-term political consequences of popular mobilisation, his government failed to enlist the full resources of the nation. During the six months following the declaration of war, a period of 'phoney war' when there was little active fighting, the production of luxury goods was not disturbed, prices were left largely uncontrolled, and taxes were hardly raised. The government moved slowly to overcome shortages of labour and materials for the production of munitions, while only petrol was rationed. In consequence, prices rose sharply. Overall, the official history of the war economy concludes, it was a period of 'lost opportunity'.[1]

Bevin and other trade union leaders responded to the war with mixed feelings. On the one hand, they recognised immediately that the war provided an opportunity to secure for the TUC the full recognition they had been striving for since the Mond–Turner talks. They were quick to grasp for it. Walter Citrine wrote to Chamberlain insisting that all government departments be instructed to consult the TUC and demanding representation on key committees. The trade unions 'expected at a time like the present, as a matter of right, to be taken into the fullest consultation', a TUC delegation told Chamberlain in October.[2] Bevin put forth the same message:

> We do not desire to serve on any Committee or Body as an act of patronage [he wrote shortly after the war began]. We represent

100

MINISTER OF LABOUR

probably the most vital factor in the State; without our people this war cannot be won, nor can the life of the country be carried on. The assumption that the only brains in the country are in the heads of the Federation of British Industries and Big Business is one which has got to be corrected, for, as a matter of fact, most of the delays and unpreparedness so apparent to-day are due to the reliance of the Departments of State upon the very limited advice of people who, after all, live in a very narrow world indeed. . . . The principle of equality has not yet been won, equality not merely in the economic sense, but in the conception and in the attitude of mind of those in power.[3]

Chamberlain, who had been seeking the TUC's co-operation over rearmament since 1938, hastened to assure them of the government's good will by instructing all departments to co-operate fully with them and establishing a National Joint Advisory Council (NJAC) of employers and trade unions.

On the other hand, Bevin and other union leaders feared that the war would undermine working-class living standards. As part of a TUC delegation, he lectured Chancellor of the Exchequer Sir John Simon about the need to share the burden of the war equitably, arguing for a tax rate of 50 per cent on the grounds that the 'interest-receiving classes are getting it out of industry'. When concerns were voiced about a possible wage-price spiral, Bevin denounced them as inspired by 'Montagu Norman and his henchmen'. 'The working classes are faced with two offensives', he told the TGWU, 'one by Hitler, which we must defeat, and one by the Bankers which, if the Government does not stop, will lead to the defeat of our nation. . . . The whole tendency is to create a situation which will enable the ruling class to use this war as a means of thrusting us back to a form of serfdom.'[4]

Hence Bevin determined to resist government policies that seemed to call for a depression of working-class living standards without corresponding demands on the wealthy. He told Seebohm Rowntree that his 'time has been taken up in trying to get wages commensurate with the cost of living. I am determined to keep them up to a proper level. The powers that be have won in the first round but that is only a temporary victory for them. As our people sicken of this business they will revolt against the depression of their standards.' When Keynes proposed that inflation be controlled by compulsory saving, Bevin criticised him for seeking to 'demonstrate

101

ERNEST BEVIN

to the public that the only way to pay for this war is to attack the standard of living of the workpeople'.[5] He warned that workers would respond if their standards were depressed.

The phoney war ended on 8 April 1940, when Germany overran Denmark and began to attack Norway. British attempts to aid the Norwegians failed badly, provoking a political crisis. Bitterly attacked in Parliament, Chamberlain lost a significant level of support as almost a hundred Conservatives either voted against him or abstained on a vote of confidence on 8 May. He responded by trying to broaden his government, but Labour, who hated both him – 'He always treated us like dirt', Attlee recalled – and his policies, refused to serve under him.[6] They agreed to serve, however, under someone else. Reluctantly, Chamberlain resigned on 10 May to be replaced by Winston Churchill.

Churchill immediately invited Labour to join in a new Coalition government, including Bevin as Minister of Labour and National Service. Although Churchill had long been an opponent of working-class organisation and activity, he recognised, as he told Clement Attlee and Arthur Greenwood, that 'it was vitally important that organised labour in industry should be directly represented' in his Cabinet.[7] Who could better speak for organised labour than Bevin? In fact, within a few months Bevin would become so powerful a spokesman for the vital trade union movement that he would be invited to join the small War Cabinet which was the fulcrum of power throughout the war.

Bevin's assumption of office (he had been found a safe seat in Parliament) also marked his own political evolution. In 1917 he had attacked the Labour Party for participating in the Lloyd George coalition because of the 'character of the people . . . whom it was expected to associate with'. Now, although he had denounced Churchill just over a year earlier as the leader of 'the extreme reactionaries in the Tory Party', he did not hesitate to join the government. In addition to his genuinely patriotic desire to help meet the military crisis of a war against fascism that was ideologically different from the clash of empires between 1914 and 1918, Bevin saw a unique political occasion. 'If our Movement and our class rise with all their energy now and save the people of this country from disaster,' he told a special conference of trade union executives a few weeks after his appointment, 'the country will

102

always turn with confidence . . . to the people who saved them.'[8]

Appreciating that the Ministry of Labour would provide him a key position from which to shape domestic policy, Bevin viewed the war as an opportunity to create the kind of industrial order that he had been advocating for almost two decades.[9] The corporatist ideal that he had embraced fully after the General Strike had proved problematic until now because neither the state nor business would co-operate fully with the trade union movement. Now, the war and his own position in the government ensured that co-operation. Bevin used this new partnership as the basis for the various measures he put in place to mobilise the entire country behind the war effort. He also took advantage of this moment to secure a new position in society for the trade union movement.

For Bevin, creating this reformed economic order also implied creating the enlarged sense of citizenship rights that he had demanded for the working class before the Shaw Committee over two decades previously. 'We are the last great class to rise in the world', he said. 'Throughout the world . . . the day of the common man has come.' It seems of at least symbolic importance that Bevin at the first Cabinet meeting he attended objected to the use of 'labour' in a proposed Emergency Powers Bill, 'as this would create the wrong impression psychologically by inferring that labour was separate from citizenship'.[10] In part to help obtain those citizenship rights, Bevin converted the Ministry of Labour into a major policy-making department, greatly expanding its power to defend working-class conditions and living standards. Thus, his actions throughout the war were consistent and effective because they all stemmed from a central core of beliefs which had grown out of his experiences in the previous three decades.

Mobilisation

When Bevin took over at the Ministry of Labour and National Service, he faced the immediate task of mobilising the entire population of Britain for the struggle against Nazi Germany, which was now overrunning Belgium, Holland and France. The Chamberlain government had rapidly expanded the armed services, but its direction of the workforce had been 'sporadic, indecisive and insufficient', failing to make the best possible use of the limited

ERNEST BEVIN

number of skilled workers who were the key to increased production of war materials.[11] Many of the measures that might have been introduced – dilution (the use of less skilled men or women to do work reserved for skilled men), the transfer of skilled workers from less essential jobs, and some control over wages – required the co-operation of the trade unions, but they remained understandably suspicious of the government. Bevin spoke for others besides himself when he wrote shortly after the war began that 'in their heart of hearts the "powers that be" are anti-trade union'. But his own inclusion in the Coalition government now transformed his attitude. 'I feel I have been living about fifty years in the last fortnight', he said at the end of May.[12]

Within a few days of taking office, Bevin produced a plan to overcome the labour supply problem that was holding back production. 'I came in [to office] at 2. 30 on the afternoon of Tuesday and on Wednesday at 11 o'clock I produced at least the outline of the basis of my scheme', he reported with characteristic immodesty a few weeks later. 'Then at 3 o'clock the staff gathered round me and examined it in all its details, and by Friday night we had circulated it to the rest of the departments.'[13] Of course, Bevin had not created a scheme out of whole cloth but drew on plans already in process, to which he added some important amendments. The scheme that emerged had three main elements.[14] First, Bevin centralised control over all labour supply. How much labour a firm needed, Bevin insisted, 'can in present circumstances no longer be left to the . . . discretion of the firms'. Instead, 'the general problem of labour supply and of the use to which labour is being put should be a duty resting on one Department, and one Department alone', the Ministry of Labour, which would now be given a staff of labour inspectors with authority to act on the Minister's behalf. The Ministry's work would be supplemented by a new Production Council – representing the Ministry of Supply, the Admiralty, the Ministry of Aircraft Production, the Board of Trade and the Ministry of Labour – able to oversee all factors necessary for production and to resolve disputes between competing demands.

Second, Bevin aimed to obtain increased support from workers for the war effort by removing their 'sense of grievance', as he told the Cabinet, in part by ensuring that at least the semblance of equal sacrifice was observed. He proposed that more suppliers be brought

104

MINISTER OF LABOUR

under direct government control and where this proved too complicated, that prices be fixed to limit profits, both steps being necessary to remove 'from the minds of the workpeople any suggestion that their additional energies are only directed to producing profits for others'.[15] It is unlikely any previous Minister of Labour had ever voiced this particular concern. In addition, trade unions were to be guaranteed that any trade practices they agreed to suspend would be restored after the war. 'We are not going to take advantage of your agreeing to dilution', he told the trade union representatives to the NJAC.[16]

Third, Bevin enlisted the co-operation of the employers and trade unions in carrying out the state's policies. To that end he proposed a new position, Director of Labour Supply, who, with representative employers and trade unionists, would make up a Labour Supply Board to survey the needs for labour in industry and decide how it was to be provided to meet these needs. The work of the Board would be supplemented by a new system of local supply boards able to act as a 'channel for considering and adjusting any conflicting requirements of the Production Departments' in each locality.

As this last proposal indicates, Bevin was determined to realise his corporatist ideal, that is, to secure a voluntary partnership of business, the trade unions and the state in running the war. When he met with the NJAC for the first time on 22 May 1940, he told them that he wanted to 'utilise the services and experience of the joint machinery which exists'. With the 'goodwill' of the employers and the TUC, 'a little less democracy and a little more trust in these difficult times, we could maintain to a very large extent intact the peacetime arrangements, merely adapting them to suit these extraordinary circumstances'. Both sides agreed to co-operate and to form a smaller Joint Consultative Committee (JCC), which became 'the primary instrument of government industrial policy' for the rest of the war.[17] Henceforth, the TUC had the recognition and political position that it been seeking since the Mond–Turner talks.

The Cabinet accepted most of Bevin's plan for the organisation of labour supply but overrode his reluctance to interfere with the labour market. The Emergency Powers (Defence) Bill, approved by Parliament on 22 May, gave the Minister of Labour power to direct any person over sixteen years of age to perform any service under terms which he would lay down. The Minister could also stipulate

105

ERNEST BEVIN

conditions under which industry should conduct its business, while the government could list establishments engaged in war work as 'controlled establishments' and levy an excess profits tax of 100 per cent. Using his new authority, Bevin that same day issued Defence Regulation 58A giving the Ministry of Labour full control of the nation's manpower.

As soon as this new machinery was in place, the government adopted a system to allocate labour supply according to a schedule of priorities that designated the production of different war materials as more more or less essential and granted skilled workers to firms according to their place in this priority schedule. In consequence, some industries were starved of skilled labour while others had more than they could usefully employ. By June, Bevin was complaining to the Production Council that some factories had men standing around.[18]

He determined, therefore, to bring about a more efficient allocation of skilled labour, but this immediately brought him into conflict with the Minister of Aircraft Production, the newspaper magnate Lord Beaverbrook. Taking advantage of aircraft's highest priority designation, Beaverbrook had acquired more skilled workers than his factories could use, on the grounds that they would be needed as soon as production increased. Bevin insisted that firms had to agree to relinquish skilled men who could not be usefully employed as determined by his labour inspectors, but Beaverbrook refused to comply. 'Though I have remonstrated with him he seems to be incorrigible', Bevin complained to Churchill. The issue, he told the Prime Minister, was about who was to control the labour supply and 'must be altered if I am to continue to bear the responsibilites which I understood you placed upon me. . . . If the individual firms, or individual Departments, are to be allowed to retain such labour in watertight compartments the position becomes impossible and I cannot go on.' He insisted that Churchill should lay down 'beyond a shadow of a doubt' that the use of labour had to be decided by the Ministry of Labour.[19] It is a sign both of Bevin's strength of character and importance to the Coalition that he prevailed over Churchill's close friend, as he would in future battles about the control of manpower.

Nevertheless, the underlying issue over which Bevin and Beaverbrook struggled, how to make the best use of scarce labour

106

resources, persisted, forcing a reluctant Bevin to employ ever greater measures of compulsion. In June, he issued the Restriction on Engagement Order that in selected industries forbade advertising for skilled workers or their hiring except through a trade union or an employment exchange. In August, he required those who worked in certain essential trades to register, even if they had not worked in the trade within the last ten years. In November, he increased pressure on employers to provide more training in their own establishments to facilitate the dilution of skilled labour. After telling the Production Council that the priority system gave the Ministry of Aircraft Production 'little incentive to dilute or make the best use of skilled labour we have given it, while other types of production have been starved', he moved to abandon that system in favour of one that distributed workers to overcome bottlenecks.[20]

When labour shortages nevertheless persisted, the Production Council commissioned a survey of manpower requirements from a committee chaired by William Beveridge, who presented his report in November. 'The peace-time economic and political structure of the country has been carried on with too little change', Beveridge wrote. He proposed instead a vast 'extension of state control not merely over the civilian labour market but over many other aspects of civilian life', including increased controls over wages and man-power and the introduction of many more women into factories.[21] However rudimentary, the Manpower Requirements Committee's survey provided the first full-scale picture of Britain's labour needs and resources and made possible the creation of the manpower budgets that would become the basis of all plans for labour supply after 1941.

Bevin eventually accepted most of Beveridge's recommendations for tighter controls, but more slowly and cautiously than Beveridge wanted, and this hesitancy was criticised both by the Labour Left and the Tory Right in Parliament. Bevin was convinced, however, that voluntary co-operation would produce better results than compulsion, particularly if the trade unions, which had always opposed 'industrial conscription', were not ready to accept more controls. Nevertheless, persistent shortages of skilled men led him to accept stricter regulations. In January 1941, Bevin told the Production Executive, the effective replacement of the Production Council which he now chaired, that his powers would have to be

ERNEST BEVIN

augmented to provide both 'measures for compulsion' and 'measures for the protection of labour'.[22]

Bevin then proposed to the Cabinet that he be given power to declare any undertaking a 'national work' in which no employee might leave or be dismissed without the Ministry of Labour's permission. No enterprise could qualify for this designation unless the Ministry of Labour certified that wages and conditions of work were suitable and sufficient provisions had been made for housing and feeding. Since firms would no longer receive adequate supplies of labour without such designation, this provision now gave Bevin great power to influence wages and conditions in thousands of firms. As he said, it was a way of 'enforcing . . . standards accepted by organised employers' on unorganised ones.[23] Equally important, in return for taking away the workers' right to switch jobs, Bevin insisted that they be given security in the form of a guaranteed weekly wage. 'If I have been justified by nothing else in coming into the Government', he later told Parliament about this reform, 'I feel rather pleased about that.'[24] Finally, to provide information about who exactly was doing what in the war economy, all men and women would now have to register.

Bevin's proposals were put into effect in March as the Essential Work Order (EWO) and the Registration for Employment Order. These orders ended poaching of skilled workers and stopped their drift from war industries to less essential work, gave the Ministry a far more accurate sense of available labour resources, and made it easier for Bevin to use his powers of direction. By the end of the war the Essential Work Order covered eight and a half million workers in 67,500 firms. While only a little over one million direction orders were made, the existence of such powers provided indirect pressure on workers to accept government goals voluntarily.

The changed balance of power in the workshops created by the Essential Work Order made a number of Conservatives increasingly 'cantankerous', as John Colville noted at the time.[25] In April 1941, one Tory MP called it a 'slacker's charter' that had 'induced indiscipline in industry'. Bevin responded by denouncing the 'kind of discipline' that was based on 'the ability to force your will on another by the imposition of starvation'. Relying on unemployment for discipline 'has meant [class] war', he observed.[26] A few weeks

108

MINISTER OF LABOUR

later, he publicly denounced the 'finance directorate' that ran many businesses. When Churchill then protested, Bevin replied that the working class had been libelled in Parliament and that 'he was going to defend the class that made me'.[27]

In June, Sir John Wardlaw-Milne, one of the leaders of the dissident Tory group in Parliament, wrote to Churchill directly to complain about the 'hopeless' position of the employer who had now 'lost control of his labour'. The Essential Work Order was 'really only being applied on the one side, in favour of the workers', he argued. In response, Bevin presented Churchill and the rest of the Cabinet, to whom the correspondence was circulated, with a strong lecture:

> If other things are put right slackness and absenteeism will be easily handled; if they are not an attack on slackness and absenteeism will be of no avail and will merely cause added bitterness. . . . The remarks made by Wardlaw-Milne reflect the views of a certain class of employers – some of whom have contributed largely to our present difficulties by their own undisciplined behaviour – who think the worker ought to be tied up without any corresponding restriction on the employers. This attitude is not shared by the organised employers who recognise that such restrictions cannot be made one-sided and that the workers must be safeguarded against arbitrary action by the employer. The alternative to the Order is not to deprive the worker of his safeguards but to restore his freedom, and plunge industry back into chaos.[28]

In public, Bevin repeatedly noted as well that prewar policies, which drove 'the best skilled men out of the industry and, what was worse, [drove] out the facilities as well', were the root cause of any remaining labour problems.[29]

While Bevin had no patience with employers like Wardlaw-Milne, he never aimed to act only on behalf of the working class. He expected workers to fulfil their 'duty to carry [their] side of the bargain' by not 'abusing' their guaranteed weekly wage.[30] And he constantly praised 'good' employers and managers, that is, those who worked with the unions and treated the men reasonably. In other words, he held to the old ideal of a fair day's wage for a fair day's work, although now it was to be administered within a more managed economy. His attempts to attain this goal can be seen in a brief look at his negotiations with the shipbuilding and shiprepairing

109

ERNEST BEVIN

industries over the application of the Essential Work Order. Securing adequate production from these vital industries had been particularly difficult because they had been so hard hit by the depression, causing many skilled workers to seek work elsewhere; the labour force had declined by 40 per cent between 1923 and 1935. In addition, complicated work rules – at least seventeen different trades of major importance worked in the industries – made it difficult to introduce new methods. In early 1941, Bevin met several times with both trade union and employer representatives. The transcripts of these meetings provide a vivid picture of Bevin at work.[31]

Bevin met first with representatives of the shipbuilding, engineering and related unions and appealed to them to relax their traditional trade practices, which restricted jobs to certain groups of men, and to accept work throughout the entire industry, not just a single firm. Although he was going to apply an Essential Work Order, he wanted this machinery to be 'on an agreed basis with the trade. . . . I do want the people of the Shipbuilding Industry to stay put, but to stay put on what I hope will be agreed conditions.' In return, he promised 'security' in the form of a guaranteed weekly wage. What he wanted, he said, was 'interchangeability' but he 'hate[d] to use the word'.

> Many of these difficulties and quarrels have existed in the past because of enormous conflict, because the question of giving up a particular job is probably a choice between giving it up and the dole [i.e. keeping it or the dole]. I want to remove that entirely, and, if the Government removes that, then alternatively, can you help us to get these ships out by everybody doing anything that comes along, in order to have the job turned out as quickly as we can?

After speaking directly to the unions' fear of change, he addressed their concerns about wages. He would tell employers that 'there must be no cutting of a rate, however much a man may earn'. The 'Government is going to pay' for more output, he promised, although the exact arrangements would be left to the two sides of industry because 'you are the people who know how to do it, and I would not presume . . . to try to suggest how it should be done. I have got an innate faith in your mutual ingenuity to do it when you get at it. . . .' Mixing an appeal to their patriotism and self-interest,

110

MINISTER OF LABOUR

Bevin concluded: 'I do not want to interfere with a single agreement in the trade, other than this, that the State says: We tie you to the State service, in effect . . . but, in return, we will not leave you standing idle on the stones. . . .'

The next day Bevin met with the employers to tell them he wanted a 30 per cent increase in output and that industry had to be regarded as a 'great public service, not limited by pre-war conceptions of private interest and limited individualism'. Although he intended to apply an Essential Work Order to the industry, he wanted to leave its administration mainly in the hands of the industry itself. Explaining his desire to secure a guaranteed weekly wage for the men in return for their not leaving, he repeated what he had said to the union representatives: 'I do not care how much the men earn . . . [but want] to encourage the feeling that the man gets what he produces.' But to the employers he also held out the promise of better work discipline: 'The main object I have in mind is that, if a man works hard and gives you a good output in one turn, I do not want him to have to lose the advantage of that in the next turn because somebody forgets to put him to work. I want to inculcate the idea of regularity.' When pushed by the employers, he agreed that he would have to make an example of the man who worked Sunday and then took two days off but warned them that 'if there is a big stick in the background you do not want to be brandishing it too much'. More punitive powers with tribunals would likely 'create such a political storm that you do not achieve your objective'. But ultimately, while promising the employers increased control of the workplace in return for their co-operation, Bevin appealed to their idealism, to the possibility of permanently ending restrictive trade practices and demarcation disputes:

> I am hoping that the training of our people, or at least the basic training of our people, will be on a more general basis. It is an awful crime for somebody to say to a youngster, who is not allowed to have any say in it himself, 'Go into the yard and I will sentence you to be a riveter for the rest of your life,' never giving the kid a chance to find his feet and consider where he ought to be and how much he ought to know. You develop one cell of his brain for six or seven years, and then wonder why the other cells do not work afterwards. That is your trouble. You have to face it.

111

ERNEST BEVIN

Both sides remained wary, however, reluctant to give up their prerogatives or protections, so Bevin met with them again, insisting that it was necessary to get the 'right spirit' from top to bottom of the industry. Once again, he refused to introduce more penalties for non-compliance, insisting they would get better results if 'the thing is handled properly'. 'I never went early in my life when I worked for a private employer', he said, 'and I never worked very late because I hated being late twice in one day, but since I have been a Union official I think I have been about the best timekeeper, and also a Minister. . . .' With his experience on the docks clearly in mind, Bevin insisted that the guaranteed weekly wage would be an 'incentive' to men to work:

> When this begins working, give it a month and see how the habits of men begin to change. . . . I have seen so many sections of people turn from an insecure and chaotic basis to an orderly one and it is surprising, how the thing changes. It has been nobody's business to tell him anything in the past, it will be somebody's business now. You will get some who will refuse [to turn out] but you will get an awful lot who will not waste that time. Besides, mother wants to know why he is at home when he should be out earning money.

In the end, both sides reluctantly agreed to the changes, although the trade unions still feared that Bevin's proposals gave employers what they had wanted for years. The agreement exemplified Bevin's use of corporatist means to achieve his productionist goals. The men were to get security and higher wages; the owners, increased control over the work process. That the industry still did not work as efficiently as Bevin wanted was a testimony to the heritage of class conflict and fear of unemployment that even with the war emergency he could not overcome. As he said at the time, 'We are paying a terrible price for the handicap of the last fifteen years' depression.'[32]

By the end of 1941, most of the system for mobilising and directing labour had been put in place and functioned effectively, although women had yet to be added in large numbers. Between 1940 and 1943 almost two and a half million men and women were added to the armed forces, a million and a half to the munitions industry and another 400,000 to other essential industries. Bevin's major contribution to that system was to secure the co-operation of

112

MINISTER OF LABOUR

the trade unions with what was in effect industrial conscription and to improve the standards and conditions of the working class. After the development of the manpower budget at the end of 1941, which measured the different needs of the services, the war industries and civilian industries in relation to the available sources of labour, most decisions about labour supply became a more technical matter and were increasingly funnelled through the powerful Lord President's Committee, chaired by Sir John Anderson, which Bevin joined in January 1941.

Women

Women provided vital support for the war effort, but only after each of the two wartime governments had overcome its reluctance to employ them. The Chamberlain government did virtually nothing to mobilise women's participation in the war or redistribute women in the workforce. On taking office in May 1940, Bevin negotiated an 'extended employment of women agreement' with the engineering industry. But he, too, in spite of this agreement, did little for the rest of the year to increase the number of women workers, preferring to rely on the market and women's voluntary decisions to join the war effort.

Bevin soon came under pressure, however, to increase government efforts at mobilising women. In his report on manpower requirements, William Beveridge placed a heavy emphasis on the need to recruit more women to the munitions industries to meet the planned increase in output. Above all, simply the shortage of skilled men and the desperate need for dilution pushed Bevin to act on this recommendation and to abandon his reliance on the voluntary principle. The March 1941 Registration of Employment Order, which applied to women as well as men, provided the basis for recruiting more women to the essential industries. Even so, Bevin applied compulsion only slowly. By August 1941, two million women had registered but only 87,000 had been directed to munitions work or the Women's Auxiliary Services.[33]

When the manpower survey indicated a need for one million more women, however, the government in December 1941 reluctantly decided to extend conscription to women, who were thereafter assigned to industry unless they asked to join the services.

113

ERNEST BEVIN

Although Churchill feared the effect conscription would have on morale, Bevin told the Cabinet that he 'had considered every practicable alternative before deciding to support the principle of compulsion . . . [but] no other method would suffice'.[34] The Cabinet agreed but excluded married women in order not to upset their husbands. It ignored, however, the objections of women MPs who demanded that equal pay should go along with conscription. Thus, 'in spite of the apparent humanity of Bevin's preference for voluntarism to direction', Penny Summerfield concludes in her study of women wartime workers, 'there are grounds for seeing it as quite mistaken. In terms of both efficiency and women's own experiences, the policy looks more like a continuation of the tradition of treating women as a marginal workforce than a real attempt to maximise women's co-operation with the war effort.'[35]

By early 1942, all of the administrative means to mobilise and direct women to essential work or the services had been put in place. Reluctant though the government had been to use women, the measures eventually produced substantial results. Between 1939 and 1943, the number of women employed increased from 6.2 to 7. 5 million. Over 1. 5 million went to work in essential industries, a figure that reflects the numbers of women who transferred from other industries, such as textiles or domestic work, as well as new recruits. In key industries the number of women employed increased dramatically. Women in engineering increased from 10 to 34 per cent of the workforce, for example, from 27 to 52 per cent in chemicals, and from 32 to 46 per cent in metals. In addition, over half a million women had joined the armed forces or civil defence forces. By 1943, 90 per cent of single women aged 18–40 did some form of war work. Such massive changes in women's lives, which included access to work from which they had been excluded, might have provided the basis for a transformation of their position in society, but it is clear that instead, as Summerfield has written, official policy only 'reinforced [their] unequal position'.[36] For this, Bevin bears a share of the responsibility.

Before Bevin took office, the British Federation of Business and Professional Women and the Woman Power Committee (WPC), a group of mainly Conservative women MPs who joined together in March 1940, urged greater use of women in the war and representation for women on government bodies that oversaw the use of

114

women. The WPC eventually included Liberal women MPs as well as two Labour women MPs. It failed, however, to win support from other Labour women, who remained suspicious of it. As Ellen Wilkinson told Bevin in July, it would be most undesirable if a group of mainly Conservative women were 'allowed to interfere, even if it is only in the sense of giving advice, into the conditions of the women in factories'. In particular, Wilkinson feared that the WPC would urge the appointment of professional women as forewomen, precluding working-class women from advancing. Bevin reassured her that she 'need not have the least fear that they will be an agency through which working-class women will be improperly pushed aside to make room for others'. And when he met the Woman Power Committee he 'stressed that there could be no segregation of the different types of women who entered factory employment in War-time and that the principle of equal opportunity and promotion by merit must be observed'.[37]

It was only in part out of class suspicion, however, that Bevin diverted the efforts of the WPC. He also disagreed with their goals. He rejected their recommendation that a woman be appointed to the Labour Supply Board and prevented the appointment of a woman under-secretary empowered to coordinate all issues concerned with the use of women. When Irene Ward on behalf of the WPC urged him to appoint an advisory committee on women, Bevin agreed but delayed and circumvented their desires. Instead, acting on the advice of his officials who told him 'it will be impossible to avoid a women's committee of some sort', he 'stole their thunder' by appointing a Women's Consultative Committee in March 1941 and inviting the WPC to recommend two members.[38] 'Perhaps I could help by presiding over the ladies on your behalf', Bevin's Parliamentary Secretary told him. 'I think I could resist their charms.' He was duly made chair of the committee, which was given only limited power and used mainly to apply compulsion to women rather than to gain equal pay and conditions.[39]

Although he had long accepted the notion of equal pay for equal work, Bevin resisted during this period various attempts by different women's groups to make that principle a reality. Traditionally, women had never been paid the same as men because by definition their work was regarded as less skilled and therefore not worth as much. In addition, it was assumed that men had to earn enough to

ERNEST BEVIN

support a family, whereas women supposedly had only themselves to support or were contributing to the family wage. Government policy supported this sexual division of labour. The requirement that women teachers and civil servants should resign their positions when they married was removed for the war, for instance, but in the armed forces and civil defence women still received lower pay and benefits. They were also paid less than men for war-related injuries.

In spite of pressure for equal pay – from professional women, the TUC women's conferences, and some women workers – and despite some gains, the notion persisted that women 'were first and foremost the wives, mothers and dependants of men, and women did not therefore have the same rights of remuneration for or access to work as men'.[40] Women's wage rates remained on average three-fifths of men's. One of Bevin's labour inspectors reported in 1941, for example, that 'women workers had about as much say in agreements on their wages as Czecho-Slovakia had in the Munich agreement'. To this report, Bevin's Chief Industrial Commissioner, Frederick Leggett, responded that the Ministry should do nothing. 'For men their work is a life matter. For the average woman it is regarded as a temporary necessity.'[41]

On this issue, Bevin came down squarely in favour of the status quo because he feared male workers would protest any change. He refused the request of the WPC to set women's wages by statute. He advised the Lord President's Committee not to remove the sex differential in personal injuries because it might raise the issue of equal pay and then ' industrial peace might be endangered for the rest of the war'.[42] He bluntly told the 1943 National Conference of Women that, because of the promises made to restore prewar practices, there was no guarantee women would retain their jobs after the war. When 16,000 women workers struck in 1943 for equal pay, Bevin refused to intervene and urged their return to work. In 1944, when Parliament attempted to pass an amendment to the education bill granting equal pay for women teachers, Bevin encouraged opposition. 'Any sign of weakness on the part of the Government [on the issue of equal pay] would have the worst possible effect on industrial relations', he told the Cabinet.[43] Similarly, the government blocked the 1944 campaign for equal pay mounted by various women's professional organisations as well as by the TUC women's conference. In short, as Harold Smith writes,

116

MINISTER OF LABOUR

Bevin and the rest of the government 'remained committed to traditional patterns of sex discrimination' and stymied women's attempts to win equality on a permanent basis.[44]

Coal

By far the most intractable labour problem Bevin faced during the war was in the coal industry. Securing sufficient numbers of men to provide the necessary output of coal proved immensely difficult, while increasing output from those employed proved impossible; if it were not for the miners, industrial unrest during the war would have seemed almost negligible. Part of the problem was historical, caused by the age and inefficiency of much of the coal industry, the harsh way in which the coal miners had been treated in the interwar period and the bitterness and alienation which that treatment had produced. On the eve of the war, in 1938, 781,700 miners, working in 1976 mines, produced 226,993,200 tons of coal. But only 59 per cent of this was cut by machines and only 54 per cent was conveyed to the surface by machines. And the work remained dirty and dangerous. Only half the miners had access to pithead baths, while in 1938 alone, 858 were killed, 3157 injured severely and 137,776 injured and disabled for more than three days. Where miners had once been among the most highly paid of industrial workers, now workers in eighty other industries received higher wages. In consequence, younger men tended not to enter the pits; in 1941, 40 per cent of the miners were aged forty or over.

The other part of the problem was caused by government mistakes. Remembering the political consequences caused by state control of the coalfields in the previous war, the wartime governments originally imposed only limited controls over the industry. 'In the first two years of the War especially', writes one recent historian of the coal industry, 'the government went a long way with the owners.'[45] Younger miners were allowed at first to join the services or to move to better paid work elsewhere. After Hitler had conquered the continent of Europe, British coal exports disappeared, increasing unemployment and leading still more coal miners to leave. By March 1941, in spite of a June 1940 order prohibiting the employment of coalminers in other jobs, the workforce had declined to 693,000. Allowing miners to drift to other work was a

117

ERNEST BEVIN

'serious error', for which Bevin was in part responsible, although he later contended that it had been politically impossible to prevent the loss of skilled miners given the high rate of unemployment.[46]

By the spring of 1941 the crisis caused by the growing demand for coal and the decline of productivity drove the government toward increased controls over the industry and more measures to improve the miners' morale. These consisted of three different initiatives. First, the government moved to retain the existing workforce and attract more new men. In May 1941, Bevin applied the Essential Work Order to the coal industry, thus preventing any more men from leaving. Shortly thereafter, he appealed for former miners to return voluntarily and introduced a registration scheme. Miners aged 20–60 now had to register, and some in other industries, but not the services, were recalled. In September 1941, the Cabinet decided they needed 720,000 miners, requiring not only an additional 11,000 men but also replacement for the 'wastage' of 28,000 men per annum. The problem was that 'wastage' continued to exceed recruitment. In the next year, Bevin withdrew some miners from other war industries and the forces but this failed to produce sufficient results. In late 1943, therefore, he reluctantly agreed to introduce conscription, making draftees chosen by lottery liable to work in the mines. The Bevin Boy scheme, as it soon became known, was not only unpopular but also failed to realise the numbers desired.

Second, this failure to solve the problem of productivity by simply adding more men led the government in 1942 to consider reorganising the industry. Bevin and Hugh Dalton, now President of the Board of Trade, wanted to requisition it, ostensibly to increase morale among the miners by making them feel they were not just working to enrich their old class enemies, but privately because they were 'both . . . sure that, if the owners lost control of the pits now, they would never get it back'.[47] Dalton, with Bevin's support, also tried to introduce coal rationing but was defeated by the opposition of Tory backbenchers who saw the scheme as the beginnings of full state control of the industry.[48] Instead, the government settled on a system of joint control, in which it took over the daily operation of the mines but left ownership and financial control in the hands of the owners. A new Ministry of Fuel and Power was also created to oversee the entire question of energy. Further demands during the

MINISTER OF LABOUR

next year for increased state control or direct nationalisation were definitively ruled out by Churchill in October 1943.[49]

Third, the government tried to improve the condition and wages of the miners in the hope that this would cause them to work harder. Here Bevin and Dalton had more success. They secured the appointment of a new committee to consider miners' wages on a national basis, thus restoring the miners to the negotiating position that they had lost in 1921. In addition to a substantial increase, the committee gave the miners the national minimum that they had sought for years. Nevertheless, although they again became one of the best paid industrial groups – they won substantial additional gains in 1944 after a number of strikes – miners remained bitter and alienated. Absenteeism and industrial conflict remained high because the miners still felt that they had to acquire as much for themselves as possible while they had the chance in order to guard against the wage cuts and unemployment they expected after the war. How much ongoing bitterness, rooted in the cruel treatment they had received between the wars, was contributing to the continued decline in output, and how much it was due to a decline in numbers, the ageing of the workforce, the exhaustion of seams and the lack of mechanisation cannot be determined, but there can be little doubt that the legacy of the interwar period was now being felt. A team of American engineers and economists were appalled in mid-1944 by what they found. 'Industry-wide morale is low', they wrote. 'There is a definite lack of confidence by the individual miner in his own leader, the coal owner and the Government. There is a mutual distrust between labour and management.'[50]

Wages and industrial relations

When the Joint Consultative Committee met for the first time on 28 May 1940, Bevin asked them to provide him with suggestions to remove the problem of wages from 'the field of controversy'. They replied on 12 June recommending that existing collective bargaining machinery be continued, but referring unsettled issues to binding arbitration; strikes and lockouts would be prohibited.[51] Bevin concurred and embodied their recommendations in The Conditions of Employment and National Arbitration Order, known as Order Number 1305, which also provided procedures to enforce recog-

119

ERNEST BEVIN

nised terms and conditions arrived at by a 'substantial proportion' of employers and workers to all firms in a district.

During the next year Bevin came under repeated pressure, especially from Conservatives in Parliament, to replace this system of restricted collective bargaining with full state control of wages. But he successfully repelled all such attempts to change the government's wage policy, in the process serving as a schoolmaster to the government on how to avoid working-class discontent. How could they 'fix maximum wages while one citizen works for another's profit?' he asked when the issue was raised in the Lord President's Committee. If wages were to be frozen, 'then the employer must go with it, and a socialised system be the inevitable result. . . . My colleagues must face it.'[52] Although the committee accepted the 'cogency' of Bevin's argument, a month later the Chancellor of the Exchequer, Kingsley Wood, again raised the issue, arguing that it was 'illogical . . . to continue to treat the determination of wages as a private affair for employers and the employed'. The existing system, he told the Lord President's Committee, did not provide 'sufficient protection for the interests of the State'. In response, Bevin spelled out why he insisted on maintaining collective bargaining:

> Any such suggestion about wages would . . . be met by a demand for further control over salaries, profits and overheads and for stricter measures to prevent evasion of the Excess Profits Tax. If the Government raised the wages issue, they would be faced with the pressure for comprehensive regulation of industry as a whole. There was, in his view, no room for half measures; and he invited the Committee to recognise the dangers of State intervention in wages-disputes. If the position of the employer were weakened in wage-negotiations, it would be weakened correspondingly in other industrial negotiations, and the State would become involved in all the countless negotiations on matters other than wages which were now being handled satisfactorily by the ordinary machinery of industrial negotiations.[53]

In short, the state would be stronger if wages were left to collective bargaining. Otherwise, wage questions would lead to 'political competition. . . . Disputes under such circumstances would bring industry into direct conflict with the State and a settlement would be impossible as the State cannot afford to give way.'[54] Although some of Bevin's arguments may have been rhetorical, his victory on

120

MINISTER OF LABOUR

this policy issue demonstrates both his own power and the extent to which the government feared working-class unrest.

As an alternative to state control of wages, Bevin supported a fully-fledged corporatism in which the state's goals were fulfilled by trade union leaders and employers, an arrangement that co-opted both these groups while it deflected criticism of the state. As Bevin explained in September 1942 to the Lord President's Committee:

> So long as the collective bargaining machinery, supplemented by compulsory arbitration, were retained, the Trades Unions and the employers were in the position of, so to speak, 'policing' the Government's policy. In the event of the regulation of wage rates by the Government, the Union officials would become advocates against the Government, who would have themselves to 'police' their policy. This would result in industrial unrest which might have most serious consequences.[55]

The co-operation and restraint of the trade unions over wage demands throughout the war validated what Bevin had long argued, that, given the chance, the trade unions would prove to be reliable allies of the state, not its enemies.

If Bevin's policy was designed to produce rising living standards for the working class, it also headed off political conflict that might undermine the war effort, which was always his first priority. Bevin himself consistently defended, both in public and in private, the high wages that workers could earn by working longer hours. 'If somebody gets 1,000, 2,000, or 3,000 [pounds]', he told Parliament, 'it is purely a conception, it is purely a tradition, but if a workman gets over 5 [pounds], somebody thinks the world is coming to an end. . . . It is time that this class distinction came to an end.'[56] Time and again, Bevin defended various wage demands in Cabinet, sometimes by blaming inadequate production on managerial incompetence. 'It must be borne in mind that when workers saw great extravagance in management', he told the Economic Policy Committee, 'they were unwilling to believe that additions to wage rates, which would not necessarily increase costs if labour were properly used, was seriously inflationary in its consequences.'[57] He made similar statements in public, much to the annoyance of many Tories. John Colville recorded in his diary in mid-1941, for example, that 'most Tories' were 'cross' with Bevin for 'condemning the private profit motive'.[58]

121

ERNEST BEVIN

In addition, Bevin did not hesitate to use his own power under the Emergency Regulations to insist that higher wages be awarded. When the Minister of Supply asked him to provide more labour for the drop forging industry, for example, Bevin refused. 'I am not going to compel men to take work of this [arduous and unpleasant] type', he replied, 'unless the wages are radically improved, and if they are I do not believe that any compulsion will be necessary.'[59] Bevin expected workers to work as hard as possible, but he repeatedly insisted that they were entitled to a fair reward for their efforts. One of his first acts as Minister of Labour was to insist, over the objections of Kingsley Wood and the Treasury, that wages for agricultural labourers be sharply increased before he 'would feel justified in stopping the drift from the country [by administrative order]'.[60] Frederick Leggett later said that at first Bevin's 'word was law' and that he had attempted to dictate large awards to various arbitration and wage-setting bodies. Bevin even forced the TGWU, now being run by Arthur Deakin, to reject a wage agreement that it had already accepted because he felt the award was not high enough![61]

By supporting continued bargaining over wages, Bevin and the Ministry of Labour aimed as well to reinforce the power of the official leadership of the trade unions who would otherwise have lost their major function. As Bevin explained to the Lord President's Committee, 'if Executives appeared to tie their hands in regard to wage claims they would open the way to unofficial movements led by representatives with less sense of responsibility and would tend to lose their authority. . . . The maintenance of production and industrial peace depend upon the authority of the unions in the day to day adjustment of wages and conditions.'[62] Hence Bevin opposed any shop steward or working-class action that failed to use proper union channels.

Supporting trade union executives was thus another aspect of Bevin's policy of relying on corporatist mechanisms as the main basis of the war effort. For this policy to function, however, trade unions had to be given fuller recognition by both the state and the employers than they had ever had. Bevin made this clear as soon as he took office. 'Whatever your predilections may have been about Union and non-Union,' he told the employers on the NJAC, 'the only method of discipline I can exercise is through my friends on my

122

right and I want every encouragement given to your people, in the interests of the State, to become members of their Unions, in order that I may have as good a disciplined force operating in the manner I have indicated, because it is to them I have to look for that side of it.'[63] Although many employers continued to oppose any extension of trade union organisation and power, the combination of full employment and government support provided the best opportunity for the expansion of trade unionism since the First World War.

Bevin's strategy to advance the position of the trade unions was an essentially moderate one. In general, he relied on the increased bargaining power created by wartime regulations to expand trade union organisation. By mandating the observance of recognised terms and conditions, these regulations undercut the economic incentive that firms might otherwise have to avoid trade union recognition. The cost-plus system for government contracts had the same effect. Moreover, the Essential Work Order made it much more difficult for a firm to sack workers, or even to fine them without good cause. Trade union activists therefore gained a new freedom to organise. As Arthur Exell, a shop steward at Morris Motors, observed, the Essential Work Order made them 'feel more secure in making [their] demands'.[64] Although there were 'wide variations according to local initiatives and managerial responses', by the end of the war, the trade unions had added two and a half million new members, an increase of about one-third.[65]

In some instances, Bevin used his position to pressure firms into recognising trade unions. In August 1941, for example, when three government suppliers refused trade union recognition after a court of inquiry had recommended it, he warned the Lord President's Committee that there would be 'serious danger to the maintenance of industrial peace and of satisfactory industrial relations if matters are left as they are now'. He thought it 'indefensible' that the government should not 'enforce compliance'. 'It was the policy of the Government', he said, 'to enlist the full co-operation of the trade unions in the war effort and it followed that the Government should give their whole-hearted support to the principle of negotiation and discussion between employers and trade unions.' The committee agreed that the relevant supply department should ensure that the recommendation was carried out, by compulsion if necessary.[66] This was by no means an isolated example.[67] Nevertheless,

ERNEST BEVIN

Bevin drew the line at a formal policy compelling trade union recognition, refusing the TUC's request for more direct help as ineffective and too controversial politically.[68] He also refused to accord the TUC more than equal representation with the employers' federations, much to the annoyance of Sir Walter Citrine. Still, while some of the TUC's gains would be lost after the war, with Bevin's help the trade unions thrived, gaining an access to power they had never previously had. The vast increase in the size and power of the TUC profoundly changed the institutional shape of British society in the second half of the twentieth century.

Joint production committees

That Bevin himself and the policies he followed after May 1940 gained the support of most official trade union leaders and overcame their suspicion of the government can hardly be doubted. But how far he succeeded in securing the support of the working class for increased output is more difficult to determine. Except during the Battle of Britain in the summer of 1940, the official history of the munitions industries concludes, workers 'tended to lose interest' in making an 'all out effort'.[69] Twenty years of unemployment and government callousness proved to be a weak foundation on which to build working-class enthusiasm for the war. The situation changed dramatically after the Nazi invasion of the Soviet Union evoked immense pro-Soviet sentiment among the working class, causing 'output . . . [to] improve suddenly', as William Beveridge observed.[70] Communist activists, who maintained a strong influence on the shop floor in a number of key industries, also encouraged more production after the Soviet Union's entry into the war. Their strengthened commitment to the war effort helps to account for Bevin's success in harnessing the growing unofficial shop stewards' movement which had re-emerged in the mid-1930s in the engineering and aircraft industries.

As the trade unions became increasingly involved in overseeing the government's industrial policies, restraining wage demands and encouraging harder work, shop floor organisation expanded rapidly.[71] Bevin supported this development as a way of 'avoiding discontent', as he said in Parliament. 'There should be established in all industrial establishments standing joint arrangements for regular

124

MINISTER OF LABOUR

discussion between management and properly elected representatives of the workpeople of matters in which they are mutually interested.'[72] In the spring of 1941, the Engineering and Allied Trades Shop Stewards National Council took up Bevin's suggestion and began a highly effective campaign for the establishment of joint production committees, climaxing with a large conference in London in October that received extensive publicity. Communists, who had denounced Bevin's December 1940 suggestion as a quasi-fascist 'Labour Front', now strongly supported it.[73]

In spite of an easily discernible Communist influence, Bevin supported this movement, although with a different interpretation of its meaning than Communist shop stewards placed on it. For them, joint production committees might be used to curtail managerial prerogatives, whereas Bevin saw them as a way to further the corporatist compact that remained his central reformist goal. Commenting on an initiative from Imperial Chemicals' chairman, Lord McGowan, who had written to Churchill that production committees could head off radical influence, Bevin wrote:

> We cannot shut our eyes to the fact that intelligent workers do become cognizant of management blunders – blunders which inevitably have increased in number as the result of the expansion of industry and the dearth of people who really understand the art of management. This fact makes it all the more essential to convince managements of the wisdom of relying less on conventional 'authority' and more on the willingness of the workers, which in the great majority of cases will be readily shown once they realise that they are in the confidence of the management. . . . I am very anxious to secure your support and that of my colleagues to a campaign for the establishment of what might be called a 'round table' in every factory. . . . What we need to do is to inculcate the right attitude of mind, which I think is implicit in the phrase 'round table.' Present methods tend to emphasise the two 'sides' of industry and therefore the apparently conflicting interests, whereas if we could get the 'round table' idea accepted, we should get more emphasis on the community of interest between people engaged together in a common task.[74]

A few months later, he told a conference of Regional Industrial Relations Officers that he looked forward to a 'new kind of industrial democracy' after the war where the 'gap between management and operatives' had been broken down and workers

125

ERNEST BEVIN

felt joining management was not 'being disloyal' to their tradition. Saying he wanted to 'marry' the shop stewards' movement and welfare, he told them to look at workshop organisation in an 'unbiassed manner'.[75]

At first, both sides of the engineering industry resisted the creation of joint production committees, but they changed their minds when the movement developed its own momentum. In January 1942, the Engineering Union told the Joint Consultative Committee (JCC) that the unofficial shop stewards movement was in danger of being controlled by the Communist Party. As a result, 'it was agreed on all sides, that it was necessary to establish some form of official machinery under the joint control of the employers and the Trade Unions, so as to prevent the growth of Unofficial Movements', and that Bevin should be asked to establish such committees. The TUC also weighed in to tell Bevin that there should be compulsory production committees elected from workers 'approved prior to the election by the unions'.[76] While refusing to make such committees compulsory, Bevin recommended their creation to the Cabinet as a way of increasing production. 'These committees should be so constituted and adminstered as not to prejudice either (a) the authority and responsiblity of the Trade Unions with regard to the regulation of wages and conditions of service and other matters dealt with by agreement between them and the employers, or (b) the rights of management of the employer.'[77] In March, the engineering industry agreed to the establishment of joint production committees; by 1944 over 4500 of them had been created nationwide.

In general, the committees operated the way Bevin wanted, mainly because the Communist Party remained committed to furthering production and working within established trade union structures, as opposed to expanding the class struggle. 'Most JPCs functioned as an extension/complement to existing negotiating machinery', their most recent historian concludes. 'They were not a qualitatively new leap into new terrain.'[78] Nevertheless, in some factories they helped to establish trade unionism in the face of bitter opposition and everywhere their very existence represented a lessening of managerial authority.

126

MINISTER OF LABOUR

Defence Regulation 1AA

Bevin's support for joint production committees indicates his basic desire to rely on the voluntary co-operation of the working class with the war effort. The official policy of the Ministry of Labour was to prosecute only 'subversive activity' and those strikes with 'malicious intent', on the grounds that 'a large number of workpeople cannot be sent to prison', as Frederick Leggett put it.[79] In general, this policy worked. Industrial unrest did not seriously disrupt the war effort or pose a political threat. Government subsidies lowering food prices, combined with the rise of wages and substantial overtime earnings meant that working-class living standards kept ahead of inflation. Although there were numerous strikes, they tended to be small and brief, mainly over piece rates.

In late 1943 and early 1944, however, Bevin's reliance on voluntary co-operation broke down. Between 24 January and 11 April 1944, almost two million days were lost in mining alone, while the engineering apprentices' refusal in March 1944 to accept direction to the mines threatened the government's entire labour policy. Arguing that this unrest was caused by a 'few individuals . . . who seize upon grievances to foment industrial unrest', Bevin asked for new powers to 'prosecute persons who declare, instigate or incite others to take part in a strike or lock-out which is calculated to impede the war effort. . . . '[80] The outcome was Defence Regulation 1AA, issued in late April 1944, which permitted the prosecution of anyone illegally inciting or furthering a strike; offenders could be sentenced to five years' penal servitude. The only exception was for 'anything [done] at a duly convened meeting of trade unions'.

This harsh new regulation was never actually used, possibly because the labour movement's objection to it was so strong. In the course of a blistering attack on 1AA in Parliament, Aneurin Bevan said it 'protected the trade union official who has arterio-sclerosis and cannot readjust himself to his membership'. It was 'the enfranchisement of the corporate society and the disenfranchisement of the individual. It gives status to the organised body and destroys the status of the individual citizens.'[81] Most of the Parliamentary Labour Party clearly sympathised with Bevan's criticism, since only fifty-six of them voted for the legislation, while 109 abstained.

127

ERNEST BEVIN

In responding, Bevin feebly reiterated his charge that the recent strikes had been caused by revolutionary agitators. In fact, he knew better. The secret service had told him that the strikes were 'essentially industrial and not political', while in the Lord President's Committee, Herbert Morrison, now Home Secretary, pointed out that 'there [was] little or no evidence . . . to show that their [the Trotskyist Revolutionary Communist Party's] activities have resulted in the starting of a strike or contributed to any material extent in prolonging a strike'.[82] Perhaps Bevin's belief in a conspiracy to cause industrial unrest was an 'obsession', as the official history of wartime labour policy explains it.[83] But there is another possible interpretation. Bevin must have known that the strikes were based on genuine discontents. Most of the strikers, after all, were miners whose continuing grievances he well understood. More likely, then, he saw the strikes as a real threat to the government's labour policy on the eve of the invasion of Europe. The aim of 1AA, as one Ministry official noted, was to 'strengthen the hands of Trade Unions in dealing with irresponsible elements'.[84] As Richard Croucher has put it, Bevin 'chose to promulgate a new regulation because it was apparent that what was needed was a political announcement of the government's intention to come down hard on industrial militancy in general'. Counting on the loyalty of the shop stewards, many of whom were Communists, Bevin 'astutely exposed the limitations of the militancy which had arisen'. And, in fact, the regulations were successful in 'isolating potential strike leaders' and stabilising industrial relations until the end of the war.[85]

Welfare

In accepting Churchill's offer of office in 1940, Bevin had told him that he would serve as Minister of Labour only if it were understood that the Ministry would not 'accept the status quo in the matter of the social services for which it is responsible'.[86] One of the first things he did after arriving at the Ministry of Labour was to bring the Factories Acts under his jurisdiction rather than that of the Home Office. He intended, he told the Labour Supply Board on 30 May, 'to add largely to the present arrangements both at Headquarters and throughout the country for training and general welfare'.[87]

128

MINISTER OF LABOUR

The next month he established a separate Factory and Welfare Department inside the Ministry of Labour. He also appointed a Factory and Welfare Board – composed of representatives from trade unions, employers, voluntary organisations, health services and the ministry's own staff – to 'advise him on welfare questions and to assist him in developing and stimulating health, safety and welfare arrangements inside the factory, and lodging, feeding and welfare arrangements outside the factory'. Acting on the Board's advice, Bevin also created a Central Consultative Council of Voluntary Organisations to help to provide more amenities for workers and facilities for those who had been directed to new work.

By creating this new machinery, Bevin aimed to fulfil his goal of making working-class welfare one of the central aims of his ministry. He told the Factory and Welfare Board at their first meeting that 'attention to the human problems of employment in industry had lagged behind attention to production problems but should be ahead of it, and he attached great importance to speedy action'. He then went on to list a variety of topics they should consider: the best use of works' doctors, the optimum diet for workers, the use of 'sun-ray treatment' in winter, training welfare supervisors, better lighting, ventilation and other conditions of work, communal feeding, day nurseries and recreational facilities. 'The welfare of labour [should] not be regarded as something separate from labour supply.'[88] With varying degrees of success, he attended to all of these concerns over the next three years. The Factories (Medical and Welfare Services) Order of July 1940, for example, empowered factory inspectors to direct employers of large firms to appoint doctors as well as officers responsible for welfare, while the Canteens Orders of 1940 and 1943 made provision of canteens obligatory. 'Production must be kept up and the workers must be protected as far as possible against the strains they are undergoing', he insisted.[89] One of Bevin's most appealing sides is evident here – his insistence that workers were entitled to the best conditions that could be provided, as well as to their own pleasures. In urging the shipowners to provide canteen facilities, to take one example, he told them:

> If you can let them have a wet canteen it is a great advantage. In many of the places I went to I saw conditions like this: in Liverpool I found the public houses were closed at 9 o'clock, after the 'Blitz,' and the

129

ERNEST BEVIN

result was that men were knocking off just before 9 o'clock. I have them open now until 10. It is no use ignoring these things. The Liverpool 'Coalie', when he has a throat with some dust on it wants a drink, and what is the good of pretending he does not . . . I do not mind whether they have a pint of beer, or what they do, as long as they get on with the work.[90]

As with so much else that he did in the war, many of Bevin's actions were taken with an eye to their becoming permanent and helping to reshape postwar industrial relations. In this regard, Bevin proposed that the entire Factory and Welfare Department of the Ministry be permanently expanded to include an enlarged role for factory inspectors, the 'development of the Medical Inspectorate, Personnel Management, special juvenile problems', and other issues.[91] He told Herbert Morrison, with whom he clashed frequently in Cabinet, that he wanted to 'widen' the duties of the factory inspectorate, which was important not just to workers' welfare and safety but was 'one of the biggest factors at our disposal to assist in the establishment of proper industrial relations'. His goal was not just to enforce the law but to promote 'good, healthy industrial conditions. . . . I have been planning, therefore, the creation of what is virtually an Industrial Health Inspection and Protection Department of which the main pivot will be the Factory Inspectorate.' He asked Morrison to agree to its permanent transfer to the Ministry of Labour.[92]

When Morrison resisted, the issue came before the Machinery of Government Committee, which had been created to consider possible changes in postwar arrangements.[93] 'Measures for safeguarding industrial safety, health and welfare should be regarded as an integral part of the employment policy of the Government and their administration should be associated as closely as possible with the administration of other parts of this policy', Bevin wrote in a successful defence of his plan.[94] Clearly, Bevin saw this change as part of his broader vision of a future industrial order in which workers would be treated fairly under a system of rational direction and co-operation, thus lessening the need for recourse to class conflict by both employers and workers, as the basis of the nation's industry.

130

MINISTER OF LABOUR

Dockers

Bevin had begun his trade union career as an organiser for the Dockers' Union and had made a national reputation for himself with his defence of the dockers' wage claims before the Shaw Committee. Central to all his efforts on behalf of the dockers had been his struggle to secure decasualisation of the docks, by limiting jobs to men signed up as regular dock workers, as a way of reversing the balance of power between the dockers (and their trade union) and the employers and securing higher wages. Thwarted by the port owners, Bevin now took advantage of the war emergency to achieve his most long-standing goal as a trade union leader.

Dock work was vital to the war effort. Shipping had to be loaded and unloaded as rapidly as possible, but this proved even more difficult than usual. Younger men had been drained off by the services or other industries, while bombing disrupted the ports. London was virtually closed until 1943, increasing the burden on other ports. Worse, shipping was irregular. For periods, work in the port could be quite light; then a number of ships might arrive, straining existing facilities. The history of dock work's formation also complicated the situation.

Dock work has often been regarded as the quintessential example of casual labour. The work force on the docks always exceeded the number of available jobs, since the unemployed resorted to dock work in hard times, swelling the already substantial core of regular dock workers. The work itself was irregular, depending on the traffic in the port. When the port was busy, dock workers could earn sufficient wages to support themselves. But work came only in spurts; except for very busy periods, large numbers of men remained idle. The situation was tailor-made for employers, who used the permanent labour surplus to keep wages low, forcing men to compete ruthlessly for available jobs. Because of the casual nature of their work, dockers developed only weak loyalties to their employers, whose power over them always remained visible and direct. Many of them also grew to like the casual nature of their work and their 'freedom' to work extensively or not as opportunity and need permitted.[95]

Shortly after he assumed office, Bevin became involved in various attempts to cope with the disruption in the ports. Consulted in

131

ERNEST BEVIN

August about the appointment of a commission to consider problems on the Clyde he said that he 'was firmly convinced that the employers wanted shaking up as much as the workers and that he could not attempt to coerce the Unions unless at the same time he was taking drastic action with the employers'.[96] Shortly thereafter, the government created a Ministerial Sub-Committee on Port Clearance, which Bevin soon convinced of the need for drastic reorganisation of the ports, at the centre of which was to be decasualisation. 'If it was suggested that we should not try to decasualise dock labour in the middle of a war', he told them, his 'reply was that desperate needs called for desperate remedies.'[97]

Bevin's plan, which centralised authority in the Ministry of Transport acting through regional port directors, was to be applied first to Liverpool and Glasgow and then, with changes, to other regions. It provided for the compulsory registration of all dockers who would now be required to present themselves for work twice a day, eleven times per week. In return they would be guaranteed a minimum payment, whether work was available or not. When work was available they would be paid by results, with extra payment for overtime and Sundays, and would respond to this financial incentive, it was hoped, with more work. Discipline would be enforced by a committee of management and labour, supplemented by labour officers from the Ministry. All work in the port would be controlled by a single authority, while the dockers, accustomed to working for specific employers or specialising in specific jobs, would now be required to accept any work in the port. 'This is a common sense method of dealing with a difficult situation: it substitutes organisation for chaos', Bevin argued. 'While it gives something to the men it is asking much of them. They must work as, when and where they are required under the rigorous conditions of modern warfare. In return they will be given some measure of security, the opportunity of adequate payment for increased output and, it is hoped, adequate gear.'[98] The committee approved his proposal and Bevin then issued the Dock Labour (Compulsory Registration) Order, creating a National Dock Labour Corporation with equal representation from the employers and the trade unions to supervise the dockers, and putting the rest of his plan into effect.

The dock scheme, as it was called, indicates both the strengths and limitations of Bevin's reformism. On the one hand, it ended the

132

casual system that all observers agreed was the source of the dockers' low wages and that pitted one docker against the other for the limited number of jobs. It improved dockers' living standards, gave them job security and increased the power of their union, the TGWU. It allowed for a more careful allocation of dock labour, the extent of which could now be calculated and directed more efficiently to meet various port needs. It was also a classic example of corporatism, joining the trade unions, the port owners and the state in running the docks. On the other hand, it left ownership of the docks in private hands. It exchanged security and income for greater work discipline and the loss of the 'freedom' many men cherished, as Bevin indicated at the time. 'The men (and what is perhaps equally important their wives and families) will realise that if they behave themselves and pull their weight they will be sure of permanent jobs and regular wages and that the penalty for unsatisfactory work or conduct (including absenteeism) will be dismissal from the regular labour force.'[99] The result was that the scheme, which did so much for the dockers, also increased their resentments and failed to allay their long-standing class hostility. In succeeding years, the dockers went from among the worst paid of industrial workers to among the best, but they also became among the most strike-prone.

Caterers

Bevin intended many of the reforms that he introduced during the war to serve as the basis of a new postwar industrial order and to prevent any repetition of the unemployment and wage cutting that had followed the previous war. He thought the form of organisation embodied in the dock scheme would be 'capable of being extended in post-war years to a large number of other industries without destroying initiative or enterprise'.[100] The same was true of his creation of the Catering Wages Board in 1943. As early as November 1940, in fact, Bevin had expressed concern to his staff about the large number of catering firms being established because of the war in which wages were 'entirely unsatisfactory'. But it was another eighteen months before he acted. In May 1942, he broached the issue to the Lord President's Committee as an extension of his basic policy of establishing joint machinery for the regulation of wages. Telling the committee that thirty-six joint industrial councils had already been established since he took office, he argued that the catering trades, with almost half a million employees, needed a broader and more 'flexible' approach than a trade board could provide.[101]

A few weeks later he met with various employers' organisations – the National Federation of Fish Fryers, the Milk Bars Association, the Association of Purveyors of Light Refreshment, etc. – who expressed total opposition to the proposed changes.[102] Conservatives in Parliament denounced the attempt to introduce 'controversial' legislation unrelated to the war effort as a violation of the party truce and the tacit agreement between the parties about the limit of wartime reforms; eventually over a hundred of them voted against the government. Nevertheless, Bevin pushed ahead. Asked by the Chairman of the Brewers' Society what he should tell the licensed Victuallers and Brewers' Members who opposed the bill, Bevin replied, 'To go to hell.'[103]

In fact, the Catering Wages Act was typical of the sort of 'revolutionary conservatism' that, as we have seen, Bevin viewed as the hallmark of his reforming efforts. It created a Catering Wages Board, consisting of representatives of the state, industry and labour, and empowered to set minimum wages in trades without organised representation and, more significantly, to enforce agreed-upon standards in trades where such representation already existed. The Board could also intervene in some circumstances in the organisation of the industry and provide for paid vacations. It neither touched the ownership of the industry, nor created provisions for workplace democracy. In fact, Bevin justified the reform to Parliament as a continuation of past policy, not a socialist measure. But the act curbed owners' prerogatives to do as they pleased and recognised that workers had a right to some say in the way the industry was run. 'I take the view . . . that those persons who invest their lives and careers in the industry are putting capital into it just as much as the employer who invests his money', Bevin told Parliament.[104]

Bevin wanted the Catering Wages Board to serve as a model for future joint industrial councils that could preserve industrial stability during the turmoil that he expected to develop after the war. 'I am one of those who do not separate pre-war, war and post-war. . . .

One is an intensification of another; what you do in one has a great effect on the other', he told Parliament. After the previous war, joint industrial councils had collapsed, he contended, 'not through the good employer breaking away, but through the bad employer undermining and undercutting the whole edifice'. The Catering Wages Board would 'protect the good employer. . . . against the man who wants to cut him out by unfair competition'.[105] Certainly, as we have seen, Bevin had long sought to forge a partnership with progressive capitalists, but such rhetoric also served to justify his imposition of as much change as he could either by administrative order or by legislation.

Reconstruction

During the course of the war much of the British public moved in differing ways to the left politically and came to demand that the 'people's war', as it was increasingly called at the time, should produce a people's peace. Perhaps more than any other Labour member of the Coalition, Bevin contributed to this shift in opinion. Unlike other Ministers, who broadcast after the 9 o'clock news on Sunday, Bevin chose to broadcast after the 1 o'clock news, when he could speak to 'his' people, 'sitting down nice and comfortable to their Sunday dinner'. He gave hundreds of speeches that in various ways called for a 'new economic order'. As he said in 1940, 'We will never tolerate again the masses of unemployed or [the] poverty that has hitherto existed.'[106] He repeatedly criticised the shortcomings of an unregulated capitalism and called for a society in which 'social security' would be the 'main motive of all our national life', a society in which 'citizenship and security are synonymous terms'.[107] Even when Churchill sent him a 'very friendly hint' not to make speeches critical of private enterprise, Bevin refused to desist, arguing that 'real Conservatives would agree with him. . . . There is no hope of carrying the British people with us for a long war if they have to return to unemployment at the end.'[108]

Often, he contended that the war had made a new order inevitable because 'social action' had replaced 'individualism' and 'competition'.[109] But at the same time, Bevin, like most other Labour leaders, expected the Conservatives to be returned to power after the war. More practically, therefore, he worked to put in place

ERNEST BEVIN

as many reforms as his Tory partners in the Coalition would tolerate. 'There is nothing I am doing without I am keeping an eye on its possible value when this war is over', he said.[110] This meant above all putting in place legislative and administrative reforms that would prevent a recurrence of the depression, unemployment and conflict of the post-1918 period. As we have seen, many of the actions he took for the sake of the war – having administration of the Factories Acts moved to his ministry, expanding the number of joint industrial councils, reorganising dock and catering work, expanding welfare facilities in factories, supporting joint production committees – were also taken with an eye to their continuation in the postwar period. 'Can I now, out of the experience of the war', he asked his staff in October 1942, 'produce a new industrial code of conduct, inspection, enforcement, and welfare?'[111] Both at the Ministry of Labour and through his membership of the Cabinet's Reconstruction Committees, Bevin worked assiduously to create this new industrial order.

His efforts in this regard were remarkably varied, and had both a visionary and a practical side. He argued, for example, for national housing and national hire-purchase corporations that could create 'garden cities' for everyone by providing inexpensive mortgages and credit to finance household goods.[112] He 'consistently favoured the collective management of domestic work both as a temporary method of coping with wartime exigencies and as a model for permanent change in the future'.[113] He told Parliament that there should be a 'service under which a woman, whether in Poplar or in the West End, who wants domestic help can get it'.[114] And he defended the Catering Wages Bill in part on the grounds that 'communal feeding will be one of the great services for the people of this country in the future'.

But at the heart of Bevin's efforts for the future were his plans for a new industrial order. On one level, these were profoundly unrealisitic, envisioning a world without class conflict in which fully unionised workers co-operated with enlightened owners to manage the economy rationally, a world in which labour worked not out of 'force of hunger' but 'as an obligation to the State', while the State in turn accepted 'an obligation to them'.[115] No longer divided over basic economic issues, Parliament would become a 'great national housekeeper'.[116] 'May not this war . . . produce not only a

136

MINISTER OF LABOUR

comradeship in the trenches, but a great comradeship in the field, the factory and the workshop?' he asked.[117] This was a dream, as Angus Calder has rightly pointed out, 'mocked by the central facts of [the] capitalist economy. Industry remained the property of private owners, who would not share any real power with their wage- earners; and . . . "progressive" managers . . . were [mainly] concerned to "lead", and to manipulate, the workers beneath them.'[118] Most Tories in Parliament, too, were hardly ready to join this new world, while most workers continued to maintain a hostile view of owners and had no intention of renouncing restrictive practices.

Nevertheless, Bevin's plans for a new industrial order were also deeply practical, intending to ensure that workers would never be treated as they had been before the war and that their living standards would improve. For the organised labour movement, Bevin wanted to maintain major elements of the industrial relations system that he had put in place during the war. He told the Lord President's Committee that compulsory arbitration was a 'possible post-war machine' that would allow them to avoid repeating the situation that had followed the last war when the trade unions sought higher wages and the Treasury deflation.[119] 'If I do nothing else in this House', he told Parliament, 'I hope I shall create such confidence in arbitration that, during the transitional period follow-ing the war . . . it will allow this resettlement to be carried out in an orderly and stable manner.'[120] In the event, compulsory arbitra-tion was maintained for another five years, while the TUC retained its place in policymaking circles until Margaret Thatcher's counter-revolution of the 1980s.

Although Bevin was confident that the trade unions would be in a new position of strength, he feared that the entire 'wages structure' of the unorganised trades might 'collapse . . . after the war', as he told the JCC in 1944. 'When controls were removed all the work of the last five years might disappear.'[121] To prevent this development, Bevin sought to extend the principle embodied in the Catering Wages Act by creating what came to be called wages councils. He proposed this reform to the Lord President's Commit-tee in late 1943, and then to the JCC, telling them he wanted 'to safeguard good employers against bad employers who depressed standards of wages and conditions and prevented good employers

137

from progressing in improvements as quickly as they otherwise would because of undercutting'.[122] Although the employers strongly opposed his plans, Bevin insisted to the Reconstruction Committee that they should go ahead with legislation. It represented, he said, 'the minimum necessary for avoiding a period of serious wage instability and sectional strikes after the war. . . . Industrial progress and contentment depended largely on allowing the best employers to take the lead, and it was important that their efforts to improve conditions should not be impeded by small recalcitrant groups.' The government had an obligation to 'prevent the collapse of the wages structure through lack of effective regulation and through unfair competition between employers'. Although they expressed some hesitations, in the end the committee authorised Bevin to proceed.[123]

The Wages Councils Act of 1945 expanded the power of existing trade boards that were now to be called wages councils. It gave government the power to establish new ones as well as to enforce existing voluntary agreements on all parts of a trade. The councils themselves would be able not only to set wages but also to advise about conditions, training and other aspects of the industry. By 1950 it covered over four million workers, mainly in the retail trades. Bevin told Parliament it would prevent 'quick, unmeasured and violent changes in the wage system', and act as a 'great brake . . . [to] force economic considerations upon those who handle finance and industry at that very critical moment [at the end of the war]'.[124] There were to be no repetitions of the events that followed the last war.

Thus, like many others, Bevin expected there would be a difficult transition period after the war, with widespread unemployment. For those workers who might lose their jobs, Bevin campaigned for adequate unemployment benefits and for a system whose first priority was 'to avoid [demoralisation]'. 'The social security service should be not merely eleemosynary but diagnostic and remedial', he argued.[125] To this end, he worked successfully to expand training facilities to prevent workers being stuck in economically decaying areas. 'The aim should be to make use of the knowledge which the Government will have of the future trend of industry to make workers fit and available for the new or expanded industries which we expected to come into being.'[126] As the Minister primarily

MINISTER OF LABOUR

responsible for most of the government's demobilisation plans, Bevin made sure these included retraining and resettlement schemes and grants for continuing education, as well as guarantees of civilian employment.[127] Similarly, because he saw training as part of a more broad-based plan to expand education for all to age sixteen, Bevin provided strong support for R. A. Butler, who oversaw the passage of the Education Act of 1944.

Until late 1942, neither the public nor Parliament paid much attention to Bevin's or the Labour Party's concerns for the postwar world. As long as the outcome of the war remained in doubt, public debate focused almost entirely on the way the war was being run. However, as the tide of battle turned in 1942–3 – with the entry of the United States into the war, the Soviet victory at Stalingrad and the British victory at El Alamein – public and parliamentary attention shifted strongly toward the shape of the postwar world. The issue was brought sharply into focus by the publication in December 1942 of the Beveridge Report, which proposed a comprehensive system of social security premised upon full employment, family allowances and universal health care. This dry report became an immediate best seller, indicating the degree to which most people in Britain had determined not to be cheated after this war as they had been after the previous one.

In spite of the public response, Churchill and most of the Conservative Party remained reluctant to endorse Beveridge's proposals. There was a feeling inside the party, R. A. Butler observed, 'that Beveridge is a sinister old man, who wants to give away a great deal of other people's money'.[128] Fearing they would lose an election if the Coalition broke up, Labour leaders in public loyally supported the decision not to endorse the Beveridge Report, much to the annoyance of most Labour backbenchers who demanded a firmer commitment to reform. Bevin lectured the Parliamentary Labour Party on the political dangers of their opposition and when that failed 'began to shout, protest, and threaten', according to Dalton.[129] When they nevertheless persisted in voting against the government, he withdrew from party affairs for over a year.

Bevin's tantrum indicates more than his ambiguous relationship to the Labour Party. In fact, he accepted the government's case for not implementing the Beveridge Report. After Viscount Simon, the Lord Chancellor, presented an extensive defence in the House of

139

ERNEST BEVIN

Lords of the government's refusal to be 'hustled', Bevin told him he 'whole-heartedly agree[d] with all that you said and express my admiration and appreciation of the way in which you put the Government's case'.[130] Nevertheless, although loyal to the Coalition's decision about Beveridge, privately, Bevin, along with Attlee and Morrison, pushed hard for a firmer Coalition commitment, as they put it, to the 'formulation of policy on those urgent questions of reconstruction on which work must be done before the end of the war'.[131] Given the continued strength of public opinion, Churchill and his Conservative colleagues had to relent and in November 1943 created a new Ministry of Reconstruction as domestic reform rose to the top of the political agenda.

Given his commitment to extensive plans for reconstruction, Bevin's lukewarm attitude to the Beveridge Report was curious. In part, he seems to have suspected that Beveridge intended to usurp trade union functions. Like most other trade unionists, he was a late convert to family allowances, for example, which he feared would undermine wages. Perhaps more important, the plan was really quite moderate, involving mainly a rationalisation and integration of existing services. Bevin found this inadequate. He told the Labour Party party that 'social security – a phrase first used by [me] – was something more than the Dole'. He would 'resist to the end the establishment of a Ministry merely to do that'. Beveridge, for example, did not mention the guaranteed weekly wage, which Bevin thought essential to social security.[132] Bevin also disliked Beveridge's notion of job training, which he found too reminiscent of the old workhouse test, whereas he insisted that any training scheme had to avoid the stigma associated with unemployment. 'It was essential to [my] conception that persons receiving such training should not regard themselves as unemployed.'[133] But much of Bevin's response seems to have been personal. He had disliked Beveridge for a long time and their interactions at the start of the war had only confirmed this hostility. Beveridge had been contemptuous of Bevin, who had responded by pushing him out of the Ministry of Labour to direct the famous enquiry on social insurance that, ironically, made his fame. Perhaps Bevin was simply jealous, as his remarks to the Labour Party about social security may indicate.

Because Beveridge had premised his plans on full employment, the question of employment policy now became central to debates

140

MINISTER OF LABOUR

about the future. Bevin, of course, had long accepted Keynesian ideas and the notion, as he put it, that 'there was a clear responsibility on Government to take whatever measures were required to provide employment . . .'.[134] Perhaps to overcome the traditional conservatism of the Treasury he wanted to convert the Ministry of Labour into a department in which 'man-power, handled through this Department, will be the key guide to the employment situation. In other words, it will be a Ministry of Employment, and not Unemployment.'[135] He had in mind the creation of much more extensive statistical information that could predict the employment situation, allowing the Ministry of Labour to press for countervailing government spending.

Bevin failed to make the Ministry of Labour into a Ministry of Employment, but did strongly support the famous White Paper of 1944 that for the first time committed the government to the 'maintenance of a high and stable level of employment', almost, if not quite, a fulfilment of his very first political demand that every person should have a right to a job. Although the White Paper was neither socialist nor even fully Keynesian, it still marked a 'revolution in official opinion', as Keynes himself said at the time.[136] Bevin hailed it in Parliament as a 'complete reversal of the policy of the years between the wars', one that provided a 'new set of rules in our economic life. . . . It is introducing, as against automatic control, conscious direction.' Significantly, Bevin also said that he hoped that 'craft prejudice' would be overcome now that the reason for its development, limited employment, had been overcome. 'I would like to see that old system in wages go. We want to relate wages to efficient production'.[137]

As part of his support for a full employment policy, Bevin also gave 'good backing' to Hugh Dalton in his struggle to pass legislation to control the location of industry.[138] For Bevin, the issue was a simple one, the 'whims or caprices or bad organisation of private industry' could not be allowed to destroy whole communities as they had between the wars at great social cost. Private enterprise was fine as long as it 'served [a] social purpose in accordance with the State requirements', but 'where private industry either does not, will not or cannot establish a balanced industry, then steps must be taken to do it'.[139] The Location of Industry Bill, for which Dalton was mainly responsible, did not go as far as Bevin

141

might have wanted, but it did give government extensive powers to create industry in specified Development Areas and to partially control the location of industry in other areas.

At various points during the war, Bevin, like other Labour members of the Coalition government, was criticised by the Labour Left for not pushing the cause of nationalisation hard enough. It is certainly true that Bevin loyally supported Churchill and accepted the limitations imposed by the Coalition for the sake of the war effort. It is also true that Bevin's vision of a future society was more that of a rationally managed capitalism than a social transformation of the sort that someone like Aneurin Bevan wanted. But as his views on the location of industry indicate, Bevin had no reverence for private property. He strongly supported nationalisation when industry was inefficient, but simply saw any attempt to achieve it during the war as illusory and politically disastrous. 'In my view the only real way to bring these big basic industries to serve the public is not to apologise for the State but to come right out for State ownership', he wrote Attlee in response to Morrison's proposal for a scheme of nationalisation, 'but this is not the time and this is not the Cabinet to take that course.'[140] It is also true that Bevin thought of nationalisation more in terms of efficiency than equity and had no objection to private industry as such. But he was strongly critical of the public corporation form of nationalisation that Labour had adopted. 'A country run by a series of London Transport Boards' would be, he thought, 'about intolerable. Boards like this would be unrepresentative, unresponsive and unlikely to pay much attention to public interest. . . .' In this case, Bevin's hatred of Herbert Morrison, the architect of the public corporation model, doubtless coloured his views.[141]

Bevin's accomplishments as Minister of Labour were impressive, a triumph for the corporatist views he had adopted two decades earlier. Bevin himself found his years at the Ministry deeply satisfying. He now devoted even more time to his work than he had as TGWU General Secretary. Outside of his work, his life continued unchanged. He lived quietly in a central London flat with his wife, Flo. Although somewhat more mellow, he could still be a difficult person. Hugh Dalton frequently noted Bevin's 'egotism, garrulity, and peasant suspicion'.[142] He told Chuter Ede, to take one example, that 'schoolmasters were a spoiled lot. They were the blue-eyed

MINISTER OF LABOUR

boys and girls of the family who had all the sacrifices made for them.'[143] He was also a poor Parliamentary performer. Nevertheless, these five years constitute a record of unprecedented accomplishment. His direction of the labour supply was in general successful. With his help the TUC gained a position of power and influence that it retained for the next thirty-five years. So did workers on the shop floor. Working-class living standards and conditions rose and the ground was laid for the postwar creation of the welfare state. He did not, nor did he even want to, create a New Jerusalem, but he did make many things better for 'his' people and help to expand the concept of citizenship to include the right to work, education, occupational training and security.

5 Foreign Secretary

The war in Europe ended on 7 May 1945. Shortly thereafter, the Coalition broke up and Churchill called a general election. He expected the Conservative Party to sweep to victory on the strength of his own popularity and the electorate's fears of Labour, whose 'abject worship of the state', he said, would force them to 'fall back on some form of Gestapo' to realise their 'totalitarian' goals.[1] This was a miscalculation. Public opinion had moved to the left during the war, to look favourably on the state and the social reforms it could bring. It was thus Bevin and the rest of the Labour Party who were able to respond effectively to people's hopes for security at home and peace abroad. 'Your vote', Bevin broadcast, 'will determine . . . whether or not this country will go back to unemployment, Means Tests, and all the things from which we suffered between the two wars, and whether abroad, we shall drift back to international chaos and war'.[2] Almost no one at the time, however, understood how much of a sea change in opinion had occurred. When Labour won a massive majority, securing 393 seats in Parliament to the Conservatives' 213, 'everyone was stunned with surprise', according to George Orwell. 'We never expected this to happen', Bevin said.[3] On 26 July 1945, Clement Attlee replaced Churchill as Prime Minister. The next day he appointed Ernest Bevin as Foreign Secretary.

Bevin had not expected to be appointed to the Foreign Office. He thought he would be going to the Treasury where he could oversee Labour's domestic programme, while Hugh Dalton, who actually became Chancellor of the Exchequer, had expected to be named Foreign Secretary. Early on the 27th Attlee had even told Dalton that he would 'almost certainly' be going to the Foreign Office. But in the course of the day Attlee changed his mind and decided to switch the appointments. In part, he came to fear that Bevin would clash too strongly with Herbert Morrison, the Lord President. 'If

FOREIGN SECRETARY

they were both on the home front they would quarrel all the time', he correctly pointed out. Attlee may have been influenced as well by Foreign Office officials who feared the upper-class Dalton would be too soft on the Russians, too friendly to Zionist aspirations, and not amenable to their advice. They preferred Bevin. 'I think we may do better with Bevin than with any other of the Labourites', the Permanent Under-Secretary, Sir Alexander Cadogan, noted in his diary. 'I think he's broadminded and sensible, honest and courageous. . . . He's the heavyweight of the Cabinet and will get his own way with them, so if he can be put on the right line, that may be all right.'[4] King George VI also 'begged' Attlee to 'think carefully' about appointing Dalton, whom he personally disliked. He suggested that Bevin, with whom he got on well, 'would be a better choice' for Foreign Secretary.[5] In the end, Bevin went to the Foreign Office.

Bevin approached his new job with bravado. 'You see, I've had a good deal of experience with foreigners', he told his private secretary, Nicholas Henderson, after his first session at Potsdam, 'before the last war I had to do a good deal of negotiation with ships' captains of all nationalities. These people, Stalin and Truman, are just the same as all Russians and Americans; and dealing with them over foreign affairs is just the same as trying to come to a settlement about unloading a ship. Oh yes, I can handle them.'[6] In fact, while no stranger to foreign affairs, Bevin was not as prepared to run the Foreign Office as he had been to run the Ministry of Labour. He had done some travelling – to the United States, Europe, Australia and New Zealand – and maintained extensive contacts with foreign trade unionists, having attended many of the congresses of the International Transportworkers' Federation since 1916, as well as conferences of the International Labour Organisation. His first inside view of foreign affairs, however, had come as a member of the wartime government, which schooled him in the traditional view of Britain's place in the world that he immediately displayed when he took office. To this Bevin had, typically, added one thing, a concern for 'the condition of the masses' worldwide.

Bevin's relative lack of experience may have made him more susceptible to the influence of his officials than Dalton would have been. Although Alan Bullock has insisted that Bevin 'played as decisive a part in shaping policy as any Foreign Minister in modern

145

times', Bevin, who was badly overweight and suffered the effects of smoking and at times of too much drink, was frequently ill during these years and unable to carry on.[7] In the winter of 1947, for example, he was so 'bad' that the BBC started planning his obituary. Such periods reinforced the influence of his civil servants, as did perhaps his dependence on them to write his position papers. Private secretaries came 'to pride themselves on their technique of ghost-writing' for him, Nicholas Henderson later noted.[8] Although Foreign Office officials, mainly conservative men from traditional elite circles, had expected a new Labour government to institute drastic changes, Bevin kept most of the top men on and vehemently defended this decision before the Labour Party. Hugh Dalton recorded that Bevin had 'become more devoted than any of his predecessors for a generation to the Career Diplomat and all the Old Boys in the F.O.'[9] The chief of these, Sir Orme Sargent, who succeeded Sir Alexander Cadogan in 1946 as Permanent Under-Secretary, was said at the time to represent 'the F.O. of say 1910 . . . He laughs at the United Nations as he did the League, and the Southern and Northern departments which with Reconstruction are the kernel of the F.O. take their lead from him.' As one historian has recently observed, men like Sargent would do more than just carry out Bevin's will. They shaped policy.[10]

If Foreign Office officials played an important role in shaping policy, it was above all because Bevin shared some of their key assumptions. Unlike Dalton, who later wrote about the Soviet Union that he 'would have tried very hard not to forget too soon our great war effort against Germany', Bevin brought to office a strong anti-Sovietism, sharpened by years of struggle with Communists inside the British and international trade union movements. Leo Amery had noted in his diary in February 1945 that Bevin was 'fed up with Winston over a good many things', including his softness towards the Soviet Union.[11] Bevin thought the Conservatives had thrown too many 'baubles to the Soviets', and at the Potsdam conference, to which he flew on 28 July (the first flight he had ever taken), his 'manner was so aggressive', American Secretary of State Byrnes later recorded, 'that both the President and I wondered how we would get along with this new Foreign Secretary'.[12]

Bevin's strong patriotism and belief in the British empire as 'the greatest collection of free nations' also matched the Foreign Office's view of the world and its determination to maintain Britain's world position. 'I'm not going to have Britain barged about', he told General Ismay as he arrived to take up his place at Potsdam. Pierson Dixon, his Principal Private Secretary, found 'wholly delightful' Bevin's 'assumption [at Potsdam] that, of the 3, we were still the biggest'.[13] Bevin's attitude to the empire led him to accept Foreign Office views of the national interest, as can be seen from the claim he made to the former Italian colonies in North Africa shortly after he took office:

> They flank our main line of Imperial communication by sea and air to India, Australia and New Zealand through the Mediterranean and the Red Sea and provide bases from which Egypt, the Sudan and Kenya would be attacked. We must therefore insure that they do not come under the control of any State which is potentially hostile or incapable of providing for the maintenance of orderly conditions and for their defence in peace and war. . . .

'These were words that could have been written just as well by Lord Curzon in 1919', one historian of the postwar British empire has observed. 'The reasoning was identical.'[14]

To a large extent, these attitudes demonstrate there was a continuity between Bevin's trade union work and his new job as Foreign Secretary. In both cases, he accepted the world as he found it and tried to win the best deal he could for his followers. His labourist philosophy was thus easily carried over to his new job. Now, instead of defending the interests of the transport workers or the British working class, he saw himself as the champion of the British nation. As he had since the 1930s, he rejected the idea that there could be a socialist foreign policy. Instead, he assumed that since Labour was now in power, it had to take a national and imperial view.[15]

The onset of the cold war

Bevin's time as Foreign Secretary was dominated by the development of the cold war – the collapse of the wartime alliance, the division of Europe into two armed camps and the beginning of a series of neo-colonial wars outside Europe – which created the world order that would last until the late 1980s. Britain's involvement in that struggle might be said to have originated in the wartime decision to maintain what the Foreign Office called Britain's 'world-wide mission' after hostilities ceased. Otherwise, the Foreign Office concluded, 'we would sink to the level of a second-class Power and thus, in the long run, be likely to suffer an agonizing collapse from which we should emerge as a European Soviet state, the penurious outpost of an American pluto-democracy, or a German *Gau*, as forces might dictate'. The Chiefs of Staff similarly took for granted that Britain had to retain its traditional imperial position. They assumed that Britain would play a 'leading part' in the Middle East, would secure 'stable and friendly regimes' in Indochina, Malaya and Thailand, and would be prepared to hold a line with the French and Dutch running from Indochina to Australia.[16] In short, there was a general consensus, which Bevin shared, that, as Churchill had said, 'we mean to hold our own'.[17] Four possible obstacles stood in the way of this goal.

The most important of these was Britain's economic weakness. Six years of war had cost the country a quarter of its prewar wealth. Britain had been forced to sell £1,100 million of overseas investments and incur over £3,000 million of new external debts, reducing its invisible income by half. Exports had shrunk to about one-third of their prewar total, while the merchant fleet that could carry them had been reduced by 30 per cent. Overall, Britain had lost about 40 per cent of its overseas markets, mainly to American competition.[18]

Even had its economic position been stronger, however, Britain would have had a difficult time holding its own after the war. Throughout the Third World, nationalist movements, sometimes Communist-led, had grown in strength, both in areas under direct or indirect British control and in territories controlled by other European powers whose continued colonial position now seemed necessary to the stability of the British empire. For Britain, the most immediate threat was the Indian independence movement, which, if successful, could deprive her of the facilities and the quarter of a million troops still helping to maintain Britain's position throughout the Far East. After India, Britain depended most on its massive base at Suez, but unrest in Palestine and growing nationalist sentiment in Egypt threatened this bastion of British power, too.

In Europe, where Britain had for centuries supported a balance of

FOREIGN SECRETARY

power to prevent one country from dominating the continent, the Soviet Union, even though it had suffered catastrophic losses in the war, was potentially too powerful to restrain. Although policy-makers appreciated that the Soviet Union was much too weak to have any immediate aggressive intentions, the expansion of its power in Eastern Europe as a result of the war, combined with the growth of Communist parties in all European countries, particularly France and Italy, seemed ominous to some of them even before the war ended. 'Has not the moment come to speak plainly to the Soviet Government, to show our resentment, and to formulate what we consider our rights?' Orme Sargent asked in April 1945.[19]

Given this situation, the British had only one place to turn for help, the United States, which had emerged from the war as by far the strongest military and economic power in the world. In spite of their close wartime alliance, however, relations between Britain and the United States were uneasy. American policy-makers had long disliked and resented British colonialism and regarded the sterling bloc, which tied present and former colonies to Britain economically, as a threat to the open world economy that they saw as the key to future American prosperity and world peace. Such attitudes complicated the Foreign Office's desire to 'make use of American power for the purposes which we regard as good', as one official had put it toward the end of the war.[20]

British policy-makers, fearful the Americans might withdraw into isolation as they had after the previous world war, often saw their American counterparts as naive, having to be convinced to 'shoulder the burden of wider responsibility that is now hers', as Lord Halifax, Britain's ambassador to the United States, put it in late 1945.[21] In fact, American policy-makers were fully aware of the 'preponderant power' of the United States and determined to maintain it by shaping a world conducive to American prosperity, one with an open international economy, where the raw materials of Third World countries remained accessible to the West, and the economic and military power of Europe remained in friendly hands.[22] The American elite were also more sympathetic to Britain and the contribution it might make to American security than British policy-makers at first appreciated. They were simply determined to exact a price – acceptance of American economic and foreign policy goals, especially the end of all closed trading blocs – in return for their

149

ERNEST BEVIN

support of Britain's world role.

Britain's involvement in the cold war emerged from the way Ernest Bevin and the Foreign Office negotiated Britain's relation to these four obstacles to Britain's world position – its own economic weakness, potential Soviet strength, actual American power, and Third World nationalism. It took less than a year from the end of the Second World War for cold war patterns to be set in place that would last until the end of the 1980s.

The starting point of Bevin's diplomacy in these years was what John Kent has aptly called an 'imperial vision of Britain'.[23] Central to that vision was Bevin's determination to retain what he called Britain's 'political predominance' in the Middle East, which provided oil vital to the British economy and military facilities key to Britain's position in the world. Seeing the British empire as a 'beneficent force', he assumed that Middle Eastern countries would understand their own need for British 'guidance' and accept a new partnership with a Britain that would now commit itself to 'schemes of economic development which would benefit the common people'.[24] For all its good intentions, this was a strategy, as William Roger Louis has noted, that preserved the status quo by 'more often than not [allying Britain] with the forces of reaction . . .' and pitting Britain against nationalist forces which potentially threatened its privileged position in the region.[25]

This imperial vision also led Bevin at first to seek closer ties to France, as part of an attempt to create a grouping of West European states able to act independently of both the United States and the Soviet Union. His 'long-term policy was to establish closer relations between this country and countries on the Mediterranean and Atlantic fringes of Europe', he told his advisers in August 1945. Enrolling the 'lesser colonial powers' as 'collaborators' with Britain, as Orme Sargent put it, entailed not only potential economic cooperation with them but also a commitment to restore their colonial possessions. Bevin gave his 'unequivocal . . . support of French rights in regard to Indo-China'.[26] Such support meant that in late September, General Gracey, the British commander on the spot, was allowed to use force, including re-armed Japanese troops, to drive the Vietminh – the broad based, Communist-led, resistance movement – from Saigon and to suppress a revolt in the countryside in order to restore French control over the southern half of

150

FOREIGN SECRETARY

Vietnam.

Similarly, Bevin instructed that in Indonesia 'no recognition should be given to any authorities not approved by the Netherlands Government'.[27] The British position here, however, was more difficult than in Indochina because nationalist forces were stronger and the terrain more intractable. In consequence, Bevin urged the Dutch to explore 'talking points' with the nationalist forces. In October, however, the British, again with the aid of the Japanese, clashed with those forces, but suffered such heavy losses that they realised they could not restore the Dutch to power with the same ease as they had the French. It was a dilemma. If they withdrew, 'the peoples of India, Ceylon, Burma, and Malaya would undoubtedly draw the inference', the Foreign Office concluded, 'that by using a sufficient degree of violence it was possible to attain complete independence'. But the alternative, committing sufficient troops to suppress the 'extremists', as the Cabinet's Defence Committee called them, seemed equally beyond their means.[28] In the end, then, Bevin and the Foreign Office decided to sustain a part of their commitment, until they could hand over responsibility to the Dutch, but not to assume control over all of the islands.

The strain of maintaining such global commitments as those in Indochina and Indonesia, as well as elsewhere in Asia and the Middle East, decisively shaped Britain's relations with the United States. As the war drew to a close, John Maynard Keynes repeatedly pointed out that without American aid Britain would face a 'financial Dunkirk', requiring 'a sudden and humiliating withdrawal from our onerous responsibilities [abroad] with great loss of prestige and an acceptance for the time being of the position of a second-class Power, rather like the present position of France'.[29] Given the unexpected American decision in May 1945 to cut off Lend Lease aid as soon as the war ended, there seemed little alternative. In September, Britain asked the United States for financial help.

Bevin had some initial suspicions of the United States because he feared that full acceptance of the American programme of multilateral trade and sterling convertibility might 'limit our autonomy in domestic economic policy and force us into courses we thought mistaken or disastrous. . . .'[30] Hence, along with other members of the Cabinet, he initially resisted American demands that a loan had to be interest-bearing and include a commitment to make sterling

151

convertible a year after it was signed. In the end, however, neither Bevin nor the rest of the government were willing to contemplate the restrictions on their domestic programmes and overseas commitments that they assumed would follow if they tried to go it alone. The loan helped Labour to implement its domestic programme and to avoid hard choices, while setting the future pattern for Anglo-American relations by 'increasingly cast[ing] Britain as an American client', as the editor of the official documentary history of this period has observed.[31]

Negotiating a loan was only one part of Bevin's determined attempt to obtain American support for British diplomatic goals in the months immediately after the war ended, 'to tie up the United States to the maximum extent in the defence of the British Commonwealth', as he told the Defence Committee.[32] Such support seemed increasingly necessary to him as his suspicions of the Soviet Union rapidly mounted. He found alarming not just Soviet actions in Eastern Europe, but particularly its apparent threat to the British position in the Mediterranean and the Middle East. Bevin was strengthened in this outlook by the Foreign Office, which encouraged him to regard Soviet actions, such as their interest in opening the Straits and securing a base there, as indicative of a much wider ambition, a desire to control Turkey and Greece.

The imperatives of British policy were clearly on display at the Council of Foreign Ministers (CFM), which met for the first time in London in September 1945. At that meeting, Bevin staked out a claim to the former Italian colonies, particularly Cyrenaica, a part of present-day Libya, that he thought 'would greatly increase the security of our vital strategic interests in the Middle East', and possibly serve as an alternative base to Suez. To his dismay, the Soviets also put in a claim to some of these colonies. At the same time, although Bevin told the Soviets that 'British claims in that area had been put forward on the same basis as the Russian claims in Eastern Europe, namely security – a perfectly legitimate basis', he joined American Secretary of State Byrnes in refusing to recognise the government the Soviets had installed in Romania. 'The time has come when we must face up to the question whether or not we are prepared to acquiesce in this block of countries remaining definitely in the Russian sphere of influence', he told Byrnes.[33]

While the Soviets concluded from the conference that Britain and

FOREIGN SECRETARY

the United States were attempting to 'give orders' to them and 'did not want to give [them] anything', what the British saw was indications of Soviet expansionism. Echoing a traditional Foreign Office view of Anglo-Russian rivalry, and with no hint of self-consciousness about Britain's own territorial claims, Pierson Dixon wrote that 'this is the opportunity for a power on the make to grab territory and stake out interests beyond the limit of war-time conquests'. The Russians, who were intensely jealous of 'our position in the Mediterranean', aimed to 'sap' the British position there, he concluded. For the moment, however, Bevin decided that 'wisdom lies in giving time for things to simmer down and for the Soviet government to show its hand more clearly'.[34]

Although the London meeting of the CFM broke up without agreement, it had brought the United States and Britain closer together, a key goal of Bevin's foreign policy. British 'stocks in the United States appreciate when those of the Soviet Union decline', Lord Halifax observed.[35] Shortly thereafter, however, Secretary of State Byrnes, without consulting Bevin, attempted to smooth out Soviet–American relations. Bevin was furious but agreed to attend a meeting in Moscow lest the 'Americans . . . give away our interests to the Russians for the sake of a settlement', as Pierson Dixon noted.[36] Bevin still thought Soviet policy 'disturbing' and told Byrnes that

> It looked as if the Russians were attempting to undermine the British position in the Middle East. This could be seen in their attitude towards Greece, Turkey and Persia, all three points where the U.S.S.R. rubbed with the British Empire. . . . The world seemed to be drifting into the position of 'three Monroes.' . . . Russia seemed to be aiming at the formation of a 'Monroe' area from the Baltic to the Adriatic on the west, to Port Arthur or beyond on the east.[37]

He did not tell Byrnes, however, as he had the Cabinet, about his resentment of exclusive American actions in the Far East and South America, or his concern that Soviet and American 'power politics naked and unashamed' could leave the British isolated with a vast area to defend if the United States clashed with the USSR.[38] And, although combative in talks with Stalin and Molotov, he now agreed to sign a peace treaty with the new Romanian and Bulgarian governments.

153

The Moscow meeting of the CFM in December 1945 raised the spectre of Bevin's worst fear, a Soviet–American *rapprochement* that would leave Britain 'exposed to Soviet pressure', as Britain's ambassador in Moscow, Clark Kerr, put it. The fear, however, proved short-lived. Secretary of State Byrnes returned to the United States after the conference to find that President Truman had become 'tired of babying the Soviets'. A month later, opinion in Washington about the Soviet Union coalesced around the views put forth by Soviet expert George Kennan in his famous Long Telegram from Moscow. Denying that 'conditions outside of Russia' had anything to do with the Soviets' 'neurotic' view of the world, Kennan argued that Soviet Communism was determined to destroy the 'traditional way of life' of the United States. In consequence, peace with the USSR could never be attained.[39]

The Soviet Union *was* a cruel dictatorship; its control of Eastern Europe reprehensible; and its diplomacy often clumsy and heavy handed. Nevertheless, Kennan's interpretation of it as an expansionist force was 'dubious', as Anders Stephenson has correctly observed, overstating both 'Moscow's intentions and capabilities' and ignoring contradictory evidence of Soviet desires to maintain the wartime alliance and of its desperate weakness.[40] Soviet actions could sometimes seem ominous – as in Iran or Poland – but they could also be conciliatory – as in Hungary, Czechoslovakia and Finland. But after 1946 such positive signs were increasingly ignored or explained away.

In fact, it is arguable that the rapid breakdown of co-operation after the war had as much to do with the changing actions of Britain and the United States as with anything that the Soviets did. Although both countries recognised Soviet security concerns in Eastern Europe, they wanted to preserve Western economic access to the region and to prevent Soviet dominance. The British feared for their own position in the Mediterranean and Middle East, while the United States feared that a closed Eastern Europe would undermine their goal of an open world economy. Both felt apprehensive that Soviet control of Eastern Europe could encourage Communist forces elsewhere, in part by making the economic recovery of Western Europe more difficult. In these circumstances, they reinterpreted wartime agreements in an anti-Soviet way, in particular, as Melvyn Leffler has argued, using the agreement reached at Yalta as a 'convenient lever to try to pry open Eastern Europe and to resist Soviet predominance'. Bevin himself acknowledged in April 1946 that Soviet complaints about what one Czech official called 'the refusal of the USA and Britain to treat the Soviet Union as an equal' were 'near the truth' and responsible for its 'clumsy' methods, which, we might add, then served to confirm Western fears.[41]

Whoever was most to blame for the rapid deterioration of relations, it is clear that opinion in British policy-making circles also crystallised in the beginning of 1946 around the most negative possible interpretation of Soviet actions. In January, Bevin, who had been willing to reserve judgement about the Soviets, told John Foster Dulles and Senator Arthur Vandenburg of his 'fears of Russian aims' which were being pursued using the same technique 'followed with such success by Hitler'. Churchill's famous Iron Curtain speech at Fulton, Missouri on 5 March 'echoed the sentiments of all' in the Foreign Office, Pierson Dixon noted, including Bevin.[42] A few weeks after that speech, Frank Roberts, British Minister in Moscow, sent a long analysis of the Soviet Union similar to Kennan's. The 'Soviet push on all diplomatic fronts', he wrote, was 'partly an attempt to profit from the present fluid state of postwar Europe' and partly 'an almost desperate effort to seize advanced positions and dig in before the inevitable reaction against high-handed Soviet actions sets in with a return to more normal and peaceful conditions'. Unlike Kennan, however, Roberts argued that 'national security' was at 'the bottom of Soviet' policy and accounted for 'much of [its] high-handed behaviour'. Since 'security' was the Soviets' 'first consideration', their goals might be reconciled with those of the British, although with difficulty.[43]

Thus in contrast to Kennan, who thought the Kremlin sought the 'total destruction of rival power', Roberts believed a basis for compromise existed. His colleagues in the Foreign Office, however, 'decided on a course of confrontation'.[44] On 2 April, C. F. A. Warner, the head of the Northern Department, wrote a seminal memorandum, 'The Soviet Campaign Against this Country and our Response to it', in which he proposed that Britain should adopt a 'defensive–offensive policy' as part of a 'world-wide anticommunist campaign' to respond to what he saw as Soviet 'aggressiveness' threatening 'British interests all over the world'. Soviet policy, he contended, was '*offensive* . . . in so far as the Russian "religion" is

ERNEST BEVIN

dynamic and proselytising Communism'. Ignoring Soviet security concerns and possible fears, Warner argued that the Soviet Union seemed 'determined to stick at nothing, short of war, to obtain her objectives'. Shortly thereafter, in order to co-ordinate policy towards the Soviet Union the Foreign Office established an inter-departmental Russia Committee which from its inception adopted the most negative view of Soviet policy. Thus by the spring of 1946 within the Foreign Office, what one historian has called the 'clear ideological inclination to perceive the Soviet Union as both untrust-worthy and expansionist' shaped every interpretation of Soviet actions.[45]

Bevin, according to Gladwyn, 'welcomed' the Russia Committee and 'took much interest in it'.[46] He also approved Warner's memo, which was sent only to selected members of the Cabinet. Dalton, Cripps, Bevan and six others were kept in the dark. Although he refused to approve all of Warner's policy recommendations, finding the prospect of an 'all-out propaganda offensive' too 'alarming a picture', Bevin accepted the general policy analysis. Echoing Warner, he told Attlee at the end of the month that the Russians 'have decided upon an aggressive policy based upon militant Communism and Russian Chauvinism . . . and seem determined to stick at nothing, short of war, to obtain [their] objectives'.[47] Nevertheless, the Soviet Union's popularity inside the Labour movement remained much too strong for Bevin to come out openly against it. In November 1946, the Labour Left tried to amend the government's opening address to Parliament to call for a 'genuinely socialist policy'. Six months later, a small Left group wrote in *Keep Left* that '"collective security against Communism" is a betrayal of Socialist principles'. Even a year later, Harold Laski could argue that a policy of hostility to the Soviet Union would 'split the party . . . from top to bottom'.[48]

In part to protect himself from his left-wing critics, Bevin consistently denied any hostility to the Soviet Union and before 1948 never publicly admitted how set in opposition to it his policy had become. In all but one of his major policy speeches to the Labour Party conference, he stressed that he had always been a friend of the Soviet Union, often mentioning 'his' founding in 1920 of the Council of Action that had opposed British intervention against the Russian revolution. 'Is there a man in this conference',

FOREIGN SECRETARY

he asked in 1946, 'who historically did more to defend the Russian Revolution than I did?' Even in early 1947 the American embassy reported how 'every [government] move' still had to be 'carefully considered and planned from [the] point of view of protecting Bevin against Labour Party rebels and also public opinion, which desires close Soviet ties'.[49]

In private, Bevin was convinced by 1946 that the Soviet Union was an expansionist force that had to be resisted. He told the Defence Committee in October 1946 that he believed it 'was now clear that Russia sought by every means to bring about the dissolution of the British Empire' and if Britain did not resist 'all of Europe would fall under Russian influence'.[50] Bevin arrived at this conclusion, as did his advisers, by interpreting political changes throughout the globe as, increasingly, either part of a Soviet expansionist plan or as potentially beneficial to the Soviet Union. Such a view cast a mantle of anti-Communist urgency over the traditional goals of his own foreign policy. Although Bevin was genuinely committed to economic development and to recasting Britain's relationships with former dependencies on a more equal basis, 'the purpose of this transformation', as Professor Louis writes about the Middle East, 'was the perpetuation of Britain as a great "world power"'.[51] This political dynamic can be seen by looking briefly at Greece and Germany, two sites of conflict that at the time seemed to confirm Bevin's (and the Foreign Office's) view of the Soviet Union.

In Greece, Bevin and the Foreign Office saw the hand of the Soviets behind the Communist-led insurgency that began in 1946 and grew into full-scale civil war by 1947. The Greek civil war had actually developed because the country had been polarised for decades between a monarchist Right and a now Communist-led Left, a situation made murderous by the conflicting allegiances of each side during the Second World War. Although the civil war was not created by the Soviet Union, a victory for the Greek Communists in that struggle would have enhanced Soviet power and threatened Bevin's entire strategic vision, which was to 'maintain' the British 'position in Greece' as a way of sustaining 'the whole of our Middle East position'.[52] As he explained to the Defence Committee in March 1946:

157

ERNEST BEVIN

Our position in the Mediterranean serves a purpose other than a military purpose which is vital to our position as a Great Power. The Mediterranean is the area through which we bring influence to bear on Southern Europe, the soft underbelly of France, Italy, Yugoslavia, Greece and Turkey. Without our physical presence in the Mediterranean, we should cut little ice with those States which would fall, like eastern Europe, under the totalitarian yoke. We should also lose our position in the Middle East (including Iraq oil, now one of our greatest economic assets), even if we could afford to let Egypt go. If we move out of the Mediterranean, Russia will move in. . . .[53]

Churchill might have made this speech, but in contrast to Churchill, who had supported the Greek monarchy, Bevin sought to establish a moderate government that could foster a parliamentary democracy. The difficulty was that although 'real authority' in Greece after 1945 lay with the British ambassador, the Labour government lacked the financial and military resources to impose a settlement, while opposition from its own left wing limited the measures it could take against the Communists and their allies, always seen as the main enemy. Labour, Orme Sargent pointed out to the British ambassador to Greece, Rex Leeper, had to give their Greek commitment 'all the trappings of anti-Imperialist and non-Interventionist respectability', while exploring 'other and more discreet methods of achieving their object'.[54]

Labour's 'discreet method' was to respect, at least ostensibly, the independence of the Greek government, a hands-off policy that effectively aided the royalist Right by leaving it free to attack all Left forces. Bevin was eager to withdraw British troops, both to protect himself from domestic and international criticism and to deprive the Soviets of any excuse for maintaining troops in Bulgaria and Romania. Convinced that the quickest way to restore the 'stability' that would allow British troop withdrawal was through a national election, Bevin refused to heed the pleas of the liberal centre and socialist and Communist Left that a fair election could not be held under the circumstances. He insisted that balloting take place, and the election was held in March 1946. The socialists and Communists boycotted the election, bringing to power the reactionary Tsaldaris government, which, because it could claim electoral legitimacy, enjoyed British and American support.

In effect, Constantine Tsoucalas notes, a 'double structure of

FOREIGN SECRETARY

power' had been created, 'democratic in the political façade but Royalist-fascist in the forces of coercion'.[55] In the next months, Tsaldaris, whom one American official later described as 'intriguing' and 'unscrupulous', representing the 'past at its worst', set about securing right-wing control over all Greek institutions, including the trade union movement, many of whose leaders were arrested. Confronted by a situation in which right-wing violence made the parliamentary process meaningless and in which their lives were in real danger, the Communists gradually took up arms, thus putting the British in the position, as Clement Attlee pointed out, of 'supporting vested interests and reaction against reform and revolution in the interests of the poor'.[56]

At the same time as Greece started to sink into civil war, the British faced what came to seem a similar problem in Germany, where they also interpreted internal political trends as evidence of Soviet expansionism. Germany had been divided into four occupation zones at the end of the war, with the British being assigned the Ruhr, the former industrial heartland of the country. It was an area without sufficient food or supplies of its own, with large numbers of refugees, millions of disarmed German soldiers and a destroyed economy. The result was a tremendous financial burden, £74 million in 1945–6 alone.[57]

The logic of Britain's self-interest therefore soon led away from the Potsdam agreement of July 1945, which had promised the Soviets reparations from the Western zones of Germany and a voice in the rebuilding of the Ruhr, as well as making a commitment to reunite Germany at a later date. This logic was strengthened by a growing fear that the German people, moved by economic misery, might turn to Communism. Increasing Soviet control over its own zone, particularly the creation in February 1946 of the Socialist Unity Party, seemed to place the Soviets in a particularly strong position to exploit this situation. In response, the British began not only to retreat from their commitment to work with the Soviets in rebuilding the Ruhr but also to organise the British zone independently and to create a divided Germany.[58] At a key meeting in April 1946, Bevin was convinced by his officials to consider such a policy, even though, as he said, it 'meant a policy of a Western bloc and that meant war'. The alternative, Orme Sargent countered, was 'Communism on the Rhine'.[59]

159

ERNEST BEVIN

Following the lead of these officials, whose 'influence', according to Anne Deighton, was 'decisive in convincing their political master . . . to take a firm stand', Bevin spelled out for the Cabinet at the beginning of May 1946 why a divided Germany was now in British interests.[60] 'The danger of Russia has certainly become as great as, and possibly even greater than, that of a revived Germany', he wrote. The British could either work for a unified Germany or create a 'West German state or states which would be more amenable to our influence'. 'On the assumption that we are not prepared to leave the field to Russia, the question arises whether we should be best advised to maintain and develop the present policy of Potsdam or to throw it overboard and organise our own zone as an independent unit according to our own ideas. . . .' He feared that if a central government were created, the Soviets and Communism would 'exercise the stronger pull', since 'on the whole the balance of advantage seems to lie with the Russians'. But throwing over the Potsdam agreement totally would also have 'grave consequences'. It would end hopes of breaking down the Iron Curtain, 'amount to bringing Western Germany into a Western anti-Soviet bloc', produce an 'irreparable break' with them and frighten the United States, which was 'probably not ready for this'.[61] After strong debate, including dissent from Dalton, the Cabinet approved Bevin's memorandum. To avoid disconcerting the United States and domestic opinion, however, the British now adopted a 'dual policy', according to the most recent study of British policy in Germany. 'The appearance of great power co-operation was publicly maintained, but the remorseless focus of British policy was directed to securing an effective Western alliance to contain Soviet might in Germany, in Europe, and throughout the world.'[62]

At the July 1946 meeting of the Council of Foreign Ministers, the Soviets insisted that they wanted their full share of reparations and a voice in running the Ruhr before they would agree to the German economic revival that the British wanted. Bevin then announced that the British zone would be organised on its own to reduce costs, while the United States, critical of the way the British ran their zone and eager to increase its own control over Germany, offered to link its zone with that of any other power. The new Bizone, Anne Deighton has concluded, was 'an expression of the very "ganging-up" of which the Soviet Union was so afraid, and was to set in train

160

the economic and then the political division of Germany'.[63]

The final moment in the formation of a full cold war stance came at the end of 1946 and beginning of 1947 when Bevin, joined by the Foreign Office and the Chiefs of Staff, defeated Clement Attlee's bid to reorient British policy. From 1945 to 1947, the Prime Minister had repeatedly questioned the strategic assumptions of the Chiefs of Staff and the anti-Soviet views of the Foreign Office. He opposed Bevin's bid for Cyrenaica as likely to 'saddle us with an expense that we can ill afford'.[64] He thought 'it was becoming difficult to justify our staying [in] the Middle East for any reason other than to be prepared for a war against Russia'.[65] He also questioned the need for 'the financial and military burden' in Greece. Not only were they backing a 'very lame horse', a country 'dominated by a small class of wealthy and corrupt people at the top and a mass of poverty stricken landworkers at the bottom', but 'the strategic importance of communications through the Mediterranean in terms of modern warfare is very much overrated by our military advisers'. Given Britain's limited resources, he argued, containing the Soviet Union by backing 'essentially reactionary' governments was inefficient, wasteful and counterproductive, a 'strategy of despair'.[66]

Attlee was also willing to consider how the world might look from a Soviet perspective and to question whether the Soviets were as great a threat as Bevin and other policy-makers believed. He thought it 'not unnatural' that the Soviets should 'assert an equal right to have free access to the oceans'.[67] In 1946 he told the Defence Committee 'there was no one to fight', a view that Dalton found 'fresh-minded', but which Bevin and the Chiefs of Staff rejected.[68] Countries bordering on the Soviet Union could not be made strong enough to form an 'effective barrier', Attlee argued at the end of 1946.

> We do not command the resources to make them so. If it were possible to reach an agreement with Russia that we should both disinterest ourselves as far as possible in them so that they become a neutral zone, it would be much to our advantage. Of course it is difficult to tell how far Russian policy is dictated by expansionism and how far by fear of attack by the U.S. and ourselves. Fantastic as this is, it may very well be the real grounds of Russian policy. What we consider merely defence may seem to them to be preparations for an attack.[69]

The Foreign Office responded strongly to Attlee's proposal.

ERNEST BEVIN

Arguing that 'nature abhors a vacuum', Dixon contended that any British withdrawal would be filled by the Soviets. Attlee's proposed neutral zone 'would mean the loss of the British position in Egypt and Arabia as well. It would, in fact, bring Russia to the Congo and the Victoria Falls.' Worse, if the Soviets entered the Mediterranean 'we should lose our influence in Italy, France and North Africa.' In short, Attlee's policy would produce another 'Munich' and act as an 'incentive to ultimate world domination' by the Soviets. 'Even if Russian world domination can be discounted [the] bear will certainly not resist pushing [its] paw into soft places', Dixon concluded.[70]

Bevin, who at this same moment was opposing what he called the Cabinet's 'defeatist' attitude over India, responded to Attlee in language which echoed his officials. 'What you propose is a reversal of the whole policy I have been pursuing in the Middle East', he wrote. Withdrawal would 'be Munich over again, only on a world scale, with Greece, Turkey, and Persia as the first victims in place of Czechoslovakia', giving the Russians control of the Middle East's manpower and oil. Retreat would also undermine the *appearance* of Britain's role as a world power, leading Egypt to fall under Communist control and undermining Britain's position in Africa. Most important,

> The effect on our relations with the United States of America would be disastrous. We are to a large extent dependent on them economically, and without their help we cannot maintain the standard of life of our people. We are hardly less dependent upon them militarily. With great labour, we have at last succeeded in persuading them that their strategic interests are involved in the maintenance of our position in the Middle East. If we now withdraw at this moment, I should expect them to write us off entirely.

Added to this, Bevin believed British economic difficulties were only temporary, and so there was no need to negotiate with the Soviets. Linked to the Americans, he wrote, 'we shall be in a position to negotiate with Stalin from strength. There is no hurry. Everything suggests that the Russians are now drawing in their horns and have no immediate aggressive intentions.' Attlee, dependent on Bevin's support in Cabinet and on his influence with the trade union movement, gave way.[71] There was to be no turning aside from the cold war.

162

FOREIGN SECRETARY

The division of Europe

In the same week in January 1947 that Bevin ended the Prime Minister's attempt to reorient British policy, he met with British representatives in Eastern Europe to decide British policy in that region. At this meeting, the assumptions which now guided British policy were on full display, including, interestingly, the belief that Eastern Europe had not been irrevocably lost to the West. After much discussion, Bevin and his representatives ruled out any attempt to compromise with the Soviets along the lines followed at the end of the war on the grounds that the Soviets 'believed in a foreign policy of friction; they would be amazed if we ceased to oppose them in Eastern Europe, and, if we were to relax our opposition, we should have to expect increased pressure from the Russians in Western Europe and the Middle East'. Compromise was also ruled out because it would 'likely shock American opinion'. As C. F. A. Warner had pointed out a month earlier, if the British bargained with the Soviets over Eastern Europe, the United States might take a less sympathetic attitude on questions 'in which we are directly dependent on their benevolence'. Underlying this conclusion about British policy in Eastern Europe were two assumptions: that economic weakness would force the Soviets to accommodate British goals in the region; and that British economic strength and world position 'might be largely reestablished' in a few years.[72]

Ironically, Britain's economic position entered into steeper decline just as Bevin and his officials were anticipating the possibilities its revival might offer. The winter of 1947 was the worst in decades. Inadequate coal stocks reduced electrical supplies for consumers and forced factories to operate part time. Unemployment rose rapidly, while imports increased as the crisis required an even more rapid utilisation than anticipated of the American loan. The effect on Britain's foreign policy of what Bevin called this 'picture . . . of almost unrelieved gloom' was very clear – it increased dependence on the United States. In plaintive tones Bevin called on the Foreign Service to redouble its efforts to increase trade with hard currency countries, emphasising particularly the need for the 'maximum protection of British oil interests', including the 'Royal Dutch Shell Group . . . as a British interest'.

Our financial policy has necessarily increased the need to co-ordinate

ERNEST BEVIN

> our foreign policy with that of the only country which is able effectively to wield extensive economic influence – namely, the United States. . . . If the corollary of United States intervention and strength is that we find ourselves at times irked at the role of junior partner, we must recognise, nevertheless, that the partnership is worth the price. . . . Only if we were to find ourselves alone with our political objectives widely divergent from those of the United States would our financial nakedness be fully apparent to the world.[73]

The fuel crisis that began in late January 1947 precipitated Britain's decision on 21 February to ask the United States to take over responsibility for the struggle in Greece. Dalton had been pushing for some time for cuts in overseas military spending and manpower commitments but was resisted by the Chiefs of Staff and Bevin, who had reaffirmed in December 1946 that Greece and Turkey were 'essential to our political and strategical position in the world'.[74] Appalled at the effect of this policy on Labour's domestic programme, Dalton fought back. 'This huge expenditure of manpower and money on defence is making nonsense of our economics and public finance', he wrote to Attlee. The financial crisis and, possibly, Bevin's bad health – 'Bevin is in no fit condition to go on much longer', Dalton wrote in his diary – now tipped the scales in Dalton's favour and led to the historic shift in power in the region from Britain to the United States.[75]

Britain's increasing dependence on the United States and opposition to the Soviet Union further alarmed the Labour Left, which tried to force a reconsideration of the government's foreign policy at the Labour Party conference in May 1947 with a series of resolutions calling, among other things, for closer co-operation with both the Soviet Union and the United States, a united Germany, and withdrawal from supporting the 'reactionary' government in Greece. In general, as Koni Zilliacus said, the Left wanted 'to re-pledge us to our Socialist principles and to our mandate from the people'.

In response, Bevin gave his most effective performance since he had demolished George Lansbury in 1935. As Dalton noted, he 'swept away all opposition'.[76] Bevin defended his policy as disinterested idealism. In the Middle East, he said, he sought to 'encourage other great social experiments and industrial developments in that part of the world so that the wealth which is taken out of the

164

FOREIGN SECRETARY

country flows back' and aids all people. It was true, of course, that he wanted to improve living standards in the region, but that was largely wishful thinking since he had little aid to give and remained wedded to the reactionary regimes that seemed the key to continued British predominance. In private, he stressed the 'vital importance for Great Britain and the British Empire of the oil resources of this area'.[77] Similarly, he insisted that his policy aimed not to divide Germany when in fact it aimed to do exactly that. And he rejected the notion that Britain was 'subservient' to the United States, although he privately acknowledged that he had to shape British policy to avoid displeasing the Americans. Finally, and most effectively, he attacked the Left as disloyal intellectuals who had 'stabbed [him] in the back' by seeking to amend the motion on the King's speech to Parliament in November 1946 while he was away in New York. 'If you are to expect loyalty from Ministers, then Ministers – however much they make mistakes – have a right to expect loyalty in return. I grew up in the trade union movement, you see, and I have never been used to this sort of thing.'[78] It was an effective performance. Richard Crossman wrote afterwards: 'No man alive is so skilful at handling a working-class audience, mixing the brutal hammer blow with sentimental appeal. . . . He did not merely smash his critics; he pulverised them into applauding him.'[79] His victory, however, resulted as much from his control of the bloc votes of the large trade unions as from the strength of his oratory.

Remaining doubts that the Labour Left may have had were largely resolved in the next few months by Secretary of State Marshall's famous aid plan, first broached in early June 1947, which forced the Left to do what it had tried to avoid, choose sides between the United States and the Soviet Union. At the time, it still seemed to American and British policy-makers that Communist parties might triumph in the West because of their supposed ability to capitalise on continuing economic chaos. Europe's economic difficulties, exacerbated by the harsh winter of 1947, also seemed to encourage a trend towards increased measures of state control to overcome the crisis, including bilateral trading agreements to reduce dependency on American imports. This trend towards a 'greater type of autocratic state control', as Thomas Finletter, head of the Marshall Plan administration in Britain, put it, seemed to make the 'ground . . . fertile for the rise of communism' with its preference for

165

ERNEST BEVIN

collectivist rather than market solutions to social and economic problems.[80] To solve Europe's economic problem, however, required the revival of Germany, a course that aroused considerable concern in France and other countries. Among other things, Marshall's famous plan aimed to provide aid to Germany in a way that other European countries would find acceptable.

All of these problems – the slow pace of European economic revival, the need to revive Germany, the continued appeal of Communism – were solved by the Marshall Plan. By providing West European countries with massive amounts of capital, the Marshall Plan raised productivity and successfully diverted political attention from questions of ownership and distribution to economic growth. 'The mere availability of this amount of economic assistance', George Kennan noted in explaining the Marshall Plan's 'basic political purpose', 'will create, so to speak, a new topographic feature' on the 'European scene.'[81] Because aid to what was soon to be West Germany was made part of this plan, it became acceptable to the other European countries. At the same time, the plan provided tremendous leverage the United States to push European economies along the lines that it preferred, both by the direct intervention of the American administrators who oversaw all spending and by the requirements for monetary and financial measures that accepted the full logic of the capitalist market and forestalled any attempts to increase controls over trade and national investment.

Bevin saw Marshall's vague offer of aid as a potential 'life-line' for economically languishing Europe. His decisive action in the next weeks played an important role in shaping the European response to Marshall's offer, although the significance of Bevin's actions in what from first to last was an American diplomatic triumph has been overestimated by Alan Bullock.[82] On 17 June Bevin met French Prime Minister Bidault to plan a conference about the American proposal. The speed with which he responded aimed in part to prevent the United Nations Economic Commission for Europe, on which the Soviets sat, from becoming involved. Bevin realised that the Soviets could not be simply excluded without grave political repercussions, but he did not want them to participate for fear they would 'play the Trojan horse' and obstruct recovery. In fact, Bevin saw the Plan in clear cold war terms – 'the quickest way to break

166

FOREIGN SECRETARY

down the iron curtain', he told American Secretary of Commerce William Clayton on 24 June. 'Russia cannot hold its satellites against the attraction of fundamental help toward economic revival in Europe.'[83]

Having been specifically assured by Clayton that the United States would still provide aid if the Soviets were excluded, Bevin adopted a belligerent stance toward Molotov when they met in Paris at the end of the month. He rejected the Soviet Union's concerns and insisted it should join Britain and France in creating a European-wide plan for American approval. The Soviets feared that 'inquiry into the resources of European nations would violate the sovereignty of the individual countries', a reasonable concern from their point of view since American plans called for them to supply only raw materials and grain towards European recovery. Bevin, however, simply assumed that the Soviets only wanted to disrupt the still unformed Marshall Plan, so he and Bidault insisted that Molotov should either accept their approach or leave. 'This really is the birth of the Western bloc', Bevin said to Pierson Dixon.[84]

By beginning the economic revival of Western Germany, and openly trying to attract East Germany and the rest of Eastern Europe, the Marshall Plan finalised the division of Europe. But it successfully placed the blame for this result on the Soviets. By offering aid on unacceptable terms to the Soviet Union, the Marshall Plan faced them with a dilemma: accept aid, and with it the risk of the integration of the Soviet Union and Eastern Europe into the Western capitalist economy, or reject aid and face opprobrium for opposing European economic recovery. Seeing the openly stated anti-Communist goals of the Marshall Plan, the Soviets forced the Eastern Europeans to renounce their earlier interest in aid and denounced it as a Wall Street plot. In the next months, they mounted a massive attempt to disrupt the plan, brutally solidified control over Eastern Europe and created the Communist Information Bureau that denounced the Western powers. As the originators of the Plan had anticipated, the United States consequently reaped a public relations windfall.

By seizing leadership of the European response to the American offer of aid, Bevin ensured that American goals for European revival would be realised. But he failed to convince the United States that Britain had a 'special position' justifying its separate treatment. 'It

167

ERNEST BEVIN

would pay the U.S. and the world for the U.S. and the U. K. to establish a financial partnership', he told Clayton. If Britain was 'considered just another European country this would fit in with Russian strategy, namely, that the U.S. would encounter a slump and would withdraw from Europe, the U.K. would be helpless and out of dollars and as merely another European country the Russians, in command of the Continent, could deal with Britain in due course'.[85]

Clayton rejected this ploy, although it was a line the British tried to exploit again a month later when the start of sterling convertibility, as required by the 1946 loan agreement, created a fiscal crisis. The British pushed for a more immediate grant of aid and warned the United States that they would be unable to meet their 'military commitments' and would be 'forced . . . to retreat from one position to another, and further and further from the concept of a multilateral world economy'.[86] Such arguments did influence the American decision to accommodate Britain's immediate financial needs. 'If Britain should not receive some aid', George Kennan noted at the time, 'she would have no choice but to dismantle extensively her defense and imperial commitments. This would mean that serious vacuums would be created in other areas, which could be most embarassing to us and cause us many headaches. . . . Some of these vacuums are ones we might have to fill. This could cost far more than . . . aid to Britain at this time.'[87] Nevertheless, the attempt to use British weakness as a lever to secure a 'financial partnership' failed. Moreover, the aid the United States was willing to supply always had a string attached: that Britain should carry out its role in the American global design. When in late July, for example, Britain moved to pull its remaining troops out of Greece, Marshall bluntly warned that cuts in Britain's defence commitments would provoke a 'thorough re-examination of the U.S. strategic position and a reconsideration of its financial and economic commitments in Europe. A large measure of U.S. foreign policy has been predicated upon the British willingness to contribute what they can to the maintenance of stability in Europe.'[88]

The United States, of course, never seriously considered ending its commitments to Europe. On the contrary, as it came to see itself locked in a world-wide struggle with communism, it increasingly expanded those commitments to include a continuation of European

168

colonial rule, which it had strongly criticised during the war. For the British, this meant that by 1947 the United States came to agree fully with them that the 'critical problem in the contemporary world is to avert the chaos which would inevitably come of any further contractions of Britain's imperial and economic influence', as Lord Inverchapel, the British ambassador to the United States, had earlier put it.[89] This view received formal validation at the secret Pentagon talks of October and November 1947, when the United States agreed to sustain Britain's position in the Middle East as part of a general co-ordination of their worldwide military responsibilities. By presenting themselves as the vanguard of the West against Soviet expansion, the 'best window' on the Middle East, as Bevin later told American Secretary of State Acheson, the British won American support for their special position in the region, and for their claims to Cyrenaica. 'The argument that the Americans usually depended on the British to hold the line does not provide an entirely adequate explanation', the historian of the postwar British empire in the Middle East has observed, 'but on the whole the unpublished records sustain it to a remarkable degree.'[90]

Although the Pentagon talks did realise a key goal of his foreign policy by gaining American support for Britain's position in the Middle East, Bevin (and the Foreign Office) persistently overestimated their ability to control this evolving relationship with the United States. To obtain American support, Bevin stressed, often against the opposition of Dalton, the need to 'assure the Americans that we intended to maintain our economic, political and strategic position in the Middle East and the Eastern Mediterranean'. Otherwise, 'it was certain that the United States would feel compelled to distinterest herself in that area'.[91] Bevin even wanted, as he put it, 'to keep the Middle East predominantly a British sphere and to exclude the United States militarily from the area'. He therefore opposed a 'combined' Anglo-American policy on the grounds that 'this area was primarily of strategic and economic interest to the United Kingdom'.[92] This was a miscalculation. United States policy-makers had a clear vision of the world order they wanted to create, including a Middle East linked to the West. They had no intention of withdrawing if the British retreated, but of taking Britain's place, as the subsequent history of Greece, Iran, Egypt, Israel and elsewhere demonstrates.

ERNEST BEVIN

Palestine

Increasing Anglo-American co-operation in the Middle East, promoted by fear of the Soviet Union and radical political change, was subjected to severe strain by the conflict between Jews and Arabs in the British mandate of Palestine. The Balfour Declaration of 1917 had committed Britain to support 'a national home for the Jewish people' in Palestine, but only in ways that did not 'prejudice the civil and religious rights of existing non-Jewish communities'. Recognising Britain's 'dual obligation' to Jews and Arabs, Bevin initially insisted that the conflict 'must be settled by discussion and conciliation', not force.[93] It was not, however, a situation open to compromise. Zionist leaders were determined to create a Jewish state, while the Arabs bitterly opposed this goal as a threat to their own existence.

Because of a number of his public statements and his opposition to Zionist goals, Bevin was accused at the time of being anti-Semitic, a charge denied by Alan Bullock and other historians who contend that he was merely heavy handed and insensitive. Certainly, Bevin's belief that Jews could be convinced to resettle in Europe showed a lack of understanding of the emotional impact of the Holocaust, as did his warning that if Jews wanted 'to get too much at the head of the queue' for resettlement they would enflame anti-Semitism. Similarly, his irritated observation that Americans agitated for Jewish immigration to Palestine because 'they did not want too many Jews in New York' had a point – immigration restrictions excluded most Jews from going to the United States – but it was not tactful.[94]

It is also the case, however, that Ernest Bevin held anti-Semitic views. We have already seen the connection he drew between Jews and finance. He did the same for Communism. Warning Zionist leaders of the political dangers of an all-Jewish state, he said that 'it was significant that the only constituency in the United Kingdom which, on a population basis, was in a position to return a Jewish Member of Parliament had, in fact, returned a Communist'. He thought that Israel might become 'another China'.[95] Various of his colleagues privately noted what Ian Mikardo called 'the pejorative and often vulgar language of many of Bevin's references to Jews'. Christopher Mayhew, Bevin's Parliamentary Under-Secretary wrote

170

in his diary in May 1948 that he

> must make a note about Ernest's anti- semitism. . . . There is no doubt
> in my mind that Ernest detests Jews. He makes the odd wisecrack about
> the 'Chosen People'; explains Shinwell away as a Jew; declares the Old
> Testament is the most immoral book ever written. . . . He says they
> taught Hitler the technique of terror – and were even now paralleling
> the Nazis in Palestine. They were preachers of violence and war –
> 'What could you expect when people are brought up from the cradle
> on the Old Testament?' . . .[96]

Some of Bevin's bitter responses can be explained as anger at Zionist
terrorism and frustration that the 'Jews showed no readiness to
reach a reasonable compromise', as he saw it, and therefore
undermined his Middle East policy. There can nevertheless be no
denying Bevin's prejudices, although there is no evidence that they
shaped his policy towards Palestine, which derived above all from
his concern for what he called Britain's 'position as a world power
. . . with its world obligations'.[97]

Accepting the position of the Foreign Office and the Chiefs of
Staff that Palestine was a strategic key to Britain's position in the
Middle East, Bevin sought to negotiate a compromise solution to the
Arab–Zionist conflict above all because it seemed the only way to
maintain Britain's position in the region. 'Abdication in Palestine
would be regarded as symptomatic of our abdication as a Great
Power', Harold Beeley, who became Bevin's closest adviser on
Palestine, wrote in July 1945, 'and might set in motion a process
which could result in the crumbling away of our influence throughout the region.'[98] At the same time, Bevin *was* genuinely sympathetic
to the Palestinians' case. 'Under the Jews the Arabs would have no
rights but would remain in a permanent minority in a land they had
held for 2,000 years', he complained to a Zionist delegation. In
Parliament, where much of the Labour Party was sympathetic to the
Zionist cause, he repeatedly insisted that the Arabs had a 'case which
has got to be considered. . . . It is sometimes forgotten that the
Arabs are in the world . . . because there is so much propaganda on
the other side'.[99]

Immediately after the war, the Arab-Zionist conflict centred on
whether to allow another 100,000 Jews to enter Palestine. Bevin
refused on the grounds that it would only open the door to more

ERNEST BEVIN

immigration and anger Arab opinion, both in Palestine and elsewhere, at Britain's expense. His insistence that Jewish refugees should be treated as one part of a world refugee problem to which all states had to respond seemed insensitive and harmed Britain's standing in world opinion, particularly in the United States.

Although by 1947 Britain had a force of 100,000 troops on the ground, at an annual cost of £40 million, it lacked the resources and the will to impose a solution in the face of Jewish terrorism and Arab resistance. Bevin tried therefore to enlist American support for British policy, even though others in the Cabinet and Foreign Office feared that inviting American co-operation would only undermine Britain's exclusive position in the region. In the event, however, this effort failed. In spite of misgivings in American policy-making circles, and against recommendations from joint committees that endorsed Britain's attempts to create a binational state, President Truman sided with the Zionists, endorsing their demand for an immediate entry of 100,000 immigrants and the partition of Palestine. 'The United States had queered our pitch in Palestine', Bevin ruefully concluded.[100]

Having belatedly 'discovered', as Dalton observed, 'that the Arabs want an Arab state and the Jews want a Jewish state, and that these two desires are irremediably in conflict', Bevin began to consider turning the problem over to the United Nations.[101] He hesitated, however, because Palestine seemed so vital to Britain's position in the region. He feared that 'the impression seemed to be growing that we had lost the ability, and, indeed, the will, to live up to our responsibilities', he said in January 1947, just as final plans were being made to withdraw from India. Retention of Palestine 'was strategically essential to the maintenance of our position in the Middle East', without whose 'oil and other potential resources, he saw no hope of our being able to achieve the standard of life at which we were aiming in Great Britain'.[102] He made therefore one last attempt to secure agreement between the Arabs and Jews, but it proved abortive.

After the failure of these last Arab-Jewish talks in London, the Cabinet agreed on 18 February 1947 to turn the issue over to the United Nations on the assumption that it would oppose partition, which still seemed to Bevin a disaster. 'The risk cannot be excluded that it would contribute to the elimination of British influence from

172

FOREIGN SECRETARY

the whole of the vast Moslem area lying between Greece and India', he told the Cabinet. 'This would have not only strategic consequences it would also jeopardise the security of our interests in the increasingly important oil production of the Middle East.'[103] But a majority of the United Nations, hostile to British colonialism and under strong American pressure, voted for partition. In response, the Labour government decided to withdraw from Palestine by 15 May 1948. The alternative of enforcing partition, which was 'manifestly unjust to the Arabs', Bevin told the Cabinet, would 'precipitate an Arab uprising' and require another division of troops. 'We should be engaged in suppressing Arab resistance in Palestine, and thus antagonising the independent Arab States, at a time when our whole political and strategic system in the Middle East must be founded on co-operation with those States.' On the day Britain formally withdrew from Palestine, Israel declared its independence, which it secured after a year-long war with its Arab neighbours. Bevin admitted defeat to Parliament in the final debate on the issue on 26 January 1949. The British goal had been to 'persuade Jews and Arabs to live together in one State as the Mandate charged us to do', he said. 'We failed in this. The State of Israel is now a fact.'[104]

Behind the decision to give up responsibility for Palestine lay the gnawing fact that, as Bevin said, 'The Palestine situation was poisoning relations between the United States and Great Britain'. American leaders, as usual, did not hesitate to make this clear to Bevin. 'Unless a satisfactory settlement was reached there [Palestine]', Marshall warned him, 'any common policy in the Middle East would be much more difficult to achieve.'[105] Bevin might complain that 'this great issue had been handled more with the electoral situation in New York City in mind than the large issues of foreign policy which were involved', and warn that the West 'would lose not only the good will of the Arab peoples but of all Moslems who might thereby go over to the wrong side in any future crisis', but in the end his concern for American support outweighed any other consideration.[106]

Overall, Bevin's policy in Palestine demonstrated that Britain could only get its way in the world with American backing, which on this occasion had not been forthcoming. The American attitude, Bevin bitterly noted, was 'let there be an Israel and to hell with the consequences' as well as 'Jewish expansion whatever the conse-

173

ERNEST BEVIN

quences'. But as Minister of State Hector McNeil reminded him, Britain 'no longer had the means nor the military resources to command this whole area by ourselves'. Keeping on the right side of the United States had to take precedence. 'It is essential even when the Jews are the most wicked and the Americans most exasperating not to lose sight of this point.'[107]

Junior partner in the Pax Americana

Although Bevin's policy in Palestine had been shaped by his underlying desire not to endanger British relations with the United States, he still hoped that Britain could avoid having to accept permanently the role of junior partner to the world's only super-power. 'I am sure we must free ourselves of financial dependence on the United States of America', he wrote to Attlee in September 1947. 'We shall never be able to pull our full weight in foreign affairs until we do so.'[108]

Bevin's continuing but unsuccessful attempt to restore Britain's ability to act independently in the world can be seen in a number of different areas. As part of a small committee of ministers, he participated in the secret decision of January 1947 to build a British atomic bomb. He and the handful of other ministers who met without consulting either the Cabinet or Parliament assumed that Britain, as a great power, had to have atomic weapons as a deterrent. Britain 'could not afford to acquiesce in an American monopoly of this new development', Bevin concluded.[109] Both Bevin and Attlee also thought that possession of atomic weapons would increase Britain's influence with the Americans, whom they still feared might revert to isolationism.[110] In fact, that influence proved illusory. The Americans, as they had since the end of the war, refused to treat Britain as an equal, while the Labour government remained so eager to show that Britain was a worthy atomic partner that it agreed in January 1948 to provide the United States with uranium and other materials and give up the right, agreed on during the war, to approve any American use of atomic weapons in exchange for technical co-operation which, according to the official historian, 'amounted to very little'.[111]

The desire to free Britain from the United States was evident, too, in the Labour government's increased efforts to increase exports from the colonies, whose raw materials were an important source of dollar earnings. Bevin had long dreamed of developing Africa as the new centre of the British empire. An African strategy would 'modernise the whole character of our defence as well as our trade and bring into British orbit economically and commercially a great area which is by no means fully developed yet', he wrote in March 1946.[112] In July 1947, he told Attlee that colonial development was 'more vital than ever now'; he had begun an enquiry of 'all the essential raw materials which the United States is short of . . . in order that we can develop an independent position with the United States instead of being supplicants'.[113] Almost a year later Bevin was still thinking in these terms. American aid, he told the Cabinet in March 1948, should be used to 'gain time' until attaining a position for Britain and Western Europe 'independent both of the US and the Soviet Union'. If Africa were developed, 'we could have [the] US dependent on us and eating out of our hand in four or five years. . . . [The] US is very barren of essential minerals and in Africa we have them all.'[114]

Such thinking indicates that Bevin's policy was not just a response to changes in the balance of power but had its own neo-imperial agenda. A developed Africa would be linked to expanded ties to the Middle East, serving now as a replacement for India, whose loss Bevin had only reluctantly accepted. (Bevin had played no part in the negotiations that led to the granting of independence to India.) In 1946, Bevin had 'favoured a policy of remaining in the whole of India', for fear Britain would otherwise 'lose considerable prestige in the Far East and in Europe'.[115] Even in January 1947 he opposed rapid withdrawal from India and urged Attlee to 'take a stronger line'. 'Within the British Empire', he wrote, 'we knuckle under at the first blow and yet we are expected to preserve the position. It cannot be done and I beg of you in all sincerity, even if it does involve a certain risk, to take it, and I believe the world will respect us.'[116] The sensible Attlee gave short shrift to Bevin's suggestion that they should stay in India, though not to the imperial vision that inspired it.

In the wake of Indian independence, Bevin told his aides early in 1948 that he planned to 'develop Aden and Somaliland as forward bases' and to use the Sudan to protect Egypt and provide 'an important source of manpower'. Mombassa would be a 'vital rear

ERNEST BEVIN

base', and Cyrenaica a 'second-best' addition or alternative to Egypt. The Lebanon might also be a 'forward base' and perhaps Akaba.[117] He also planned to create a new alliance system of Egypt, Iraq and Transjordan that would allow Britain, as he put it, to 'exploit the manpower resources of the Middle East by means of joint defence boards set up under treaties between H. M. G. and each of the states concerned. . . . Thus we should have one great Middle Eastern Army. This was the more necessary now that we could longer count on India as a manpower reserve.'[118] The problem with this plan was that it took no account of growing nationalist sentiment and of the reluctance of Middle Eastern countries to play their part.

Even Bevin's renewed turn to closer European co-operation, although taken with an eye to a perceived Soviet threat, was initially aimed at becoming independent from the United States. He told French Prime Minister Ramadier in September 1947 that 'with their populations of 47 million and 40 million respectively and with their vast colonial possessions', France and Britain could, 'if they acted together, be as powerful as either the Soviet Union or the United States'.[119] After the Council of Foreign Ministers failed once again to reach agreement on anything in December 1947, Bevin began to act on his plan to 'organize the Western States into a coherent unity', as he had put it to his officials a few months earlier. He now proposed to Secretary of State Marshall 'the formation of some form of union, formal or informal in character, in Western Europe backed by the United States and the Dominions' to 'create confidence in Western Europe that further Communist inroads would be stopped'. This would not be a 'formal alliance' between Europe and the United States, Bevin said, but 'an understanding backed by power, money and resolute action. It would be a sort of spiritual federation of the West.'[120]

In January 1948, Bevin informed the Cabinet of his plans, telling them that the Soviets, 'actively hostile to British interests everywhere', were 'exerting a constantly increasing pressure which threatens the whole fabric of the West'. 'The success of Russian expansionist plans would threaten, if not destroy, the three main elements of Commonwealth defence, the security of the United Kingdom, the control of sea communications, and the defence of the Middle East.' He thought Britain would 'be hard put to it to stem

176

FOREIGN SECRETARY

the further encroachment of the Soviet tide' without 'some form of union in Western Europe', for which Britain should take the lead. 'The countries of Western Europe which despise the spiritual values of America will look to us for political and moral guidance. . . . ' Britain, in other words, was to provide the link between Europe and the United States.

> Provided we can organise a Western European system . . . backed by the power and resources of the Commonwealth and the Americas, it should be possible to develop our power and influence to equal that of the United States of America and the U.S.S.R. We have the material resources in the Colonial Empire if we develop them, and by giving a spiritual lead now we should be able to carry out our task in a way which will show clearly that we are not subservient to the United States of America or the Soviet Union.[121]

He was not yet thinking of a formal military alliance but a union based on shared ideals and the acceptance of British leadership.

American policy-makers welcomed this development while making clear they wanted the Europeans to take the initiative before they would provide increased support. The Europeans' tentative steps towards closer unity – there was disagreement about the French desire to protect against Germany rather than the Soviet Union – became a rapid march after the Communist seizure of power in Czechoslovakia in late February 1948, which evoked memories of the Nazis and seemed to confirm the worst fears about the Soviet Union. Bevin now told the Cabinet that the Soviet Union intended to 'extend its hold over the remaining part of continental Europe' and eventually over 'the whole World Island'. Rhetorically asking his colleagues whether 'our policy should not now be broadened so that we can proceed urgently with the active organisation of all those countries who believe in parliamentary government and free institutions', he argued that 'evidence of irresolution and divided counsels' could produce a 'lack of the will to resist which may have terrible results'.[122] Only two weeks after his warning to the Cabinet, Britain signed a defence treaty with France, Belgium, Holland and Luxemburg.

Bevin saw the Brussels Pact as a step toward his goal of securing an American commitment to the defence of Europe, as well as a way to ease French fears about the revival of Germany. Shortly after its

177

formation, he proposed that Britain, the United States and Canada should join to form an 'Atlantic security system'. This introduced a new way of thinking about the issue of European defence. Instead of simply linking the United States to a European system it adopted a different regional view. From this idea grew the much broader North Atlantic Treaty Organisation (NATO) that began in April 1949 and whose creation Bevin saw as his most significant achievement.

The talks that eventually culminated in NATO began in Washington in the summer of 1948, just as events in Germany threatened to bring the Soviet Union and the West into actual conflict. After the break-up of the Council of Foreign Ministers in December 1947, Bevin had negotiated a new agreement about the Bizone that provided for increased American financial support. But such aid, as it had since 1946, had a price, the abandonment of Britain's reformist economic goals, which included plans for a capital levy and the nationalisation of German heavy industry. In February 1947, Bevin had told the Cabinet that the government should push ahead with socialisation 'regardless of American reactions'.[123] Now these goals were abandoned in accord with American desires. As Brian Robertson, the British military governor in Germany, pointed out, 'He who pays the piper calls the tune'.[124]

Beginning in February 1948, Belgium, Holland, Luxemburg, Britain, the United States and France held a series of talks in London designed to speed the economic revival of Germany and prepare the way for the creation of a West German state. This created two problems. The French were reluctant to accept a revived Germany and the Russians would view it with fear and possibly try to prevent its creation. The division of Germany, in other words, made even more urgent the need for a new defence system. The talks that led to the creation of NATO began in part to meet these two needs. The French, Bevin told Marshall, had to have 'some additional hope of a really workable Security System if they are to be induced to accept the plan for Germany'.[125]

When the Western powers in June instituted a currency reform in the Western zones and Berlin as an essential step toward reviving Germany, the Soviets responded by blockading the routes into Berlin in an attempt to prevent the creation of a Western-oriented, German state. Although it was a response to what must have seemed

178

FOREIGN SECRETARY

threatening Western actions, the Berlin blockade only confirmed the dominant view of Soviet aggressiveness and further contributed to the decision to create a new military alliance, one that could also provide increased diplomatic leverage in cold war struggles.[126] The Western powers countered with the famous Berlin airlift, which stymied the blockade and overcame Soviet resistance to the creation of West Germany.

Bevin worried about the Western ability to defend Berlin but encouraged a strong Western stance. 'The Western Powers must no longer be subservient to the Soviet Union', he told other foreign secretaries in July.[127] One day after the blockade began he invited the United States to station bombers in Britain in order to show the Soviets, as he put it, 'that we mean business'.[128] The basing in England of American B-29 bombers capable of carrying atomic weapons aimed to convince the Russians not to interfere with the airlift to Berlin. Bevin said that his goal in accepting American bombers was to be in a 'strong position' and 'not to be, as we had previously been, at the mercy of Molotov'.[129] Such a statement seems to indicate that Bevin's acceptance of American bombers was designed to increase British autonomy by making Britain more able to resist the Soviet Union. Arguably, however, it had the opposite effect, because Bevin and the others who made this decision failed to win any right to approve the American use of atomic weapons, a failure that indicates Britain's growing client status. When the issue came up again in 1950, Bevin and other responsible officials failed to mention it for fear, according to the official history, 'that a letter on the subject might cause suspicion and offence'. As the Foreign Office noted at that time, 'The primary aim of our foreign policy must be to keep the United States firmly committed in Europe. . . . We must face the fact that this island is strategically well placed as an advanced air base and we must accept that role.'[130]

By increasing the possibility that tension with the Soviet Union could spin out of control and lead to war, the Berlin crisis underlined the need for a new defence organisation. Nevertheless, ominous as the Berlin blockade seemed, Bevin still thought that the main threat from the Soviet Union was not military, but economic and psychological, that Europe would turn to communism out of despair and lack of confidence or that the Soviets would somehow exploit continued economic difficulties for their own ends.[131]

179

ERNEST BEVIN

Europe, Bevin thought, lacked confidence and will, without which it could never recover. 'The loss of [national self-respect] is at the root of France's present troubles', Bevin told the Cabinet.[132] American support for Europe's defence would provide the key to renewed confidence. It 'would put heart into the whole of Western Europe', he said. It would also have a 'profound influence in dealing with the long standing German problem', and thus win French agreement to the revival of Germany, without which European economic recovery would stall.[133]

The possibility of a more formal American commitment to Europe raised the same questions as the Marshall Plan: What was Britain's relationship to the other European countries? Was Britain just another European country or did it have a special relationship with the United States as well as with its present and former colonies? Initially, Bevin wanted Britain to take a leading role in organising European unity. In March 1948, he and Stafford Cripps, now Chancellor of the Exchequer, told the Cabinet that Britain was 'the only country than can give a lead' to promote European recovery. Failure to do so could leave them pensioners of the United States, with 'disintegrating political and social results'. Accepting that closer ties could create a 'profound change' in the British economic system, they argued that it was 'only by changes in and reintegration of our economies that we can have our economic freedom'. But even though they thought at this time there was 'no option' for Britain than closer links to Europe, they remained deeply ambivalent, since such links should 'not weaken' Britain's 'connection with the Commonwealth'. Closer ties also had 'risks', association with 'partners in Western Europe whose political condition is unstable and whose actions may be embarrassing to us'.[134]

During 1948 pressure for greater European unity grew both from the United States, which saw unity as a key to economic recovery, and from other European countries. For a variety of reasons, Bevin resisted these pressures to speed up the pace of change. Inside Britain, the cause seemed to be endorsed by the Conservatives and therefore acquired partisan overtones. There was also a certain provincialism in Bevin's view of Europe. He thought the French, for example, lacked 'any sense of civic responsibility, while the Government for their part show little capacity to give leadership, tackle the problems of the day and inspire public confidence'.[135]

180

FOREIGN SECRETARY

Above all, Bevin and the rest of the government gave up their original attempt to lead Europe toward unity because of their calculation about Britain's self-interest. Europe seemed too weak economically and militarily, and Bevin lost faith that it could evolve with Britain into an independent third force in the world. 'We must not run risks which would jeopardise our chance of survival if the attempt to restore Western Europe should fail', Bevin and Cripps advised their colleagues in January 1949.[136] Closer ties to Europe also seemed to threaten the financially more important connection to the Commonwealth and the sterling area as well as the government's ability to control financial policy. Labour had by now created a new welfare state and Bevin feared that a larger European entity might interfere with it. Thus, for Bevin and other policy-makers, Britain's self-interest still seemed to lie in its world role, not in building a united Europe. We 'cannot accept integration in Western Europe on a scale which would impair [our] other responsibilities', Bevin said in 1949. 'Because of its overseas connexions . . . [Britain] could never become an entirely European country.'[137]

Lacking confidence in the other European countries while retaining a commitment to a world role that Britain could still not sustain on its own, Bevin turned even more ardently to the United States. Instead of 'Western Union', they now had to 'substitute the wider conception of the Atlantic community', Bevin told the Cabinet in 1949. In addition to the support it could provide against a perceived Soviet threat, American aid was vital to stamp out the growing revolutionary unrest in Europe's colonies. Loss of these colonies, Bevin told Dean Acheson, would be 'fatal' to the West since they were 'an essential part of Europe's economic existence'.[138] Accepting what later came to be called the domino theory, Bevin encouraged the United States to take a more active role in aiding French attempts to reimpose its rule over Indochina. The French, he told them, 'stand in Indo-China in one of the key positions for the defence of the free world against Communism'.[139] Sustaining the French position in Indochina seemed essential to the British position in the region, particularly in Malaya, its most prosperous colony and the site now of a revolutionary insurgency. 'We would naturally prefer to defend Malaya by defending Indochina', one key British official explained in August 1950.[140]

Bevin regarded the creation of NATO in April 1949, which he

181

had been urging since March 1948, as the capstone of his diplomatic strategy. By linking the United States to Europe, NATO assured French acceptance of a revived Germany, which was essential to European recovery, as well as the containment of the Soviet Union, which was vital to European confidence. Within this new treaty organisation, Bevin and his advisers believed that British interest lay in positioning Britain, along with Canada and the United States, as what the Foreign Office called the 'real core of the anti-Communist coalition', an unofficial inner group whose existence 'should be kept entirely from the Latins – to say nothing of the journalists'.[141] To maintain this status as first among (European) equals, Bevin and his advisers thought, Britain above all had to remain willing to sustain its world position so that the United States would continue to find it a useful investment. Otherwise, the Foreign Office concluded, 'partnership [with the USA] might well be broken, with grave effects, especially on the priority accorded to the United Kingdom in the field of economic help'.[142] In spite of Stafford Cripps's criticism that 'the implications' of this Foreign Office position seemed 'to be much nearer permanent subservience to the U.S.A. than anything else', Bevin made the 'special relationship' with the United States and the Atlantic alliance the centre of British policy.[143] 'Since it [NATO] is the kernel of their policy, it must also be the kernel of ours', Bevin told the Cabinet in May 1950.[144]

Bevin thought Britain could act, ideally, as an intermediary between the rest of Europe and the United States. In reality, Europe now proceeded to develop on its own. The French, whom Bevin thought showed no capacity for leadership, launched in May 1950 the European Coal and Steel Community, which eventually gave rise to the European Economic Community. After the 1949 sterling crisis, the United States had accepted that Britain could not be forced to unite with the other European countries and that it had to accept Britain's special economic needs.[145] But American policy-makers continued to refuse to regard Britain 'as entirely different from the other European powers', as they made clear in bipartite meetings in May 1950, and proved quite willing to accept French leadership on the continent.[146] In retrospect at least, Bevin's failure to join with the Europeans in favour of a largely mythical special relationship with the United States was perhaps his most serious failure of vision during this entire period.

182

FOREIGN SECRETARY

Although not willing to accord the British a special status, American policy-makers still wanted them to continue and even expand their military commitments. A number of factors in 1949 – the triumph of Communism in China, Soviet development of atomic weapons, the continued slowness of European economic recovery, the need to reconcile France to an independent and economically revived West Germany, and the expansion of revolution in the Third World – convinced American leaders that massive rearmament was needed to meet these problems, as well as what they saw as a dangerous loss of confidence.

> What was needed now was a determined effort by the Western Powers to show that they were not prepared to give way under the pressure of Russian communism [Acheson told the British]; on the contrary that they were determined to strengthen and consolidate their position. In the old days the British fleet by a show of force had been enough to maintain the peace of the world. It was just as essential now to be able to demonstrate to the peoples of Asia, as also to the Satellite Powers, that the West was strong, organised, and determined to maintain its way of life.[147]

He therefore pressured Britain to increase defence spending, which the British, who already devoted a greater percentage of their income to the military than any other Western country, resisted unless the United States would provide substantial aid. Bevin told the American ambassador in September 1949 that the proposal for increased defence spending 'seemed to rest on the totally false assumption that we could undertake enormous unknown and unlimited liabilities'.[148]

Eventually, Bevin, who viewed the Soviet Union as a 'predatory expansionist power' that required the West to 'build up its strength', agreed to a vast increase in military spending, but only after the Korean War began in June 1950. Although precipitated by the North Korean invasion of South Korea, and regarded as another example of Soviet expansion, that war, like the one in Greece, was really a civil war, as historians Jon Halliday and Bruce Cumings point out, between a 'revolutionary nationalist movement, which had its roots in tough anti-colonial struggle, and a conservative movement tied to the *status quo*, especially to an unequal land system'.[149] Both Britain and the United States, however, saw the hand of the Soviet Union behind the struggle and feared that it

183

ERNEST BEVIN

marked a prelude to Soviet thrusts elsewhere. For American policy-makers, the war also provided the occasion to overcome political resistance to their already planned expansion of the defence budget, while for the British it provided the occasion to show that they were worthy partners of the United States. Sending troops to Korea, which the Chiefs of Staff opposed, would be a 'useful demonstration of the United Kingdom's capacity to act as a world power', the Cabinet noted.[150]

Bevin and the rest of the Labour government, fearing that they would otherwise be 'treated as merely one of the European countries', as Attlee put it, now agreed to the American demands for a more massive increase in military spending than they thought Britain could afford.[151] Aneurin Bevan warned his colleagues to no avail that social and economic improvement, not militarisation of the Atlantic alliance, represented the best defence against Soviet communism. They would have done well to listen. By diverting scarce resources from private industry, the rearmament programme hastened Britain's economic decline as competitors increased their market share of the exports Britain was unable to supply. By driving up the price of raw materials and overheating the economy, it also created a sterling crisis that undermined the credibility and resolve of the government, which had been narrowly re-elected in 1950. Equally important, the rearmament programme divided the Labour Party, which never regained the degree of support or unity that it had had from 1945 to 1950. 'The transformed defence commitment', Kenneth Morgan has observed, 'marked a profound watershed in British political history.'[152]

Throughout his tenure as Foreign Secretary, Bevin had health problems, which the strain of office and his destructive habits – he worked non-stop, and ate, drank and smoked to excess – made worse. His periodic breakdowns grew more frequent as time went on. By early 1950, one of his private secretaries later recorded, Bevin was 'clearly past his best. . . . The random wisdom, often hard to comprehend . . ., was gradually disappearing into a more and more confused articulation and periods of physical strain, when he would sit, hardly attentive now, with pendulous stomach and great head lolling upon his chest.'[153] In January 1951, Bevin was stricken with pneumonia. Under the circumstances, he should have resigned on his own, but he lived only for his work and wanted to

184

FOREIGN SECRETARY

die in office. By March, however, Attlee felt compelled to ask him to resign. By ill chance, Attlee informed Bevin of this decision while a party for his seventieth birthday was in progress at the Foreign Office. It was a sad end to his career. 'I've got the sack', Bevin told his wife later that day.[154] Just over a month later he died, on 14 April 1951.

Conclusion

Most historians have celebrated Bevin's accomplishments as Foreign Secretary, particularly for successfully maintaining Britain as a major player on the world stage in spite of economic weakness. Alan Bullock writes glowingly of Bevin's 'grand design' to revive and unite Western Europe, including West Germany, and obtain American support for it. Certainly, as much as any single person, Bevin was responsible for creating the North Atlantic system that provided the military organisation for the West for the next four decades. In so far as that system created the basis for a stable balance of power and therefore maintained peace inside Europe, it ranks as a major accomplishment. If it is assumed that the Soviet Union did threaten to take over the entire continent of Europe, or that British withdrawal from its imperial position would have produced a dangerous instability, then Bevin's accomplishments as Foreign Secretary are impressive.

But those assumptions are questionable. The Soviet Union was primarily a political, not a military threat and, badly damaged by the war, initially sought some sort of accommodation with the West. To be sure, the dictatorial nature of the Soviet Union and its increasingly brutal control of Eastern Europe, coupled with the postwar strength of Communist parties in Western and southern Europe, aroused real fears. Political conflict was probably unavoidable. Nevertheless, even though Bevin's and others' fears of the Soviets were strong, the massive militarisation of the West was excessive and would seem to have had as much to do with American determination to project the preponderant power of the United States worldwide as with any military threat from the Soviet Union. The creation of NATO and the rearmament of 1950–1 started an arms race that wasted vast resources which might have been better devoted to human development. It underwrote and justified as a

185

ERNEST BEVIN

defence of freedom the numerous neo-colonial wars in the Third World that fastened reactionary governments on unwilling populations and cost millions of lives. It also hastened Britain's economic decline by diverting resources from domestic economic development and helping to create a series of balance of payments crises that prevented sustained economic growth. The cold war was a tragedy, not a triumph.

Bevin's view of the world was in many ways backward-looking. He believed that because he was in charge and had good intentions British imperialism had changed – 'We have ceased to be an imperial race. We dominate nobody', he said in 1949 – but this was not a view shared by an increasing number of people in Asia, the Middle East and Africa who were still ruled, directly or indirectly, by Britain. In reality, aside from the socialist gloss he put on it, his imperial vision differed only slightly from that of Lord Curzon or Winston Churchill. 'My whole aim', Bevin wrote to Atlee, 'has been to develop the Middle East as a producing area [in agriculture and oil] to help our own economy and take the place of India.'[155] Underlying Bevin's support for the cold war was an imperial vision that shaped his attitude to the Soviet Union and determined his decision to link Britain to the United States.

The object of Bevin's policy was to preserve Britain's freedom of action. But did it do that? Bevin, like his Foreign Office advisers, believed that he could control the partnership with the United States. 'The United States was a young country and the administration was only too apt to take unreflecting plunges. We made it our business to restrain them', Bevin told Nehru in 1950.[156] This was an exaggeration. When, for example, Bevin suggested that the United States should compromise in Korea by trading acceptance of Communist China's membership in the United Nations for North Korean withdrawal from South Korea, Acheson rebuffed him with a warning that the 'the implications of your message and its possible consequences on the relationship between your country and mine might be very serious indeed'.[157] It was the sort of response the British might have delivered to an uppity client in the nineteenth century and made perfectly clear who was the dominant partner in this relationship. It was the United States, with its own clear vision of the postwar world, that determined the shape of Anglo-American relations.

FOREIGN SECRETARY

Bevin and other British policy-makers believed that if they acted in certain ways the United States would treat them as equals and support their independence, but this, too, was an illusion. The United States was never willing to provide Britain with sufficient aid to regain the ability to function autonomously in the world. Moreover, by relying on the United States to underwrite a world role that Britain was unable to sustain on its own, Bevin, and in this case the rest of the Labour government, isolated the country from Europe for the next twenty years. This surely represents the great lost opportunity of the period, one that perhaps irreparably delayed Britain's adaptation to changed international circumstances, particularly to the need for economic modernisation.

In so far as Bevin himself was responsible for these foreign policy choices – to interpret ambiguous evidence of Soviet intentions in the most negative way, to encourage the division of Germany and Europe, to accept the militarisation of the cold war with all its waste and destruction, to support a recharged European imperialism and the wars needed to sustain it, to make Britain virtually a client of the United States and isolate it from Europe – it seems arguable that there is less to celebrate in this last phase of his career than has hitherto been assumed. Although it can only be speculation, it is intriguing to consider whether the more iconoclastic Dalton would have been better able to respond to Clement Attlee's imaginative response to Britain's postwar situation, a response that was far truer to Labour's internationalist ideals, and more realistic.

Conclusion

The trade union movement formed the centre of Errest Bevin's life and achievement. It made possible his rise in life, gave purpose and direction to his early religious and socialist ideals, and shaped his mature views. 'Can the diplomats and governing classes show us anything so wonderful as this movement which was built out of nothing', he said to the dockers in 1920. . . . 'Its capital was an ideal, the desire to fight against evil.'[1] Almost everything he did after joining the Dockers' Union in 1910 was calculated in some way to increase the power of the trade union movement and make it better able to defend the working people it represented.

Bevin was not the only labour leader who understood, as he put it, that 'the fundamental basis of power is conscious Trade Union membership', but no one proved better able to put this idea into practice.[2] It was Bevin's energy and practical ability that proved decisive in creating the Transport and General Workers' Union, a massive accomplishment of which he was justifiably proud. Bevin's ideal of a trade union as a 'disciplined army' could be overly bureaucratic and hierarchical, and could at times clash with traditions of workplace autonomy; but this ideal grew out of his experience as a trade union organiser – where he saw only too clearly the lack of real unity among transport and dock workers and the resulting weakness in the face of the owners' ruthless use of power – as well as out of the harsh economic climate of the interwar years. Bevin deserves considerable credit not only for creating the TGWU, but also for establishing it on what proved to be a lasting basis. Had he done nothing else, he would have earned a permanent place in modern British history for his role in founding the TGWU and steering it through its first years.

Although Bevin's central organisational goal as a trade unionist remained fixed, his strategies changed over time. Always filled with anger at the exclusion of the working class from full membership in

CONCLUSION

British society and at that society's failure to accept the trade union movement, he could often be belligerent and even at times flirt with direct action. Until the General Strike, he sometimes thought that the 'capitalist system . . . [was] going to its death', as he put it in 1921, or at least that organised trade union power could compel changes in the way management treated workers. Increasingly, however, his need to 'deal with facts as they are' led him to conclude that what was later called corporatism – the co-operation of business, the unions and the state – provided the most effective route for working-class advancement. Particularly after the failure of the General Strike convinced him that capitalism was not about to give way to socialism, he, along with Walter Citrine, successfully steered the TUC along this path. 'We have to deal with our business on business lines and whilst working under a capitalist system we have to have regard to it accordingly', he told A. J. Cook in 1927.[3] After the Mond–Turner talks of 1928–9, he never wavered from this approach.

Throughout the barren 1930s this corporatist strategy had only partial success outside the confines of the TGWU, signally failing to help unemployed workers or those who were not union members. At times, it also overrode rank and file activism and undercut the attempts of militants to expand trade union membership. As Minister of Labour during the Second World War, however, Bevin made corporatism a success. The mechanisms he then put in place not only mobilised the working class for the war effort with a minimal amount of unrest, but also encouraged a vast expansion of the trade union movement and ensured what seemed, at least until Margaret Thatcher's reign, the permanent institutionalisation of its power. Working-class living standards, working conditions and opportunities steadily improved as a result of his work. This was an impressive confirmation of the betterment in workers' lives that corporatist arrangements could achieve.

Underlying Bevin's embrace of corporatism was his strong belief that economic and social problems could be solved with good will and rational direction, 'a complete combination of management, science and men'.[4] Labour organisation made corporatism possible because without large trade unions and employers' federations, such co-operation would have proved impossible. The real villain for Bevin was not management, but the 'King Johns of Finance', as he

189

ERNEST BEVIN

called them, who manipulated industry without regard to the needs of those engaged in it.[5] All others in industry, he thought, had a shared stake in improving production and in working together.

As such sentiments indicate, Bevin after his early years ceased to be a socialist in the conventional sense of focusing primarily on questions of ownership. 'I want to test every expedient by that standard', he said in 1930, whether it can 'maintain the standard of living and even to see it progress – That is the object of industry, is it not?'[6] Bevin's labourism, his willingness to accept the existing framework of society, does not, however, mean that he simply embraced existing capitalist institutions. He had an ideal of a better society, one that had its origins in his youthful religious nonconformity, but that took precise shape from his work as a trade unionist. Workers, he never stopped insisting, contributed as much to society as anyone else. 'Nothing exists except through the producer; that is where wealth comes from', he told Parliament, no doubt to the annoyance of his Tory listeners.[7] Workers therefore had a right to employment and security, to a decent minimum standard, and to be regarded as equal members of society. That ideal could be realised because the state, he believed, had the capacity (and the obligation) to solve remaining social problems and provide the material basis for expanded citizenship rights for everyone. 'I believe the day is not far distant when we shall say about poverty, unemployment and all the other things that have ailed us in this country and have been part of our economic regime, that it is as much a disease as illiteracy was', he said at the start of the Second World War.[8] Planning, public ownership where necessary and co-operation among the institutional representatives of both business and labour could attain these goals. This was neither the socialism his critics on the Labour Left envisioned, nor the capitalism most Tories wanted, as shown by their opposition to him as Minister of Labour.

Bevin's emphasis on the representation of organised interest groups, that is, trade union leaders, rather than workplace democracy, as the key to working-class empowerment could leave some workers dissatisfied, as the busmen in the 1930s and the dockers after the Second World War demonstrate. In spite of the increased power of the trade union movement, the wage relationship itself remained problematic. Bevin was too optimistic at times as well

CONCLUSION

about the possibility of converting business to an ideal of 'service' and the willingness of employers to put working-class welfare ahead of profits. He was not naive, however. Many of the reforms he sponsored in these years were designed precisely to force more selfish employers to conform to the standards of the more progressive ones, or to ensure that trade unions were in a permanently stronger position to defend workers.

As a socialist, Bevin understood in theory that capitalism was both unjust and inefficient, but it clearly took him time in practice to appreciate that the traditional ruling elite had no special wisdom that entitled them to govern. 'Superiority is claimed by the middle class in the realms of Government, when, as a matter of fact, their work is a monument of incompetence', he said in 1935. 'Their claim is not justified, for some of the greatest geniuses and people of great managerial capacity have sprung from the ranks of the working people.'[9] Surely, one of the geniuses Bevin had immodestly in mind was himself. And with some justification. Walter Citrine later said that he had 'never met his [Bevin's] equal . . . in wage negotiations and the general things affecting Trade Unions'.[10] An able administrator, skilled negotiator, possessed according to one of his secretaries at the Ministry of Labour of the 'most remarkable memory of any man I have ever known', Bevin was right to see himself as the equal of any representative of the traditional governing class.[11]

Bevin was at his best when denouncing the incompetence of traditional elites and defending working-class talents and rights, a stance which grew out of his own experience. At the same time, his insistence on working-class abilities may also indicate the emotional wounds inflicted on him by poverty, class distinction and lack of education. As we have seen, Bevin had difficulty tolerating criticism or acknowledging the work of others, talked about himself constantly and exaggerated his own accomplishments, even though they were widely recognised and honoured. It is possible that such traits indicate an underlying emotional insecurity, a great need to inflate his own ego or violently ward off those who seemed to challenge it. Whatever the source of this behaviour, it made up Bevin's least attractive side. He sometimes bullied his opponents and critics, constantly personalised disagreement as a form of treachery and fell at times into what can only can be called egomania. 'When our Government was trying to stamp out your Revolution, who was it

191

ERNEST BEVIN

that stopped it? It was I, Ernest Bevin. I called out the transport workers and they refused to load the ships . . . ', he said to Soviet Foreign Secretary Molotov.[12] 'I formed the International Transport Workers' Union', he told the Labour Party.[13] 'My union', 'my paper', 'my policy' – it was a strangely individualist stance for someone so genuinely committed to a collective movement.

At times, this individualism led Bevin into a sort of paternalistic attitude toward the working class that would seem more appropriate to a Tory leader. No one, after all, more ably defended working-class ways or working-class abilities. But he expected workers to 'appreciate' what he had done for them and to respond by giving 'good output'. He had, of course, done a great deal, but it was something he accomplished with the working class, through their loyalty and sacrifices, not just on his own.

Bevin's attitude to the traditional ruling elite, whose incompetence he so often castigated, was similarly contradictory. A supporter of the monarchy, he criticised Edward VIII during the abdication crisis of 1936 for 'letting down the country'.[14] He got on well with George VI, whom he found to be a 'very decent man'.[15] Such attitudes may simply mark him as sharing widely held working-class views about the monarchy, similar perhaps to his prejudices against Jews and Catholics. Bevin, one of his closest Foreign Office advisers later noted, 'had all kinds of awful prejudices'.[16] But he was also a 'warm admirer of Eton and Harrow', main breeding grounds of the class privilege and class distinction that he so denounced.[17] Alan Lascelles, private secretary to George VI, recorded in his diary that at one wartime dinner, 'various Ministers started a round of old-school-tie chaff. . . . Ernie . . . fetched a gargantuan sigh, and said in my ear "I always wish I'd been at one of them places".'[18] Such stories suggest that Bevin's desire to be accepted played an unconscious role in his own political formation.

Although Bevin's move in 1945 to the Foreign Office marked a real break in his career, his approach to the new job created a continuity with the work he had done as a trade union leader. As he had done earlier, Bevin tried to make a realistic assessment of 'facts as they are' and obtain for his followers the best deal possible under the circumstances. Now, however, he saw himself defending not just the working class but all of Britain. As Alan Bullock has aptly pointed out, once the Labour Party was 'accepted as the constitu-

192

CONCLUSION

tional government of the country . . . he found it natural to take a national rather than a class view of his responsibilities'.[19] For Bevin, the best way to protect British national interests – its world position, the basis of Britain's economic well-being and the perceived threat from the Soviet Union – was to draw closer to the United States and pull back from Europe. Whether this was the best or even the only policy he could have chosen remains open to question, according to how British national interests are defined and how the threat from the Soviet Union is assessed, but it set the course of British foreign policy for the next two decades.

Had Bevin died in 1945, he would never have been lionised as he was only six years later. As a trade union leader, he would have been recognised only for his contributions to the working class, not something *The Times* or its readers usually prized. His work as Minister of Labour was of lasting importance, but much of it had been controversial. Many Conservatives disliked what he had done and remained unreconciled to the new power of the TUC. It was thus Bevin's years as Foreign Secretary that likely account for the praise showered upon him at his death as embodying 'characteristically British qualities'.

In these years, Bevin's proud nationalism came to the fore, displacing his earlier criticisms of the ruling class's incompetence. 'I know there are lots of people who believe that the British race – and I am beating no patriotic drum – is finished with, is down and out, and is done for', he told the TUC in 1930. 'I do not believe it. I believe that we have a culture, we have an ability, we have a craftmanship that can still render great service to the world in return for the food we eat, and for the goods we make.'[20] He was as strongly positive twenty years later. Bevin's nationalism carried an implicit message: the criticism of British society and British imperialism that generations of labourites had made was no longer true. His own successful career, which climaxed with Labour's rise to power in 1945, seemed to demonstrate that Britain could be made into a more inclusive and fair society, while his career as Foreign Secretary put a social democratic gloss to a traditional goal – preserving Britain's position as a world power and its predominance in areas such as the Middle East. Bevin's celebration of Britain was thus profoundly reassuring, particularly for those groups that the labour movement had been opposing since its inception. It was this,

193

it can be suggested, that accounts for his apotheosis after his death.

Bevin's legacy as Foreign Secretary, as we have seen, is open to debate. From the Foreign Office point of view, it was an immense success, preserving Britain's great power status, and helping to contain the threat from the Soviet Union, a judgement many historians have endorsed. It might also be said, however, that Bevin unintentionally hastened Britain's decline by delaying its coming to terms with reduced power, tying it to an expensive world position that interfered with economic growth, and turning it away from the most effective available path to economic modernisation, membership in the European community. Indeed, the history of Britain since the late 1960s can be seen, at least in one respect, as an attempt to undo much of this legacy, particularly to shrink British commitments east of Suez and focus on Europe.

In contrast, Bevin's legacy as a trade union leader and as Minister of Labour remains as vital today as half a century ago. Trade unions remain the major institutional defence of workers, and the TGWU continues to fulfil that function in ways that would have pleased Bevin. His ideal of working-class rights to employment, a decent wage, and social security – all to be secured by state regulation of the economy – remains as necessary in post-Thatcherite Britain, with its almost three million unemployed, as it was before the Second World War. This aspect of Bevin's work remains both radical and humane, a lasting contribution to the working people of Britain and an ideal that still needs to be achieved.

Notes

Preface

1 John Saville, 'The Ideology of Labourism', in *Knowledge and Belief in Politics: The Problem of Ideology*, edited by Robert Benewick et al., London, 1973, pp. 215–16.

Chapter 1

1 Trevor Evans, *Bevin of Britain*, New York, 1946, p. 16; *The Times*, 16 April 1951, p. 6. The account in this chapter is based on the various biographies of Bevin cited in the Bibliography.
2 Samuel Gompers used this phrase, as did George VI's secretary. Mark Stephens, *Ernest Bevin: Unskilled Labourer and World Statesman*, Stevenage, 1981, p. 30; Alan Lascelles Diary, 24 October 1942, Bevin Papers, II, 9/3, Churchill College, Cambridge.
3 Alan Bullock, *The Life and Times of Ernest Bevin*, vol. I: *Trade Union Leader 1881–1940*, London, 1960, p. 2. Hereinafter cited as LT.
4 Evans, *Bevin*, p. 32.
5 Dockers Triennial Delegate Conference, 1920, Mss. 126/DWR/4/3/2, Modern Records Centre, Warwick. Hereinafter cited as MRC.
6 Cited by Bullock, *LT*, I, p. 69.
7 'Generally', TUC General Secretary Walter Citrine later observed, Bevin 'was serious-minded and even morose at times'. 'Bevin – The Man I Knew', Citrine Papers, I, 7/3, London School of Economics.
8 Bullock, *LT*, I, p. 16.
9 S. Bryher (S. Bale), *An Account of the Labour and Socialist Movement in Bristol*, Part I, London, 1929, p. 7.
10 Bryher, *Socialist Movement in Bristol*, Part II, pp. 54, 3.
11 Bristol Right-to-Work Committee, *Report 1908*, pp. 1–2, Bevin Papers, II, 7/2.
12 Bullock, *LT*, I, p. 20.
13 Bryher, *Socialist Movement in Bristol*, Part III, p. 3.
14 *Ibid.*, pp. 2–3.

Chapter 2

1 *Dockers' Record*, October 1920, p. 11.

NOTES TO PP. 9–20

2 Eric Hobsbawm, 'The "New Unionism" in Perspective', *Workers: Worlds of Labor*, New York, 1984, p. 156.

3 TUC, *Annual Report*, 1927, p. 298.

4 *Dockers' Record*, February 1916, p. 7; Meeting of Triple Industrial Alliance, 21 June 1917, Mss. 127/NU/1/1/5, MRC.

5 TUC, *Annual Report*, 1919, p. 243.

6 General Labourers' National Council and NTWF, Special Conference on Amalgamation, July 1914, p. 47, Mss. 126/NTW/4/1/6, MRC.

7 E. J. Hobsbawm, 'National Unions on the Waterside', in *Labouring Men: Studies in the History of Labour*, paperback ed., Garden City, New York, 1967, p. 255.

8 Speech to 1935 Biennial Delegate Conference, Bevin Papers, I, 7/2; Bevin to Deakin, 23 December 1942, Bevin Papers, I, 7/2.

9 Syndicalists argued for escalating conflict with employers as a way to educate workers and build organisation and support for a revolutionary general strike, out of which would come a new form of industrial democracy, with industries under the control of their workers and the state reduced to administrative functions. The syndicalist ideal of joining workers into 'one big union' affected Bevin and many other trade union leaders who still opposed conflict.

10 Conference on Amalgamation, p. 22, Mss. 126/NTW/4/1/6, MRC.

11 Cmd. 936, *Parliamentary Papers* (Hereinafter *PP*), 1920, XXIV, p. 495.

12 'The Reconstruction of Industry', *The Athenaeum*, May 1917, pp. 227–30.

13 TGWU, Biennial Delegate Conference, 1935, Bevin Papers, I, 1/7.

14 TUC, *Annual Report*, 1915, p. 337; NTWF, Annual General Council Meeting, 1916, Mss. 126/NTW/4/1/19, MRC; TUC, *Annual Report*, 1916, pp. 220–1.

15 NTWF, Annual General Council Meeting, 1917. See Bullock, *LT*, I, p. 48; Meeting of Triple Industrial Alliance, 21 June 1917, Mss. 127/NU/1/1/5, MRC.

16 Cited by Bullock, *LT*, I, p. 69.

17 Conference at Ministry of Labour, 26 March 1918, Williams to George Askwith, 16 April 1918, Devonport to Lloyd George, 9 April 1918, LAB 2/127/1, Public Record Office, London (hereinafter cited as PRO); *Transport and General Workers' Record*, March 1932, p. 241. Hereinafter cited as *Record*.

18 Meeting of Triple Alliance, 21 October 1916, Mss. 127/NU/GS/3/97vii, MRC; Bevin to D. C. Cummings, 25 August 1917, LAB 2/124/2, PRO; *Record*, March 1936, p. 172.

19 *British Labour and the Russian Revolution*. Reprint of *What Happened at Leeds*, Nottingham, n.d. [1974].

20 'The Reconstruction of Industry.'

21 Cited by Bullock, *LT*, I, p. 67; NTWF, Annual General Council Meeting, 1916, Mss. 126/NTW/4/1/19, MRC.

22 TUC, *Annual Report*, 1917, p. 227.

23 National Federation of General Workers, Annual General Council Meeting, 14–15 August 1919, p. 87, Mss. 126/NFGW/4/1/2, MRC. By 1920 he sat on fourteen Whitley councils.

24 Elie Halévy, *The Era of Tyrannies*, Garden City, New York, 1965, p. 181.

25 'The Need of a Re-organised Labour Movement', *Daily Herald*, 14 July 1919; 'Overproduction and the Inevitable Revolution', *Dockers' Record*, June, 1919.

NOTES TO PP. 20–30

26 *The Times*, 7 June 1919.
27 *The Times*, 12 January 1920.
28 Delegate Conference, 1920, p. 36, Mss. 126/DWR/4/3/2, MRC.
29 Bullock, *LT*, I, p. 136.
30 Cited by Stephen White, *Britain and the Bolshevik Revolution: A Study in the Politics of Diplomacy, 1920–1924*, New York, 1980, p. 48.
31 Dockers' Union, Delegate Conference, 1919, Mss. 126/DWR/4/3/2, MRC; Labour Party, *Conference Report*, 1920, p. 144. Hereinafter cited as *LPCR*.
32 Bevin, 'The Old must Give Place to the New', *Dockers' Record*, June/July, 1921, pp. 3–4.
33 'The Need of a Re-organised Labour Movement'.
34 TUC, *Annual Report*, 1920, p. 320. As he put it in October 1919: 'It is possible for the movement to organise without strikes, but in order to do so, and to save itself from waste, it must increase its collective bargaining power, and go on doing so.' *Daily Herald*, 8 October 1919, cited by B. C. Roberts, *The Trades Unions Congress 1868–1921*, Cambridge, Mass., 1958, p. 337.
35 Testimony to the Port of London Labour Committee [the Roche Committee], 12 May 1919, submitted by Bevin to the Shaw Committee and published as an appendix to its report. Cmd. 937, *PP*, 1920, XXIV, p. 36.
36 Minute by Mr Ramsbottom, 5 July 1919, LAB 2/638/6, PRO.
37 National Industrial Conference, Speeches, 27 February 1919, MUN 5/152/300/74, PRO; *Manchester Guardian*, 30 June 1920, Mss. 126/EB/AS/1/5, MRC.
38 Cited by Rodney Lowe, 'The Government and Industrial Relations', in *A History of British Industrial Relations*, vol. II: *1914–1939*, edited by Chris Wrigley, Brighton, 1987, p. 191.
39 Triple Alliance, 24 September 1920, Mss. 127/NU/GS/3/97/xxxi, MRC.
40 Bullock, *LT*, I, pp. 108–9.
41 23 September 1920, Mss. 127/NU/GS/3/97xxx, MRC; 22 September 1920, Mss. 127/NU/GS/3/97/xxix, MRC.
42 NTWF, Annual General Council Meeting, 1921, p. 30, Mss. 126/NTW/4/1/11, MRC; International Transport Workers' Federation Congress, *Report*, 1921, p. 73.
43 Mss. 126/NTW/4/1/11, pp. 32–3, MRC.
44 *The Diary of Beatrice Webb*, edited by Norman and Jeanne Mackenzie, Cambridge, Mass., 1984, III, p. 377.
45 14 July 1919, Mss. 126/EB/TU/5/1, MRC.
46 Cmd. 936, *PP*, 1920, XXIV, p. 127.
47 *Ibid.*, pp. 44, 491, 496.
48 *Ibid.*, pp. 190, 186.
49 *Ibid.*, pp. 24, 186, 189.
50 *Ibid.*, pp. 99, 197, 28, 496.
51 *Manchester Guardian*, 28 February 1919.
52 Cmd. 936, pp. 498, 11.
53 *Ibid.*, pp. 10–11.
54 Cmd. 937, p. 33.
55 *Ibid.*, p. 35.
56 Cmd. 936, p. 490.
57 *Ibid.*, p. 38.

197

NOTES TO PP. 30–40

58 Cmd. 937, p. 31.
59 Cmd. 936, p. 24.
60 *Ibid.*, pp. 178, 340, 497.
61 *Ibid.*, p. 497.
62 *Ibid.*, p. 490.
63 *Ibid.*, pp. 27, 426.
64 *The Times*, 21 February 1924.
65 Conference on Amalgamation, 1914, p. 48, Mss. 126/NTW/4/1/6, MRC.
66 Speech, May 1919, Mss. 126/EB/AS/1/1, MRC.
67 *Ibid.*; Memo by MF, 'The Amalgamation of the T.G.W.U.', 13 April 1928, Mss. 126/EB/TG/10/8, MRC. The fullest account is Ken Coates and Tony Topham, *The History of the Transport and General Workers' Union*, Oxford, 1991, pp. 772–838.
68 Minutes of Delegate Conference, 1 December 1920, Mss. 126/EB/TG/2/9i, MRC; *Dockers' Record*, December 1920, pp. 14–15.
69 NTWF, General Council Meeting, 1920, Mss. 126/NTW/4/1/10, MRC.
70 Coates and Topham, *Making*, p. 831.
71 Jack Jones, *Union Man*, London, 1956, p. 32.
72 *Winston Churchill: The Struggle for Survival, 1940–1965*, London, 1966, p. 67.
73 *The Second World War Diary of Hugh Dalton*, edited by Ben Pimlott, London, 1986, p. 636.
74 'Bevin – The Man I Knew', Citrine Papers, I, 7/3.
75 Conference, 4 June 1925, Mss. 127/NU/GS/3/97xxxix, MRC; Jack Jones, 'Ernest Bevin, Revolutionary by Consent', *Employment Gazette*, March 1981, p. 101.
76 Citrine, *Men and Work: An Autobiography*, London, 1964, pp. 179, 78. During the General Strike, Stanley Baldwin thought Bevin might 'picture himself as the Napoleon of the trade union movement'. Tom Jones, *Whitehall Diary*, edited by Keith Middlemas, London, 1969, II, p. 38.
77 Remarks at Shornells Conference, 23 March 1927, Mss. 126/EB/TG/6/19, MRC.
78 Transcript of radio show of 23 April 1957, Citrine Papers, I, 7/3; Alfred Chandler, *ibid.*
79 *Union Man*, p. 33.
80 *Record*, August 1923, March 1922.
81 *Manchester Guardian*, 5, 6, 7 and 9 July 1923.
82 *Record*, August 1923.
83 *Manchester Guardian*, 10 July 1923.
84 *Record*, September 1923.
85 F. W. Leggett, 23 January 1924, LAB 2/1039/14/IR1724, PRO.
86 Bevin, 'The Old must Give Place to the New'.
87 Dockers' Delegate Conference, 1920, Mss. 126/DWR/4/3/20, MRC.
88 *The Times*, 18 February 1924.
89 Kenneth Morgan, *Consensus and Disunity: The Lloyd George Coalition Government 1918–1922*, Oxford, 1979, p. 63.
90 Cited by G. A. Phillips, *The General Strike*, London, 1976, p. 55.
91 July 1925, Mss. 126/EB/GS/4/10, MRC. He thought that the coalowners' offer, if accepted, 'would have a detrimental effect upon the whole of the working class of this country' (*ibid.*).

198

NOTES TO PP. 41–49

92 General Secretary's (Third) Quarterly Report, 1925.
93 *Record*, July 1925, p. 277. My emphasis.
94 Biennial Delegate Conference, July 1925, Mss. 126/EB/GS/4/10, MRC; Third Quarterly Report, 1925.
95 Biennial Delegate Conference, 1925.
96 Bevin, 'The Miners' Dispute and the General Strike, 1926', *Record*, May–June 1926.
97 TUC, 'The Mining Situation, Report of a Special Conference of Executive Committees of Affiliated Unions, 29–30 April, 1 May', Mss. 126/EB/GS/5/9, MRC.
98 *Ibid.*
99 Bevin, 'Statement to Area Secretaries', 27 May 1926, Mss. 126/EB/GS/7/32, MRC.
100 TUC, 'The Mining Situation'.
101 TUC, 'The Mining Situation'; Bevin, 'The Miners' Dispute', *Record*, May–June 1926; 'Paper on Finance', 18 February 1927, Mss. 126/EB/TG/6/20, MRC.
102 Lord Citrine, *Men and Work*, pp. 178–9.
103 Statement to Area Secretaries; Citrine, *Men and Work*, p. 196.
104 Statement to Area Secretaries. Bevin later argued that they 'had accomplished the purpose for which the strike was called', namely 'to secure the carrying on of negotiations on a proper basis' (Bevin to his officers, 28 May 1926, Mss. 126/EB/GS/7/33, MRC; Statement to National Docks Group, 22 July 1926, Mss. 126/EB/GS/8/25i, MRC).
105 Statement to Area Secretaries.
106 Statement to National Docks Group; Minutes, 17 June 1926.
107 Statement to Area Secretaries.
108 *Ibid.*
109 Statement to National Docks Group.
110 Bevin, 'The Miners' Dispute and the General Strike, 1926', p. 243.
111 *Record*, January 1927, p. 179; Bevin to Weir, 19 May 1927, Mss. 126/EB/IP/1/22, MRC.
112 *Record*, January 1927, p. 180.
113 General Secretary's (First) Quarterly Report, 1928.
114 G. W. McDonald and Howard Gospel, 'The Mond–Turner Talks, 1927–1933: A Study in Industrial Co-operation', *Historical Journal*, XVI, 1973, p. 819.
115 Mond to Citrine, 23 November 1927, Mss. 126/EB/TU/2/2, MRC.
116 Biennial Delegate Conference, July 1925, Mss. 126/EB/GS/4/10, MRC; TUC, *Annual Report*, 1927, pp. 315–16.
117 Special Meeting of the General Council, 24 January 1928, Trades Union Congress records, 262, London. Hereinafter cited as TUC.
118 Conference of General Officers, 19–21 February 1927, Harold Clay, 'The Industrial Upheaval: Its Effects and Lessons', Mss. 126/EB/TG/6/18, MRC.
119 TUC, *Annual Report*, 1928.
120 Bevin to R. B. Walker and A. A. Findlay, 2 June 1926, Mss. 126/EB/GS/7/39i, MRC.
121 TUC, *Annual Report*, 1931, p. 364; TUC, *Annual Report*, 1929, p. 385.

199

NOTES TO PP. 49–61

122 TUC, *Annual Report*, 1928, p. 447.
123 TUC, *Annual Report*, 1928, p. 448.
124 TUC Industrial Committee, 'Trade Union Recognition', TUC, 262.
125 'Statement on Melchett–Turner Unemployment Report', Mss. 126/EB/ TU/11/13, MRC.
126 TUC, *Annual Report*, 1929, p. 385; General Council, Minutes, 8 November 1928, TUC, 262.
127 General Council Minutes, 8 November 1928.
128 Conference Minutes, 12 January 1928, TUC, 262; Interim Joint Report on Unemployment.
129 General Council Minutes, 26 June 1928; A. J. Cook, *The Mond Moonshine*, London, 1928, p. 11.

Chapter 3

1 General Secretary's First Quarterly Report, 1925; General Secretary's Report, February 1930; General Secretary's Report, March 1935.
2 *LPCR*, 1925, p. 184; for domestic policy, see Elizabeth Durbin, *New Jerusalems: The Labour Party and the Economics of Democratic Socialism*, London, 1985.
3 *LPCR*, 1929, p. 186.
4 *LPCR*, 1930, p. 198.
5 Economic Advisory Council, 16 April 1931, TUC, 567.
6 Peter Clarke, *The Keynesian Revolution in the Making 1924–1936*, Cambridge, 1987, p. 81.
7 Rough Notes, 26 May 1931, Mss. 126/EB/FI/40/10, MRC.
8 *Minutes of Evidence Taken Before the Committee on Finance and Industry*, London, 1931, Vol. I, qq. 3830, 3832, 3836.
9 Private Sessions, 20 and 21 November 1930, Mss. 126/EB/FI/34/4–5, MRC.
10 Rough Notes, 26 May 1931, Mss. 126/EB/FI/40/10; Private Session, 7 November 1930, Mss. 126/EB/FI/33/5, MRC.
11 Memo, 22 January 1930, Mss. 126/EB/FI/7/1, MRC.
12 Bevin to Macmillan, 30 January 1931, Mss. 126/EB/FI/37/4, MRC.
13 Questions 3347, 7845.
14 Questions 4127, 3510.
15 *Record*, March 1936.
16 Private Session, 21 March 1930, Mss. 126/EB/FI/14/5, MRC.
17 Questions 2261, 1973.
18 Question 8676; Private Session, 7 November 1930.
19 *Macmillan Committee Report*, Cmd. 3897, *PP*, XIII, 1930–1, par. 9; Addendum I, pp. 209–10.
20 Rough Notes, 26 May 1931, Mss. 126/EB/FI/40/10, MRC.
21 Philip Williamson, 'A "Bankers' Ramp"? Financiers and the British Political Crisis of 1931', *English Historical Review*, XCIX, 1984, p. 791.
22 *Labour Magazine*, X, December 1931, pp. 343–7; Meeting of the National Executive of the Labour Party and General Council, 20 August 1931.
23 Meeting, 20 August 1931, Bevin Papers, 7/8; Philip Williamson, *National Crisis and National Government*, Cambridge, 1992.

200

NOTES TO PP. 61–71

24 General Secretary's Report, August 1931; David Marquand, *Ramsay MacDonald*, London, 1977, p. 622.
25 Andrew Thorpe, 'Arthur Henderson and the British Political Crisis of 1931', *Historical Journal*, XXXI, 1988, pp. 124–5; General Secretary's Report, May 1931.
26 *Record*, November 1931, p. 112.
27 Bevin to his permanent officials, Mss. 126/EB/TG/10/10, MRC; *Record*, December 1931, p. 144.
28 Archie Potts, 'Bevin to Beat the Bankers: Ernest Bevin's Gateshead Campaign of 1931', *Bulletin of the Northeast Group for the Study of Labour History*, XI, 1977, pp. 28–38.
29 General Secretary's Report, November 1931.
30 F. M. Leventhal, *The Last Dissenter: H. N. Brailsford and his World*, New York, 1985, p. 195.
31 Bevin to Brailsford, 7 June 1926, Mss. 126/EB/GS/8/1i, MRC; Bevin to Brockway, 13 April 1926, Mss. 126/EB/IL/1/3, MRC; *Manchester Guardian*, 1 November 1927, Mss. 126/EB/AS/2/10, MRC.
32 Bevin to Brockway, n.d. [June, 1926], Mss. 126/EB/GS/8/5, MRC.
33 Margaret Cole, 'The Society for Socialist Inquiry and Propaganda', in *Essays in Labour History, 1918–1939*, edited by Asa Briggs and John Saville, London, 1977, pp. 194–6.
34 Bevin to J. R. Bellerby, 23 May 1931, Cited by Bullock, *LT*, I, p. 501.
35 SSIP, 'Aims and Methods', Fabian Society Papers, Oxford, J2/6.
36 'The Election Issue – Capitalism versus Socialism', *ibid*. The manifesto was signed by Bevin, Cole and D. N. Pritt.
37 'Reorganisation of Government Departments and Ministerial Functions', 22 January 1932, Fabian Society Papers, J38/2.
38 Bevin to Cole, 29 September 1932, Cole Papers, 3/5/E, Box 5, Folder 6B, Nuffield College, Oxford.
39 Margaret Cole, 'Society', p. 200; Bullock, *LT*, I, p. 531.
40 Kingsley Martin, *Editor: The 'New Statesman' Years, 1931–1945*, Chicago, 1968, p. 49.
41 *Politicians, Socialism and Historians*, London, 1980, p. 125.
42 *Ibid.*, p. 125.
43 Lascelles Diary, 20 August 1943, Bevin Papers, II, 9/3.
44 TUC, *Annual Report*, 1927, p. 298.
45 TUC, *Annual Report*, 1936, p. 342.
46 *The Labour Party's Political Thought, A History*, London, 1985.
47 *Record*, July, 1936.
48 General Secretary's Report, November 1936.
49 Cmd. 936, p. 489.
50 *The Times*, 29 September 1924, p. 9.
51 *Manchester Guardian Supplement*, 1 November 1927, Mss. 126/EB/AS/2/10, MRC.
52 General Secretary's Report, February 1930; Bevin to Henderson, 4 June 1926, Mss. 126/EB/GS/7/44i, MRC.
53 Henry Pelling, *A Short History of the Labour Party*; LPCR, 1935.
54 *LPCR*, 1931, pp. 191–2; TUC, *Annual Report*, 1931, pp. 408–11, 464–5.
55 TUC, *Annual Report*, 1935, p. 295.

201

NOTES TO PP. 72–82

56 Alan Booth and Melvyn Pack, *Employment, Capital, and Economic Policy: Great Britain, 1918–1939*, New York, 1985.
57 TUC, *Annual Report*, 1930, pp. 257–61, 282–7.
58 Durbin, *New Jerusalems*, p. 204.
59 TUC, *Annual Report*, 1925, p. 494.
60 Evans, *Bevin*, pp. 71–2.
61 *Record*, March, 1928, p. 240; 'The Written Word', *Dockers' Record*, November 1919, p. 10.
62 Durbin, *New Jerusalems*, p. 77; *LPCR*, 1932, p. 212.
63 Bevin to Milne-Bailey, 21 December 1931, TUC, 574.1.
64 *LPCR*, 1931, p. 172.
65 Cmd. 9236, *PP*, 1918, XIII, p. 18.
66 TUC, *Annual Report*, 1917, p. 301; TUC, *Annual Report*, 1919, pp. 275–6; TUC, *Annual Report*, 1921, pp. 247–8.
67 *LPCR*, 1931, p. 191; TUC, *Annual Report*, 1931, p 465.
68 *Dictionary of National Biography 1951–1960*, p. 105.
69 TUC, *Annual Report*, 1933, pp. 161–2.
70 *LPCR*, 1932, p. 190.
71 Durbin, *New Jerusalems*, p. 246.
72 *Record*, February 1929, p. 208; General Secretary's Report, May 1938.
73 Report, May 1938.
74 General Secretary's Report, March 1935.
75 TUC, *Annual Report*, 1937, p. 70; General Secretary's Report, November 1936.
76 Ross Martin, *TUC: The Growth of a Pressure Group*, Oxford, 1980, pp. 216, 236.
77 Stephen Jones, 'The British Trade Unions and Holidays with Pay', *International Review of Social History*, XXXI, 1986, pp. 40–67.
78 'Social Welfare and Industrial Relations 1914–1939', in *A History of British Industrial Relations*, vol. II: *1914–1939*, edited by Chris Wrigley, Brighton, 1987, p. 236.
79 Cited by Noreen Branson and Margot Heinemann, *Britain in the 1930s*, New York, 1971, pp. 131–2.
80 Discussion with Basil Sanderson, 3 November 1936, cited by Bullock, *LT*, I, p. 592.
81 *LPCR*, 1925, p. 183; Daniel F. Calhoun, *The United Front: The TUC and the Russians 1923–1928*, Cambridge, 1976.
82 Booth and Pack, *Employment*, pp. 94–5.
83 'May Day 1937', in *Essays in Labour History, 1918–1939*, edited by Asa Briggs and John Saville, London, 1977, p. 241.
84 Richard Croucher, *We Refuse to Starve in Silence: A History of the National Unemployed Workers' Movement*, London, 1987; Peter Kingsford, *The Hunger Marchers in Britain, 1920–1939*, London, 1982; Ralph Hayburn, 'The National Unemployed Workers' Movement, 1921–36: A Re-appraisal', *International Review of Social History*, XXVIII, 1983, pp. 279–95; Frederic Miller, 'The British Unemployment Assistance Crisis of 1935', *Journal of Contemporary History*, XIV, 1979, pp. 329–52.
85 Hayburn, 'Re-appraisal', p. 293.
86 Wal Hannington, *Unemployed Struggles*, New York, 1973; facsimile of London, 1936.

NOTES TO PP. 82–97

87 TUC, *Annual Report*, 1933, p. 273.
88 Miller, 'Unemployment Assistance', pp. 337, 338, 344.
89 *Record*, July 1936; General Secretary's Report, November 1936.
90 General Secretary's Report, March 1935; TUC, *Annual Report*, 1934, p. 268.
91 *Aneurin Bevan*, New York, 1963, p. 159.
92 Ken Fuller, *Radical Aristocrats: London Busworkers from the 1880s to the 1980s*, London, 1985, p. 69.
93 Bullock, *LT*, I, p. 520.
94 General Secretary's Report, February 1933.
95 *Record*, June 1934, p. 253.
96 Nina Fishman, 'The British Communist Party and the Trade Unions, 1933–45: The Dilemmas of Revolutionary Pragmatism', Unpublished Ph.D. Dissertation, University of London, 1991, pp. 364, 162–78. I am endebted to Dr Fishman for making her dissertation available to me.
97 *LPCR*, 1934, pp. 156–7.
98 Cited by James Hinton, *Protests and Visions: Peace Politics in Twentieth–Century Britain*, London, 1989, p. 93.
99 General Secretary's Report, November 1933.
100 Transcript of radio show of 23 April 1957, Citrine Papers, I, 7/3.
101 Francis Williams, *Ernest Bevin*, London, 1952, p. 196.
102 *LPCR*, 1935, pp. 153–80.
103 General Secretary's Report, May 1936.
104 Jonathan Schneer, *George Lansbury*, Manchester, 1990, pp. 161–76.
105 General Secretary's Report, November 1936.
106 General Secretary's Report, March 1937.
107 NCL verbatim report, 25 August 1936, cited by Tom Buchanan, *The Spanish Civil War and the British Labour Movement*, Cambridge, 1991, p. 60.
108 Hugh Dalton, *The Fateful Years*, London, 1957, p. 139.
109 Eric Shaw, *Discipline and Discord in the Labour Party*, Manchester, 1988, pp. 24–6. For a contrasting view, see Ben Pimlott, *Labour and the Left in the 1930s*, London, 1977.
110 *LPCR*, 1934, pp. 138–41.
111 *LPCR*, 1936, p. 169.
112 Buchanan, *Spanish Civil War*, p. 30.
113 Labour Movement Conference, 28 October 1936, Cited in *ibid.*, p. 46.
114 *LPCR*, 1936, p. 175.
115 TUC, *Annual Report*, 1936, p. 385.
116 Buchanan, *Spanish Civil War*, p. 226.
117 TUC, *Annual Report*, 1936, p. 388.
118 *LPCR*, 1937, p. 209.
119 *Ibid.*, p. 207.
120 *Ibid.*, p. 211.
121 *The Collected Essays, Journalism, and Letters of George Orwell*, edited by Sonia Orwell and Ian Angus, New York, 1968, I, p. 396.
122 General Secretary's Report, May 1936; TUC, *Annual Report*, 1935, pp. 354–7.
123 *Record*, October 1935, p. 55.
124 *Record*, January 1938, p. 154.
125 *LPCR*, 1939, pp. 243–5; 'The Future of the Commonwealth', 16 March

NOTES TO PP. 97–106

1939, Mss. 126/EB/BC/20/7, MRC.
126 'The Future of the Empire', *Spectator*, 3 February 1939; Bevin, 'Impressions of the British Commonwealth Relations Conference, 1938', *International Affairs*, XVIII, January 1939, p. 63. In 1940, Bevin suggested an international consortium, including the United States, Japan and India, should develop a United Provinces of Africa (Talk, 29 February 1940, Bevin Papers, II, 3/1).
127 *LPCR*, 1939, p. 243.
128 *Record*, March 1939, p. 224.
129 *Record*, April 1939, pp. 256–7.
130 Memo by FNT, 18 July 1939, responding to TUC memo of 17 April 1939, T 172/1917, PRO.
131 28 June 1939, PREM 1/325, PRO.
132 General Secretary's Report, March 1938.
133 General Secretary's Report, March 1937.

Chapter 4

1 W. K. Hancock and M. M. Gowing, *British War Economy*, London, 1949, p. 149.
2 Citrine to Chamberlain, 15 September and 27 September 1939, Meeting, 5 October 1939, PREM 1/430.
3 'Our Tasks in War-time', *Record*, October 1939, pp. 142–3.
4 TUC deputation, 21 December 1939, T 172/1917; *Record*, February 1940, pp. 242–3.
5 Cited by Paul Addison, *The Road to 1945*, London, 1945, pp. 58–9; *Record*, April 1940, p. 299.
6 Addison, *Road to 1945*, p. 61.
7 Cited by Ross Martin, *TUC: The Growth of a Pressure Group, 1868–1976*, Oxford, 1980, p. 267.
8 Special Conference of Trade Union Executives, 25 May 1940.
9 In *Adjusting to Democracy: The Role of the Ministry of Labour in British Politics, 1916–1939*, Oxford, 1986, Rodney Lowe has shown that the Ministry had been growing in power before the war and was not the unimportant home department that Alan Bullock thought it to be. See Alan Bullock, *The Life and Times of Ernest Bevin*, vol. II: *Minister of Labour, 1940–1945*, London, 1967, p. 119. Hereinafter, *LT*, II.
10 Speech to Fife Federation of Divisional Labour Parties, 2 May 1943, Bevin Papers II, 1/13; W. M. (40) 1, 22 May 1940, CAB 65/7.
11 H. M. D. Parker, *Manpower: A Study of War-time Policy and Administration*, London, 1957, p. 77.
12 'Our Tasks in War-time'; Special Conference of Trade Union Executives.
13 Parker, *Manpower*, p. 88.
14 Bevin, 'Supply of Labour', 20 May 1940, W. P. (40) 142, CAB 66/7; Parker, *Manpower*, pp. 87–96.
15 W. M. 149 (40) 11, 31 May 1940, CAB 65/7.
16 22 May 1941, LAB 10/651.
17 *Ibid.*; Keith Middlemas, *Politics in Industrial Society*, London, 1979, p. 278.
18 'Utilisation of Spare Capacity', P. X. (40) 21, 19 June 1940, LAB 76/38.

204

NOTES TO PP. 106–119

19 Bevin to Churchill, 1 July 1940, PREM 3/259.
20 Meeting, 9 October 1940, LAB 76/37; P. X. (40) 76, 4 December 1940, LAB 76/38; Joint Meeting, Economic Policy Committee and Production Council, 9 July 1940, LAB 76/37.
21 CAB 67/8; José Harris, *William Beveridge A Biography*, Oxford, 1977, p. 371.
22 8 January 1941, LAB 76/39.
23 Production Executive, 25 February 1941, LAB 76/39; 'Heads of Labour Policy', W. P. (G) (41) 8, 18 January 1941.
24 *Parliamentary Debates*, 4 December 1941, 376:350.
25 *The Fringes of Power: 10 Downing Street Diaries*, New York, 1985, p. 401.
26 *Parliamentary Debates*, 2 April 1941, 370:1030, 1074.
27 Bevin to Churchill, 9 May 1941, PREM 4/83/1A.
28 Bevin to Churchill, 27 June 1941, W. P. (41) 71, CAB 66/17.
29 *Parliamentary Debates*, 2 April 1941, 370:1076.
30 Broadcast, 5 September 1943, BBC Archives.
31 The meeting began on 12 February 1941. The transcripts are in LAB 8/381.
32 Bullock, *LT*, II, pp. 60–2; Correlli Barnett, *The Audit of War: The Illusion & Reality of Britain as a Great Nation*, London, 1986, Chapter 6.
33 Penny Summerfield, *Women Workers in the Second World War: Production and Patriarchy in Conflict*, London, 1984, pp. 34–5.
34 W. M. 110 (41) 1, 10 November 1941.
35 Summerfield, *Women Workers*, p. 36.
36 *Women Workers*, p. 185. See also Harold Smith, 'The Effect of the War on the Status of Women', in *War and Social Change*, edited by Harold Smith, Manchester, 1986.
37 Wilkinson to Bevin, 3 July 1940; Bevin to Wilkinson, 23 July 1940; Meeting, 7 January 1941, LAB 26/59.
38 Harold Smith, 'The Womanpower Problem in Britain during the Second World War', *Historical Journal*, XXVII, 1984, pp. 925–45; Summerfield, *Women Workers*, p. 44.
39 26 February 1941, LAB 26/59.
40 Summerfield, *Women Workers*, p. 179.
41 V. Holmes, Minute, 4 March 1941, Leggett, Minute, 20 March 1941, LAB 8/378.
42 20 November 1942, CAB 71/7; see also Harold Smith, 'The Problem of "Equal Pay for Equal Work" in Great Britain during World War II', *Journal of Modern History*, LIII, December 1981, p. 652.
43 W. M. (44) 42, 28 March 1944, CAB 65/41; Smith, 'Equal Pay', p. 669.
44 Smith, 'Womanpower', p. 945.
45 Barry Supple, *The History of the British Coal Industry*, vol. 4: *1913–1946: The Political Economy of Decline*, Oxford, 1987, p. 499.
46 M. W. Kirby, *The British Coalmining Industry, 1870–1946: A Political History*, London, 1977, p. 171; E. V. Newbegin, 'Labour in the Coal-Mining Industry', LAB 76/18; *Parliamentary Debates*, 13 October 1943, 392:942–4.
47 Hugh Dalton, *The Fateful Years: Memoirs, 1931–1945*, London, 1957, p. 391.
48 R. A. Butler said they were 'afraid that it will mean that they won't get enough [coal] for their country houses' (cited by Ben Pimlott, *Hugh Dalton*, London, 1985, p. 353).
49 *Parliamentary Debates*, 13 October 1943, 392:920–34.

205

NOTES TO PP. 119–126

50 Cited by Supple, *History*, p. 561, n. 1.
51 'The Settlement of Questions Concerning Wages and Working Conditions During Wartime', P. X. (40) 31, 5 July 1940, CAB 71/1.
52 Notes by Minister, 19 December 1941, Meeting, 24 December 1941, LAB 10/161.
53 Wood, 'Wages Situation and Inflation', L. P. (42) 13, 15 January 1942, CAB 71/8; Meeting, Lord President's Committee, 23 January 1942, CAB 71/6.
54 'Wages Policy', L. P. (41) 216, 22 December 1941, CAB 71/5.
55 24 September 1942, CAB 71/7.
56 *Parliamentary Debates*, 29 July 1941, 373:1359. Wage rates rose 53 per cent during the war; living costs, 44 per cent, and earnings, 85 per cent (Middlemas, *Politics*, p. 279).
57 19 July 1940, CAB 72/3. W. M. 270 (40) 4, 14 October 1940, CAB 68/9.
58 *Fringes of Power*, p. 298; Kingsley Wood told Dalton that 'many of his people dislike Bevin and accuse him of playing politics and attacking the employers'. *Fateful Years*, p. 251.
59 Bevin to Andrew Duncan, 1 January 1941, LAB 10/260.
60 W. M. 149 (40), 31 May 1940, CAB 65/7.
61 Meeting of F. Leggett and A. V. Judges, 19 June 1951, LAB 76/3.
62 'Wages Regulation in Relation to the Budget Statement on the Cost of Living', L. P. (41) 73, 16 May 1941, CAB 71/3. See also 'Wages Policy', L. P. (41) 216, 17 December 1941, LAB 10/161.
63 22 May 1940, LAB 10/652.
64 'Morris Motors in the 1940s', *History Workshop*, no. 9, spring, 1980, p. 91. See also Jones, *Union Man*, pp. 95–6.
65 Stephen Tolliday, 'Government, Employers and Shop Floor Organisation in the British Motor Industry', in *Shop Floor Bargaining and the State*, edited by Stephen Tolliday and Jonathan Zeitlin, Cambridge, 1985, p. 115.
66 'Refusal of Firms Engaged on Government Work to Negotiate with Trade Unions', L. P. (41) 136, 20 August 1941, CAB 71/4; Meeting, 26 August 1941, CAB 71/2.
67 See, for example, LAB 10/155; W. M. 89 (41) 8, 4 September 1941.
68 'Trade Union Recognition', unsigned memo circulated to conference of Regional Industrial Relations Officers, 11 March 1943, LAB 10/155; Bevin to E. P. Harries, *ibid.*
69 P. F. Inman, *Labour in the Munitions Industries*, London, 1957, p. 369; Richard Croucher, *Engineers at War*, London, 1982; See Barnett, *Audit of War*, pp. 65–7, 121–3, 154–6.
70 *The Times*, 17 March 1942.
71 Angus Calder, *The People's War*, New York, 1969, p. 393.
72 *Parliamentary Debates*, 19 December 1940, 367:1327.
73 Kevin Morgan, *Against Fascism and War: Ruptures and Continuities in British Communist Politics, 1935–41*, Manchester, 1989.
74 Bevin to Churchill, 9 July 1941, CAB 92/55.
75 'Remarks to Conference of Regional Controllers and Regional Industrial Commissioners', 10 September 1941, LAB 12/294.
76 Minute, n. d., TUC to Bevin, 14 January 1942, LAB 10/213.
77 Memo, n. d., LAB 10/213.
78 Fishman, 'British Communist Party.'

206

NOTES TO PP. 127–136

79 M. Bevan, Minute, 29 October 1941, LAB 10/153; F. Leggett, 'Prohibition of Strikes', September 1940, LAB 10/153.
80 'Unofficial Strikes. Powers of Prosecution', L. P. (44) 64, 4 April 1944, CAB 71/16.
81 *Parliamentary Debates*, 28 April 1944, 399:1072.
82 H. Emmerson, Minute, 29 September 1943; Emmerson, Minute, 23 November 1943, LAB 10/281; 'Use of Regulation 18B Against Fomenters of Strikes', L. P. (44) 67, 12 April 1944, CAB 71/16.
83 Parker, *Manpower*, p. 471.
84 Croucher, *Engineers*, p. 241.
85 *Ibid.*, pp. 242–3.
86 Bevin to Churchill, 13 May 1940, Bevin Papers, II, 9/1.
87 LAB 76/41.
88 10 June 1940, LAB 14/425.
89 15 October 1940, *ibid.*
90 LAB 8/381.
91 T. W. Phillips to Sir Alexander Maxwell, 21 April 1942, LAB 12/269.
92 18 June 1942, LAB 12/269.
93 Morrison to Bevin, 22 July 1942, LAB 12/269.
94 'Administration of Factory Acts and Cognate Matters', October 1944, LAB 12/269.
95 Gordon Phillips and Noel Whiteside, *Casual Labour*, Oxford, 1985; David Wilson, *Dockers – The Impact of Industrial Change*, Bungay, Suffolk, 1972.
96 Minute, A. Higham (?), 21 August 1940, LAB 8/262.
97 Ministerial Sub-Committee on Port Clearance, 23 December 1940, 7 January 1941, CAB 72/26.
98 Joint Report by Minister of Labour and Minister of Transport, 'Port Clearance', L. P. (41) 2, 11 January 1941, CAB 71/3.
99 *Ibid.*
100 *Parliamentary Debates*, 4 December 1941, 376:1340.
101 [illegible] to F. Leggett, 5 November 1940, CAB 11/1675; 'Regulation of Conditions of Employment in the Catering Trades', L. P. (42) 107, 2 May 1942.
102 Meeting, 28 May 1942, CAB 11/1675.
103 Kevin Jefferys, ed., *Labour and the Wartime Coalition: From the Diary of James Chuter Ede, 1941-1945*, London, 1987, p. 113.
104 1 April 1943, 388:393.
105 31 March 1943, 388:276.
106 Williams, *Bevin*, p. 226; Broadcast, 26 October 1940, BBC Archives.
107 Speech at the Rotary Club, 20 November 1940; Speech, 10 December 1940.
108 Churchill to Bevin, 25 November 1940; Bevin to Churchill, 26 November 1940, PREM 4/83/1A.
109 Speech at Manchester, 12 October 1940.
110 Bevin Papers, II, 6/57.
111 Minister's Note on Post-War Policy, 19 October 1942, LAB 10/248.
112 CAB 82/2, R. P. (42) 20, 17 June 1942.
113 Summerfield, *Women Workers*, p. 185.
114 *Parliamentary Debates*, 23 February 1943, 387:113.
115 10 October 1943, Bevin Papers, II, 1/3.

NOTES TO PP. 136–143

116 *Parliamentary Debates*, 29 April 1941, 371:372.
117 Broadcast, 17 February 1941.
118 *People's War*, p. 392.
119 'Wages Policy', L. P. (41) 22 December 1941, CAB 71/5.
120 *Parliamentary Debates*, 21 October 1942, 383:2061–2.
121 10 October 1944, LAB 10/653.
122 Meeting, 10 February 1944, LAB 10/653; 'Regulation of Wages and Conditions of Employment. Legislation to Meet Post-War Requirements', L. P. (43) 293, 22 December 1943.
123 Meetings, 6 September 1944, 6 November 1944, CAB 87/6; Meeting, 6 November 1944, CAB 87/6; 'Wages Regulation – Legislation to Meet Post-War Condition', R (44) 182, 25 October 1944, CAB 87/9.
124 16 January 1945, 407:70.
125 'Sanctions Applicable to the Recalcitrant or Workshy following Exhaustion of Unemployment Insurance Benefits', P. R. (43) 64, 20 September 1943, CAB 87/13. 'Unemployment Insurance', R (44) 34, 29 February 1944, CAB 87/7; 11 October 1943, CAB 87/12.
126 'Training Benefit', P. R. (43) 91, 1 November 1943, CAB 87/13.
127 See, for example, 'Reallocation of Man-power Between the Forces and Civilian Employment During the Interim Period Between the Defeat of Germany and the Defeat of Japan', R (44) 140, 14 August 1944, CAB 87/9.
128 Cited by Kevin Jefferys, *The Churchill Coalition and Wartime Politics, 1940–1945*, Manchester, 1991, p. 122.
129 *The Second World War Diary of Hugh Dalton*, edited by Ben Pimlott, London, 1986, p. 554.
130 Bevin to Simon, 26 February 1943, Simon Papers, 92, f. 163, Oxford University.
131 W. P. (43) 324, 20 July 1943. See also 'The Need for Decisions', 26 June 1943, CAB 66/38.
132 Jefferys, ed., *Labour and the Wartime Coalition*, p. 123.
133 Memo, 2 February 1943, P. R. (43) 4, CAB 87/12; 'Training Benefit', 1 November 1943, P. R. (43) 91, CAB 87/13.
134 CAB 87/5, 12 April 1944.
135 'Post-War Responsibility for Employment Policy', 22 June 1943, LAB 11/1711. See also LAB 10/260.
136 *Parliamentary Debates*, 21 June 1944, 401:211; Alan Booth, 'The War and the White Paper', in *The Road to Full Employment*, edited by Sean Glynn and Alan Booth, London, 1987, p. 184.
137 *Parliamentary Debates*, 21 June 1944, 401:211–31.
138 *Fateful Years*, p. 440.
139 'Location of Industry. Note Dictated by the Minister', 7 February 1944, Bevin Papers, II, 3/9.
140 Bevin to Attlee, 22 November 1944, Bevin Papers, II, 4/12.
141 *Ibid.* Chuter Ede recorded in his diary that Bevin was 'very bitter' about Morrison, who he thought 'took the officials' view about everything'. Bevin predicted Morrison would 'be a Tory in five years' (Jefferys, ed., *Labour and the Wartime Coalition*, p. 169).
142 *Second World War Diary*, p. 677.
143 Jefferys, ed., *Labour and the Wartime Coalition*, p. 153.

208

NOTES TO PP. 144–150

Chapter 5

1 Alan Sked and Chris Cook, *Post-War Britain: A Political History*, Harmondsworth, 1984, pp. 20–1.
2 Broadcast, 22 June 1945. Copy in TUC Library.
3 *The Collected Essays, Journalism and Letters of George Orwell*, edited by Sonia Orwell and Ian Angus, III, p. 395; Nicholas Henderson, *The Private Office*, London, 1984, p. 22.
4 David Dilks, ed., *The Diaries of Sir Alexander Cadogan*, London, 1971, p. 776.
5 All quotations from Pimlott, *Dalton*, pp. 408–22, whose account of Dalton's and Bevin's appointments is definitive.
6 Henderson, *Private Office*, p. 22.
7 Alan Bullock, *Ernest Bevin: Foreign Secretary, 1945–1951*, New York, 1983, p. 102. Hereinafter cited as *FS*.
8 A. P. Ryan, Memo, 30 January 1947, BBC archives, Acc. No. 32746; Henderson, *Private Office*, p. 36.
9 *LPCR*, 1946, p. 165; Hugh Dalton, *High Tide and After: Memoirs, 1945–1960*, London, 1962, p. 104.
10 Charles Webster Diary, 3 February 1946, cited by Raymond Smith, 'Introduction', *British Officials and British Foreign Policy*, ed. John Zametica, Leicester, 1990, p. 2. See also Raymond Smith, 'A Climate of Opinion: British Officials and the Development of British Soviet Policy, 1945–7', *International Affairs*, LXIV, 1988, pp. 631–47.
11 Dalton, *High Tide and After*, p. 14; John Barnes and David Nicholson, eds., *The Empire At Bay: The Leo Amery Diaries 1929–1945*, London, 1988, p. 1030.
12 James L. Gormly, *The Collapse of the Grand Alliance 1945–1948*, Baton Rouge, Louisiana, 1987, p. 25; Byrnes, *Speaking Frankly*, p. 79.
13 Bullock, *FS*, p. 25; Piers Dixon, *Double Diploma: The Life of Sir Pierson Dixon*, London, 1968, p. 170.
14 William Roger Louis, *Imperialism at Bay*, Oxford, 1978, pp. 555–6. The memorandum was by Bevin and Colonial Secretary George Hall.
15 Bullock, *FS*, p. 109.
16 Hubert Miles, Baron Gladwyn, *Memoirs*, London, 1972, p. 117; 'World Strategic Survey', 5 February 1945, FO 371/50774/U1090; 'Policy Required to Secure British Strategic Interests in the Eastern Mediterranean and Middle East', 27 March 1945, FO 371/50774/U73; 'Security of British Commonwealth and Empire Interests in South East Asia and the Pacific', 30 December 1944, FO 371/50774/U36.
17 Louis, *Imperialism at Bay*, p. 200.
18 Sked and Cook, *Post-War Britain*, p. 26; Henry Pelling, *Britain and the Second World War*, paperback edition, Glasgow, 1970, pp. 275ff.; A. J. P. Taylor, *English History 1914–1945*, Oxford, 1965, p. 599.
19 Graham Ross, ed., *The Foreign Office and the Kremlin: British Documents on Anglo-Soviet Relations, 1941–45*, Cambridge, 1984, p. 201.
20 Terry Anderson, *The United States, Great Britain, and the Cold War, 1944–1947*, Columbia, Mo., 1981, pp. 12–13.
21 Halifax to Bevin, 12 December 1945, *Documents on British Policy Overseas*, Series 1, IV, London, 1987, p. 2. Hereinafter cited as *DBPO*.
22 Melvyn Leffler, *A Preponderance of Power: National Security, the Truman Adminis-*

209

NOTES TO PP. 150–155

tration and the Cold War, Stanford, Cal., 1992.

23 John Kent, 'Bevin's Imperialism and the Idea of Euro-Africa', in *British Foreign Policy,1945–1956*, edited by Michael Dockrill and John W. Young, New York, 1989, p. 47.

24 'Middle Eastern Policy', C. P. (45) 130, 28 August 1945; William Roger Louis, *The British Empire in the Middle East, 1945–1951*; F. S. Northedge, 'Britain and the Middle East', in *The Foreign Policy of the British Labour Governments, 1945–1951*, edited by Ritchie Ovendale, Leicester, 1984, pp. 149–80.

25 Louis, *British Empire*, p. 18.

26 *DBPO*, Series 1, V, p. 16; Sean Greenwood, 'Ernest Bevin, France and "Western Union": August 1945–February 1946', *European History Quarterly*, XIV, 1984, pp. 319–38; 'Stocktaking After VE Day', 11 July 1945, *DBPO*, Series 1, I, pp. 181–7; Lloyd C. Gardner, *Approaching Vietnam*, New York, 1988, p. 73.

27 Cited by Christopher Thorne, *Allies of a Kind: The United States, Britain, and the War Against Japan*, New York, 1978, p. 682.

28 Robert J. McMahon, *Colonialism and Cold War: The United States and the Struggle for Indonesian Independence, 1945–49*, Ithaca, N.Y., 1981, pp. 91, 108; Defence Committee, 10 October 1945, CAB 69/7.

29 'Our Overseas Financial Prospects', 13 August 1945, *DBPO*, Series 1, III, pp. 29–37.

30 J. M. Keynes, Memorandum, 15 August 1945, *ibid.*, pp. 44–9. Keynes was expressing support of Bevin's view.

31 M. E. Pelley, Introduction, *DBPO*, Series 1, III, p. xxiv; Pimlott, Dalton, pp. 439–40.

32 'U. S. Request for Bases', 29 November 1945, D.O. (45) 38, CAB 69/7.

33 Memorandum by Bevin and Hall, 25 August 1945, *DBPO*, Series 1, II, pp. 26–35; 23 August 1945, *DBPO*, Series 1, II, p. 15.

34 Memoranda, 24 September 1945, 2 October 1945, *DBPO*, Series 1, II, pp. 349–50, 473; Jonathan Knight, 'Russia's Search for Peace: The London Council of Foreign Ministers, 1945', *Journal of Contemporary History*, XIII, 1978, pp. 137–63.

35 Cited by Anderson, *Cold War*, p. 91.

36 *Double Diploma*, p. 199.

37 Record of Conversation, 17 December 1945, *DBPO*, Series 1, II, pp. 733–6.

38 Memorandum by Mr Bevin on the Foreign Situation, 8 November 1945, *DBPO*, Series 1, III, pp. 310–13.

39 Kerr to Bevin, 8 December 1945, FO 800/501; Leffler, *Preponderance of Power*, p. 48; Kenneth Jensen, ed., *Origins of the Cold War: The Novikov, Kennan, and Roberts 'Long Telegrams' of 1946*, Washington D. C., 1991.

40 Anders Stephanson, *Kennan and the Art of Foreign Policy*, Cambridge, Mass., 1989, p. 50.

41 Melvyn Leffler, 'Adherence to Agreements: Yalta and the Experiences of the Early Cold War', *International Security*, XI, summer 1986, p. 106; Sean Greenwood, 'Frank Roberts and the "other" Long Telegram', *Journal of Contemporary History*, XXV, 1990, p. 118.

42 DBPO, Series 1, IV, pp. 67–9; Raymond Smith, 'A Climate of Opinion: British Officials and the Development of Soviet Policy, 1945–7', *International*

210

Affairs, LXIV, 1988, p. 638.

43 Jensen, ed., *Origins of the Cold War*; John Zametica, 'Three Letters to Bevin: Frank Roberts at the Moscow Embassy, 1945–46', in *British Officials and British Foreign Policy 1945–50*, edited by John Zametica, Leicester, 1990, pp. 39–97.

44 Zametica, 'Three Letters to Bevin', p. 87; Greenwood, 'Frank Roberts', pp. 103–22.

45 'The Soviet Campaign Against this Country and our Response to it', 2 April 1946, FO 371/56832/N6344; Ray Merrick, 'The Russia Committee of the British Foreign Office and the Cold War, 1946–47', *Journal of Contemporary History*, XX, 1985, pp. 453–68; Anne Deighton, *The Impossible Peace: Britain, the Division of Germany, and the Origins of the Cold War*, Oxford, 1990, p. 234.

46 *Memoirs*, p. 227.

47 Mr Lambert, Minute, 22 August 1946, FO 371/56788/N11471; Raymond Smith, 'Climate of Opinion'; FO 800/501; Bullock, *FS*, p. 234.

48 *Keep Left*, London, 1947, p. 35; Laski, *Russia and the West: Policy for Britain*, London, 1947.

49 *LPCR*, 1946, p. 167; 841.00/2–247, Department of State, Record Group 59 (hereinafter cited as DS, RG 59).

50 16 October 1946, CAB 131/1.

51 Louis, *British Empire*, p. 15.

52 Bullock, *FS*, p. 160; G. M. Alexander, *The Prelude to the Truman Doctrine: British Policy in Greece, 1944–1947*, Oxford, 1982.

53 Memorandum, 13 March 1946, D. O. (46) 40, CAB 132/2.

54 John Iatrides, *Greece in the 1940s*, Hanover, N. H. and London, 1981, p. 149; Sargent to Leeper, 9 November 1945, FO 800/276.

55 *The Greek Tragedy*, Baltimore, Md., 1969, p. 97.

56 Attlee to Bevin, 5 January 1947, FO 800/476.

57 Robert Carden, 'Before Bizonia: Britain's Economic Dilemma in Germany, 1945–46', *Journal of Contemporary History*, XIV, 1979, pp. 535–55.

58 Sean Greenwood, 'Bevin, the Ruhr and the Division of Germany: August 1945–December 1946', *Historical Journal*, XXIX, 1986, pp. 203–12.

59 Deighton, *Impossible Peace*, p. 63.

60 Deighton, *Impossible Peace*, p. 78.

61 'Policy Towards Germany', C. P. (46) 186, 3 May 1946.

62 Deighton, *Impossible Peace*, pp. 6–7.

63 Deighton, *Impossible Peace*, p. 108.

64 23 July 1945, *DBPO*, Series 1, I, pp. 573–4; 1 September 1945, CP (45) 144, CAB 129/1.

65 Smith, 'Climate of Opinion', p. 643.

66 5 January 1947, FO 800/476; 1 December 1946, FO 800/475.

67 Attlee to Churchill, 23 July 1945, *DBPO*, Series 1, I, pp. 573–4.

68 Raymond Smith and John Zametica, 'The Cold Warrior: Clement Attlee Reconsidered', *International Affairs*, LXI, spring 1985, pp. 237–52.

69 Attlee to Bevin, 1 December 1946, FO 800/475.

70 Memo, 9 December 1946; Dixon, undated note for meeting of 8 January 1947, FO 800/475.

71 Bevin to Attlee, 9 January 1947, *ibid.*; Smith and Zametica, 'Cold Warrior', p. 251; Trevor Burridge, *Clement Attlee: A Political Biography*, London, 1985, pp. 188–9.

NOTES TO PP. 167–172

72 See FO 371/65964.
73 'Effect of our External Financial Position on our Foreign Policy', 12 February 1947, FO 371/62420/UE678.
74 Lawrence Wittner, *American Intervention in Greece, 1943–1949*, New York, 1982, p. 64; 'Policy Towards Greece and Turkey', C.P. (47) 34, 25 January 1947.
75 *High Tide and After*, p. 198; *The Political Diary of Hugh Dalton, 1918–40, 1945–60*, edited by Ben Pimlott, London, 1986, p. 391.
76 *Political Diary*, p. 393.
77 'Middle East Oil', C. P. (47) 11, 3 January 1947, CAB 129/16.
78 *LPCR*, 1947, p. 179.
79 Jonathan Schneer, *Labour's Conscience: The Labour Left, 1945–51*, London, 1987, p. 63.
80 *Hearings Before the Committee on Foreign Relations of the United States Senate, 81st Congress, on the Amendment of the Economic Cooperation Act of 1948*, Washington, D.C., 1949, p. 174.
81 Policy Planning Staff Report 23, 24 February 1948, Box 9.
82 William C. Cromwell, 'The Marshall Plan, Britain, and the Cold War', *Review of International Studies*, VIII, October 1982, p. 238; Bullock, *FS*, pp. 404–5.
83 *Foreign Relations of the United States*, 1947, III, p. 268. Hereinafter cited as *FRUS*.
84 Caffery to State, 29 June 1947, *FRUS*, 1947, III, p. 299; Douglas to State, 3 July 1947, *ibid.*, p. 306; Bullock, *FS*, p. 422.
85 24 June 1947, *FRUS*, 1947, III, p. 271.
86 British Aide-Memoire to Department of State, 28 July 1947, *FRUS*, 1947, III, pp. 45–8.
87 *FRUS*, 1947, III, p. 337.
88 Marshall to Douglas, 841.24568/8–147, DS, RG 59.
89 13 May 1946, FO 371/68014/AN1997.
90 Bullock, *FS*, p. 673; Louis, *British Empire*, p. 102.
91 Chiefs of Staff Committee, 21 November 1947, FO 800/476.
92 Louis, *British Empire*, p. 112; Chiefs of Staff Committee, 21 November 1947, FO 800/476.
93 *Parliamentary Debates*, 13 November 1945, 415:1927.
94 Bullock, *FS*, pp. 177, 277. Louis, *British Empire*, p. 384; Michael J. Cohen, *Palestine and the Great Powers 1945–1948*, Princeton, N.J., 1982, pp. 66–7; *LPCR*, 1946, p. 165.
95 CAB 131/85, 30 January 1947; Louis, *British Empire*, p. 570. Because so many Jewish immigrants came from Eastern Europe, Bevin thought, they would more likely be Communists.
96 Ian Mikardo, *Back-Bencher*, London, 1988, pp. 98–9; Christopher Mayhew, *Time to Explain*, London, 1987, pp. 119–20.
97 Palestine Conference, 3 February 1947, CAB 131/85, 11 September 1946, CAB 133/85.
98 Minute, Harold Beeley, July 1945, cited by Michael J. Cohen, 'The Genesis of the Anglo-American Committee on Palestine, November 1945: A Case Study in the Assertion of American Hegemony', *Historical Journal*, XXII, 1979, p. 188. Beeley became Bevin's closest adviser on Palestine.

212

NOTES TO PP. 172–178

99 Palestine Conference, 3 February 1947, CAB 131/85; *Parliamentary Debates*, 26 January 1949, 460:933–4.
100 Palestine Conference, 3 February 1947, CAB 133/85; Amikam Nachmani, '"It is a Matter of Getting the Mixture Right": Britain's Post-war Relations with America in the Middle East', *Journal of Contemporary History*, XVIII, January 1983, pp. 117–39.
101 Cited by Nachmani, 'Getting the Mixture Right', p. 133.
102 1 January 1947, CAB 131/5.
103 CP (47) 30, 14 January 1987, CAB 128/11. Cited by Ritchie Ovendale, *Britain, the United States and the End of the Palestine Mandate*, Woodbridge, Suffolk, 1989, p. 187.
104 'Palestine', 18 September 1947, C. P. (47) 259, CAB 129/21; *Parliamentary Debates*, 26 January 1949, 460: 931.
105 Conversation with Douglas, 3 August 1947, FO 800/487; Conversation, 24 November 1947, *ibid.*
106 *Ibid.*, 2 April and 28 April 1948.
107 Bevin to Franks (draft), 3 February 1949; Minute, 14 January 1949, both cited by Louis, *British Empire*, pp. 567–8.
108 Bevin to Attlee, 16 September 1947, CO 537/3047; FO 800/444.
109 Margaret Gowing, *Independence and Deterrence: Britain and Atomic Energy, 1945–1952*, I: *Policy Making*, London, 1974, pp. 20, 47.
110 Ian Clark and Nicholas J. Wheeler, *The British Origins of Nuclear Strategy 1945–1955*, Oxford, 1989, p. 50. N. J. Wheeler, 'British Nuclear Weapons and Anglo-American Relations, 1945-54', *International Affairs*, LXII, 1986, p. 71.
111 Margaret Gowing, 'Britain, America and the Bomb', in Dockrill and Young, eds., *British Foreign Policy*, p. 40.
112 13 March 1946, cited by P. Gupta, 'Imperialism and the Labour Government of 1945–51', in *The Working Class in Modern British History*, edited by Jay Winter, Cambridge, 1983, p. 101.
113 7 July 1947, FO 800/514.
114 Pimlott, ed., *Political Diary*, p. 443; John Kent, 'The British Empire and the Origins of the Cold War', in *Britain and the First Cold War*, edited by Anne Deighton, New York, 1990, pp. 178–9.
115 Nicholas Mansergh, ed., *The Transfer of Power*, London, 1970–80, VIII, p. 927.
116 Bevin to Attlee, 1 January 1947, *The Transfer of Power*, IX, pp. 431–3.
117 Note of Conversation on H.M.S. 'Victory' on 15 January 1948, FO 800/477.
118 10 January 1948, cited by Louis, *British Empire*, p. 106.
119 Geoffrey Warner, 'The Labour Governments and the Unity of Western Europe, 1945–51', in *Foreign Policy*, edited by Ritchie Ovendale, pp. 65–6.
120 Cees Wiebes and Bert Zeeman, 'The Pentagon Negotiations March 1948: The Launching of the North Atlantic Treaty,' *International Affairs*, LIX, 1983, p. 342; Lawrence Kaplan, *The United States and NATO*, Lexington, Ky., 1984, p. 50; Bullock, *FS*, p. 499; FO 800/466.
121 'Review of Soviet Policy', 5 January 1948, C.P. (48) 7, CAB 129/23; 'The First Aim of British Policy', 4 January 1948, C.P. (48) 6, CAB 129/23.
122 'The Threat to Western Civilisation', C.P. (48) 72, 3 March 1948.

213

NOTES TO PP. 179–184

123 'Socialization of German Basic Industries', C. P. (47) 37, 1 February 1947.
124 5 July 1947, FO 371/64514/C1290, PRO; Ian Turner, 'Great Britain and the Post-war German Currency Reform', *Historical Journal*, XXX, September 1987, pp. 685–708.
125 *FRUS*, 1948, III, p. 138.
126 US Chief of Staff, General Omar Bradley, said at the time that 'the whole Berlin crisis has arisen as a result of two actions on the part of the Western powers. These actions are (1) implementation of the decisions agreed in the London Talks on Germany and (2) institution of currency reform' (Leffler, *Preponderance*, p. 218).
127 Meeting of Foreign Ministers, 19 July 1948, FO 800/447.
128 Conversation, Bevin and Douglas, 25 June 1948, FO 371/70497.
129 Meeting of Foreign Ministers, 19 July 1948, FO 800/447. See also Nicholas Wheeler, 'The Attlee Government's Nuclear Strategy', in *First Cold War*, edited by Anne Deighton, p. 137; Clark and Wheeler, *Nuclear Strategy*, Oxford, 1989, pp. 127ff. Duncan Campbell, *The Unsinkable Aircraft Carrier: American Military Power in Britain*, revised ed., London, 1986, p. 27.
130 Gowing, *Independence*, pp. 311–12; Wheeler, 'British Nuclear Weapons', p. 72.
131 Leffler, *Preponderance*, pp. 261–2, 306.
132 'North Atlantic Treaty and Western Union', 2 November 1948, C. P. (48) 249; Bullock, *FS*, p. 617.
133 *FRUS*, 1948, III, pp. 79–80.
134 'European Economic Cooperation', C. P. (48) 75, 6 March 1948.
135 'North Atlantic Treaty and Western Union', C.P. (48) 249, 2 November 1948.
136 E.P.C. (49) 6, 25 January 1949.
137 *FRUS*, 1949, IV, p. 436; Geoffrey Warner, 'The Labour Government and the Unity of Western Europe, 1945–51', in *Foreign Policy*, edited by Ritchie Ovendale, Leicester, 1984, p. 71.
138 9 May 1950, FO 800/449.
139 Strang to Harvey, 6 July 1950, *DBPO*, Series 2, I, p. 254.
140 Andrew Rotter, 'The Triangular Route to Vietnam: The United States, Great Britain, and Southeast Asia, 1945–50', *International History Review*, VI, August 1984, p. 422.
141 *DBPO*, Series 2, II, p. 153.
142 *DBPO*, Series 2, II, pp. 157–72.
143 *DBPO*, Series 2, II, p. 87n.
144 C.P. (50) 118, 26 May 1950.
145 Michael J. Hogan, *The Marshall Plan*, Cambridge, 1987, Chapter 6.
146 Shuckburgh to Gore-Booth, 2 June 1950, *DBPO*, Series 2, II, pp. 388–90.
147 Conversation, 9 May 1950, *DBPO*, Series 2, II, p. 275.
148 Peter G. Boyle, 'Britain, America and the Transition from Economic to Military Assistance, 1948–1951', *Journal of Contemporary History*, XXII, 1987, p. 529.
149 Jon Halliday and Bruce Cumings, *Korea the Unknown War*, p. 10. See also Cumings, *The Origins of the Korean War*, 2 vols., Princeton, N.J., 1981–90.
150 Ra Jong-yil, 'Special Relationship at War: The Anglo-American Relationship during the Korean War', *Journal of Strategic Studies*, VII, 1984, p. 310.

NOTES TO PP. 185–193

151 Geoffrey Warner, 'The British Labour Government and the Atlantic Alliance', in *Western Security: The Formative Years*, edited by Olav Riste, New York, 1985, p. 260.
152 Kenneth Morgan, *Labour in Power, 1945–1951*, Oxford, 1984, p. 435.
153 George Mallaby, *From My Level*, New York, 1965, p. 144.
154 Bullock, *FS*, pp. 832–3.
155 Louis, *British Empire*, pp. 740–41.
156 M. L. Dockrill , 'The Foreign Office, Anglo–American Relations and the Korean War, June 1950–June 1951', *International Affairs*, LXII, 1986, pp. 459–76.
157 *Ibid.*, p. 461.

Conclusion

1 Dockers Delegate Conference, 1920, p. 136.
2 *Record*, February 1929, p. 208.
3 Remarks at Shornells Conference, 23 March 1927, Mss. 126/EB/TG/6/19, MRC.
4 BBC speech, 19 July 1947.
5 'Whither Britain?', *The Listener*, 31 January 1934, p. 178.
6 T 200/4, 21 February 1930, PRO.
7 *Parliamentary Debates*, 9 December 1943, 395:1238.
8 Speech, 10 December 1940, Bevin Papers, II, 1/1.
9 *Record*, February 1935, pp. 156–7.
10 Transcript of radio show of 23 April 1957, Citrine Papers, I, 7/3.
11 George McCorquodale, *ibid.*
12 Harold Nicolson, *Diaries and Letters 1945–1962*, London, 1968, p. 116.
13 *LPCR*, 1936, p. 204.
14 Jones, *Union Man*, p. 32.
15 Valentine Lawford, 'Three Ministers', *The Cornhill Magazine*, 1010, winter, 1956/7, p. 89.
16 Gladwyn Jebb, cited by Deighton, *Impossible Peace*, p. 14. Two additional examples: Valentine Lawford ('Three Ministers', p. 81) related how when he told Bevin that the Pope had charged him to convey blessings to him and his family, Bevin 'looked momentarily as outraged as though I had played him a practical joke'. Chuter Ede related a story about Bevin's refusal to see three Labour Party representatives who happened to be Jewish. He 'could spend his time better than in discussing Britain's future with three Yids,' Bevin was reported to have said (*Labour and the Wartime Coalition*, p. 193).
17 Sir Roderick Barclay, *Ernest Bevin and the Foreign Office*, London, 1975, p. 76.
18 Diary, April 1946, Bevin Papers, II, 9/3.
19 Bullock, *FS*, p. 109.
20 TUC, *Annual Report*, 1930, pp. 257–61, 282–7.

215

Select Bibliography

Manuscript Collections

Public records

National Archives, Washington, D. C.
  Department of State:
      Record Group 59 (General Records)
Public Record Office, London
  Cabinet
      CAB 65 (War Cabinet Minutes)
      CAB 66–8 (War Cabinet Memoranda)
      CAB 71 Lord President's Committee)
      CAB 117 (Reconstruction)
      CAB 128 (Labour Cabinet Minutes)
      CAB 129 (Labour Cabinet Memoranda)
      CAB 130 (Ad Hoc Committees)
      CAB 131 (Defence Committee)
      CAB 133 (Commonwealth and International Conferences, 1945–51)
      CAB 134 (Cabinet Committees)
  Foreign Office
      FO 371 (General Correspondence)
      FO 800 (Private Collections – includes Bevin, Halifax, Inverchapel, and
         Orme Sargent Papers)
  Ministry of Labour
      LAB 2 (General Correspondence)
      LAB 8 (Employment)
      LAB 10 (Industrial Relations)
      LAB 12 (Establishments)
      LAB 14 (Welfare)
      LAB 26 (Welfare)
  Prime Minister's Office
      PREM 1 (Correspondence and Papers, 1916–39)
      PREM 3 (Operations Papers, 1938–46)
      PREM 4 (Confidential Papers, 1939–46)
      PREM 8 (Correspondence and Papers, 1945–51)
  Treasury:
      T 172 (Chancellor of the Exchequer's Office)
      T 200 (Committee on Finance and Industry)

BIBLIOGRAPHY

Private papers

Clement Attlee Papers, Oxford University.
Beaverbrook Papers, House of Lords Record Office.
William Beveridge Papers, London School of Economics.
Ernest Bevin Papers, Cambridge University.
Ernest Bevin Papers, Modern Records Centre, University of Warwick.
Lord Citrine Papers, London School of Economics.
G. D. H. Cole Papers, Oxford University.
Lionel Curtis Papers, Oxford University.
Hugh Dalton Papers, London School of Economics.
Halifax Papers, York University.
Ramsay MacDonald Papers, Public Record Office, London.
John Simon Papers, Oxford University.

Other Papers

British Broadcasting Corporation, BBC Written Archives Centre, Reading.
Fabian Society, Oxford University.
Dock, Wharf, Riverside and General Workers' Union, Modern Records Centre, University of Warwick.
International Transport Workers' Federation, ITWF Headquarters, London, and Modern Records Centre, University of Warwick.
Labour Party, Labour Party headquarters, London.
Rank and File London Busmen's Movement, Modern Records Centre, University of Warwick.
National Union of Railwaymen, Modern Records Centre, University of Warwick.
Trades Union Congress, TUC headquarters, London, and Modern Records Centre, University of Warwick.
Transport and General Workers' Union, TGWU headquarters, London, and Modern Records Centre, University of Warwick.

Parliamentary papers

Cmd. 9236, 1918, XIII, 'Trusts and Profiteering'.
Cmd. 936 & Cmd. 937,1920, XXIV, 'Transport Workers – Court of Enquiry'.
Cmd. 2956,1924, XI, 'Dock Labour Dispute'.
Cmd. 3897,1930–1, XIII, 'Committee on Finance and Industry'.
Cmd. 5724, 1937–8, XII, 'Holidays With Pay'.
Cmd. 6548,1943–4, VIII, 'Re-allocation of Man-power'.

Books and Articles

Adamthwaite, Anthony. 'Britain and the World, 1945–9: A View from the Foreign Office', *International Affairs*, LXI, 1985, pp. 223–35.
Addison, Paul. *The Road to 1945*. London, 1975.
Alexander, G. M. *The Prelude to the Truman Doctrine: British Policy in Greece, 1944–*

217

ERNEST BEVIN

1947. Oxford, 1982.

Anderson, Terry. *The United States, Great Britain and the Cold War, 1944–1947.* Columbia, Missouri, 1981.

Ashby, M. K. *Joseph Ashby of Tysoe.* London, 1974.

Barclay, Roderick. *Ernest Bevin and the Foreign Office.* London, 1975.

Barker, Elizabeth. *Britain Between the Superpowers, 1945–50.* Toronto, 1983.

Barnes, John, and David Nicholson, eds. *The Empire at Bay: The Leo Amery Diaries, 1929–1945.* London, 1988.

Barnett, Correlli. *The Audit of War: The Illusion & Reality of Britain as a Great Nation.* London, 1986.

Becker, Josef, and Franz Knipping, eds. *Power in Europe? Great Britain, France, Italy and Germany in a Postwar World, 1945–1950.* Berlin and New York, 1986

Best, Richard A. *'Cooperation with Like-Minded Peoples': British Influence on American Security Policy, 1945–1949.* New York, 1986.

Booth, Alan. *British Economic Policy 1931–1949.* London, 1989.

——, and Melvyn Pack. *Employment, Capital and Economic Policy: Great Britain, 1918–1939.* New York, 1985.

Boyce, Robert W. D. *British Capitalism at the Crossroads. 1919–1932: A Study in Politics, Economics, and International Relations.* Cambridge, 1987.

Boyle, Peter G. 'Britain, America and the Transition from Economic to Military Assistance, 1948–1951', *Journal of Contemporary History*, XXII, 1987, pp. 521–38.

Branson, Noreen. *History of the Communist Party of Great Britain, 1927–1941.* London, 1985.

——, and Margot Heinemann. *Britain in the 1930s.* New York, 1971.

Briggs, Asa, and John Saville, eds. *Essays in Labour History, 1886–1923.* London, 1971.

——. *Essays in Labour History, 1918–1939.* London, 1977.

Bryher, S. *An Account of the Labour and Socialist Movement in Bristol.* London, 1929.

Buchanan, Tom. *The Spanish Civil War and the British Labour Movement.* Cambridge, 1991.

Bullock, Alan. *The Life and Times of Ernest Bevin.* Vol. 1: *Trade Union Leader 1881–1940.* London, 1960.

——. *The Life and Times of Ernest Bevin.* Vol. 2: *Minister of Labour, 1940–1945.* London, 1967.

——. *Foreign Secretary.* New York, 1983.

Burgess, Keith. *The Challenge of Labour: Shaping British Society, 1850–1930.* London, 1980.

Burridge, Trevor. *Clement Attlee: A Political Biography.* London, 1985.

Cain, P. J., and A. G. Hopkins. 'Gentlemanly Capitalism and British Expansion Overseas, II: New Imperialism, 1850–1945', *Economic History Review*, XL, 1987, pp. 1–26.

Calder, Angus. *The People's War: Britain, 1939–1945.* New York, 1969.

Calhoun, Daniel. *The United Front: The TUC and the Russians, 1923–1928.* Cambridge, 1976.

Campbell, Duncan. *The Unsinkable Aircraft Carrier: American Military Power in Britain.* London, 1986.

Campbell, John. *Nye Bevan and the Mirage of British Socialism.* London, 1987.

Carden, Robert. 'Before Bizonia: Britain's Economic Dilemma in Germany, 1945–

218

BIBLIOGRAPHY

46', *Journal of Contemporary History*, XIV, 1979, pp. 535–55.

Carew, Anthony. *Labour under the Marshall Plan*. Detroit, 1987.

Citrine, Walter. *Men and Work; an Autobiography*. London, 1964.

———. *Two Careers*. London, 1967.

Clark, Ian, and Nicholas J. Wheeler. *The British Origins of Nuclear Strategy, 1945–1955*. Oxford, 1989.

Clarke, Peter. *The Keynesian Revolution in the Making, 1924–1936*. Cambridge, 1987.

Clegg, Hugh Armstrong. *A History of British Trade Unions Since 1889*. Vol. 2: *1911–1933*. Oxford, 1985.

———. *Labour Relations in London Transport*. London, 1950.

———, Alan Fox, and A. F. Thompson. *A History of British Trade Unions Since 1889*. Vol. 1: *1889–1910*. Oxford, 1964.

Coates, Ken, and Tony Topham. *The History of the Transport and General Workers' Union*. Oxford, 1991.

Cohen, Michael J. *Palestine and the Great Powers, 1945–1948*. Princeton, 1982.

Colville, John. *The Fringes of Power: 10 Downing Street Diaries*. New York, 1985.

Cook, A. J. *The Mond Moonshine*. London, 1928.

Cromwell, William C. 'The Marshall Plan, Britain, and the Cold War', *Review of International Studies*, VIII, 1982, pp. 233–50.

Cronin, James E. *Labour and Society in Britain*. London, 1984

———. *The Politics of State Expansion: War, State and Society in Twentieth–Century Britain*. London, 1991.

Croucher, Richard. *Engineers at War*. London, 1982.

———. *We Refuse to Starve in Silence: A History of the National Unemployed Workers' Movement 1920–1946*. London, 1987.

Crowther, Anne. *British Social Policy, 1914–1939*. London, 1988.

Cumings, Bruce. *The Origins of the Korean War*. 2 vols. Princeton, 1981–90.

Dalton, Hugh. *The Fateful Years: Memoirs, 1931–1945*. London, 1957

———. *High Tide and After: Memoirs, 1945–1960*. London, 1962.

Darwin, John. *Britain and Decolonisation*. New York, 1988.

Davies, Paul. *A. J. Cook*. Manchester, 1987.

Deighton, Anne, ed. *Britain and the First Cold War*. New York, 1990.

———. *The Impossible Peace: Britain, the Division of Germany, and the Origins of the Cold War*. Oxford, 1990.

Dilks, David, ed. *The Diaries of Sir Alexander Cadogan*. London, 1971.

Dimbleby, David, and David Reynolds. *An Ocean Apart: The Relationship Between Britain and America in the Twentieth Century*. New York, 1988.

Dixon, Piers. *Double Diploma: The Life of Sir Pierson Dixon*. London, 1968.

Dockrill, M. L. 'The Foreign Office, Anglo-American Relations and the Korean War, June 1950–June 1951', *International Affairs*, LXII, 1986, pp. 459–76.

Durbin, Elizabeth. *New Jerusalems: The Labour Party and the Economics of Democratic Socialism*. London, 1985.

Edmonds, Robin. *Setting the Mould: The United States and Britain, 1945–1950*. Oxford, 1986.

Eisenberg, Carolyn. *Drawing the Line: The American Decision to Divide Germany, 1944–1949*. Cambridge, 1993.

Evans, Trevor. *Bevin of Britain*. New York, 1946.

Exell, Arthur. 'Morris Motors in the 1940s', *History Workshop*, 9, 1980, pp. 90–

219

ERNEST BEVIN

114.

Farman, Christopher. *The General Strike*. London, 1972.

Fishman, Nina. 'The British Communist Party and the Trade Unions, 1933–45: The Dilemmas of Revolutionary Pragmatism'. Ph.D. dissertation, University of London, 1991.

Foote, Geoffrey. *The Labour Party's Political Thought: A History*. London, 1985.

Fryth, Jim. *The Signal Was Spain: The Aid Spain Movement in Britain, 1936–1939*. London, 1986.

Fuller, Ken. *Radical Artistocrats: London Busworkers from the 1880s to the 1980s*. London, 1985.

Gardner, Lloyd C. *Approaching Vietnam: From World War II Through Dienbienphu, 1941–1954*. New York, 1988.

Garside, W. R. *British Unemplovment, 1919–1939*. Cambridge, 1990.

Gilbert, Bentley. *British Social Policy, 1914–1939*. Ithaca, 1970.

Gladwyn, Hubert Miles Gladwyn Jebb. *The Memoirs of Lord Gladwyn*. London, 1972.

Glynn, Sean, and Alan Booth, eds. *The Road to Full Employment*. London, 1987.

Gormly, James L. *The Collapse of the Grand Alliance, 1945–1948*. Baton Rouge, 1987.

Gowing, Margaret. *Independence and Deterrence: Britain and Atomic Energy, 1945–1952*. 2 vols. London, 1974.

Greenleaf, W. H. *The British Political Tradition*. 3 vols. London, 1983–7.

Greenwood, Sean. 'Bevin, the Ruhr and the Division of Germany: August 1945–December 1946', *Historical Journal*, XXIX, 1986, pp. 203–12.

———. 'Ernest Bevin, France and "Western Union": August 1945–February 1946', *European History Quarterly*, XIV, 1984, pp. 319–38.

———. 'Frank Roberts and the "Other" Long Telegram: The View from the British Embassy in Moscow, March, 1946', *Journal of Contemporary History*, XXV, 1990, pp. 103–123.

Gupta, P. S. *Imperialism and the British Labour Movement, 1914–1964*. London, 1975.

———. 'Imperialism and the Labour Government of 1945–51 '. In *The Working Class in Modern British History*, ed. Jay Winter, Cambridge, 1983, pp. 99–123.

Halliday, Jon, and Bruce Cumings. *Korea: the Unknown War*. London, 1988.

Hancock, W. K., and M. M. Gowing. *British War Economy*. London, 1949.

Hannington, Wal. *Unemployed Struggles*. London, 1936.

Harbutt, Fraser J. *The Iron Curtain: Churchill America and the Origins of the Cold War*. New York, 1986.

Harris, José. *William Beveridge: A Biography*. Oxford, 1977.

Hayburn, Ralph. 'The National Unemployed Workers' Movement, 1921–36: A Re-appraisal', *International Review of Social History*, XXVIII, 1983, pp. 279–95.

Healey, Denis. *The Time of My Life*. New York, 1990.

Henderson, Nicholas. *The Private Office*. London, 1984.

Hinds, Alistair. 'Sterling and Imperial Policy 1945–1951', *Journal of Imperial and Commonwealth History*, XV, 1987, pp. 148–69.

Hinton, James. *The First Shop Stewards' Movement*. London, 1973.

———. *Protests and Visions: Peace Politics in Twentieth-Century Britain*. London, 1989.

Hobsbawm, Eric. *Labouring, Men: Studies in the History of Labour*. Garden City, New York, 1967.

———. *Workers: Worlds of Labor*. New York, 1984.

BIBLIOGRAPHY

Hogan, Michael J. *The Marshall Plan: America Britain, and the Reconstruction of Western Europe, 1947–1952.* Cambridge, 1987.

Holton, Bob. *British Syndicalism, 1900–1914.* London, 1976.

Howell, David. *British Social Democracy.* New York, 1980.

——. *British Workers and the Independent Labour Party, 1888–1906.* New York, 1983.

Hunt, E. H. *British Labour History, 1815–1914.* London, 1981.

Hyman, Richard. *The Workers' Union.* Oxford, 1971.

Iatrides, John, ed. *Greece in the 1940s.* Hanover, N.H. and London, 1981.

Ingham, G. *Capitalism Divided? The City and Industry in British Social Development.* New York, 1984.

Inman, P. F. *Labour in the Munitions Industries.* London, 1957.

Ireland, Timothy P. *Creating the Entangling Alliance: The Origins of the North Atlantic Treaty Organization.* Westport, Connecticut, 1981.

Jefferys, Kevin. *The Churchill Coalition and Wartime Politics, 1940–1945.* Manchester, 1991.

——, ed. *Labour and the Wartime Coalition: From the Diary of James Chuter Ede, 1941–1945.* London, 1987.

Jensen, Kenneth, ed. *Origins of the Cold War: The Novikov, Kennan, and Roberts 'Long Telegrams' of 1946,* Washington, D.C., 1991.

Jones, Barry, and Michael Keating. *Labour and the British State.* Oxford, 1985.

Jones, Gareth Stedman. *Outcast London.* Oxford, 1971.

Jones, Jack. *Union Man.* London, 1986.

Jones, Stephen. 'The British Trade Unions and Holidays with Pay', *International Review of Social History,* XXXI, 1986, pp. 40–67.

Jong-yil, Ra. 'Special Relationship at War: The Anglo-American Relationship During the KoreanWar, *Journal of Strategic Studies,* VII, 1984, pp. 301–17.

Jupp, James. *The Radical Left in Britain, 1931–1941.* London, 1982.

Kaplan, Lawrence S. *The United States and NATO: the Formative Years.* Lexington, Kentucky, 1984.

Kendall, Walter. *The Revolutionary Movement in Britain, 1900–21.* London, 1969.

Kennedy, Paul, ed. *Grand Strategies in War and Peace.* New Haven, 1991.

——.*Strategy and Diplomacy,1870–1940.* London, 1983.

Kent, John. 'Bevin's, Imperialism and the Idea of Euro-Africa'. In *British Foreign Policy, 1945–1956,* ed. Michael Dockrill and John Young, New York, 1989, pp. 47–76.

——. 'The British Empire and the Origins of the Cold War. In *Britain and the First Cold War,* ed. Anne Deighton, New York, 1990, pp. 165–83.

Kingsford, Peter. *The Hunger Marchers in Britain, 1920–1939.* London, 1982.

Kirby, M. W. *The British Coalmining Industry, 1870–1946: A Political and Economic History.* London, 1977.

Knight, Jonathan. 'Russia's Search for Peace: The London Council of Foreign Ministers, 1945', *Journal of Contemporary History,* XII, 1978,pp. 137–63.

LaFeber, Walter. 'NATO and the Korean War: A Context', *Diplomatic History,* XIII, 1989, pp. 461–77.

Leventhal, F. M. *Arthur Henderson.* Manchester, 1989.

——. *The Last Dissenter: H. N. Brailsford and his World.* New York, 1985.

Leffler, Melvyn. 'Adherence to Agreements: Yalta and the Experiences of the Early Cold War', *International Security,* XI, 1986, pp. 88–123.

221

ERNEST BEVIN

———. *A Preponderance of Power: National Security, the Truman Administration and the Cold War.* Stanford, 1992.

Louis, William Roger. *The British Empire in the Middle East, 1945–1951.* Oxford, 1984.

———. *Imperialism at Bay: The United States and the Decolonization of the British Empire, 1941–1945.* Oxford, 1978.

Lovell, John. *Stevedores and Dockers: A Study of Trade Unionism in the Port of London, 1870–1914.* New York, 1969.

Lowe, Rodney. *Adjusting to Democracy: The Role of the Ministry of Labour in British Politics, 1916–1939.* Oxford, 1986.

McDonald, G. W., and Howard Gospel. 'The Mond–Turner Talks, 1927–1933: A Study in Industrial Cooperation', *Historical Journal,* XVI, 1973, pp. 807–29.

Mackenzie, Norman, and Jeanne Mackenzie, eds. *The Diary of Beatrice Webb.* 4 vols. Cambridge, Massachusetts, 1982–5.

McKibbin, Ross. *The Evolution of the Labour Party, 1910–1924.* Oxford, 1974.

———. *The Ideologies of Class: Social Relations in Britain, 1880–1950.* New York, 1990.

McMahon, Robert J. *Colonialism and Cold War: The United States and the Struggle for Indonesian Independence, 1945–49.* Ithaca, 1981.

Maier, Charles. 'The politics of productivity: Foundations of American international economic policy after World War II', *International Organization,* XXXI, 1977, pp. 607–33.

Mallaby, George. *From My Level.* New York, 1965.

Mansergh, Nicholas, ed. *The Transfer of Power, 1942–7.* 12 vols. London, 1970–83.

Marquand, David. *Ramsay MacDonald.* London, 1977.

Martin, Kingsley. *Editor: The 'New Statesman' Years, 1931–1945.* Chicago, 1968.

Martin, Ross. *TUC: The Growth of a Pressure Group.* Oxford, 1980.

Mayhew, Christopher. *Time to Explain.* London, 1987.

Meacham, Standish. *A Life Apart: The English Working Class, 1890–1914.* Cambridge, Massachusetts, 1977.

Middlemas, Keith. *Politics in Industrial Society: The Experience of the British System Since 1911.* London, 1979.

Middleton, Roger. *Towards the Managed Economy: Keynes, the Treasury, and the Fiscal Policy Debate of the 1930s.* London 1985

Mikardo, Ian. *Back-Bencher.* London, 1988.

Miliband, Ralph. *Parliamentary Socialism.* 2nd edition. London, 1972.

Miller, Frederick. 'The British Unemployment Assistance Crisis of 1935', *Journal of Contemporary History,* XIV, 1979, pp. 329–52.

Mommsen, Wolfgang J., and Hans-Gerhard Husung, eds. *The Development of Trade Unionism in Great Britain and Germany, 1880–1914.* London, 1985.

Morgan, Austen. *J. Ramsay MacDonald.* Manchester, 1987.

Morgan, Kenneth. *Consensus and Disunity: The Lloyd George Coalition Government, 1918–1922.* Oxford, 1979.

———. *Labour in Power, 1945–1951.* Oxford, 1984.

———. *Labour People: Leaders and Lieutenants.* Oxford, 1987.

Morgan, Kevin. *Against Fascism and War: Ruptures and Continuities in British Communist Politics, 1935–41.* Manchester, 1989.

Morris, Margaret. *The General Strike.* Harmondsworth, 1976.

Nachmani, Amikam. '"It is a Matter of Getting the Mixture Right": Britain's Post-

222

BIBLIOGRAPHY

war Relations with America in the Middle East', *Journal of Contemporary History*, XVIII, 1983, pp. 117–39.

Naylor, John F. *Labour's International Policy: The Labour Party in the 1930's*. Boston, 1969

Newton, Scott. 'The 1949 Sterling Crisis and British Policy Towards European Integration', *Review of International Studies*, XI, 1985, pp. 169–82.

——. 'The Sterling Crisis of 1947 and the British Response to the Marshall Plan', *Economic History Review*, XXVII, 1984, pp. 391–408.

Ovendale, Ritchie. *Britain, the United States and the End of the Palestine Mandate, 1942–1948*. Woodbridge, Suffolk, 1989.

——. *The English-Speaking Alliance: Britain, the United States, the Dominions and the Cold War, 1945–1951*. London, 1985.

——, ed. *The Foreign Policy of the British Labour Governments, 1945–1951*. Leicester, 1984.

Parker, H. M. D. *Manpower: A Study of War-time Policy and Administration*. London, 1957.

Peden, George. *British Economic and Social Policy: Lloyd George to Margaret Thatcher*. Oxford, 1985.

Pelling, Henry. *Britain and the Second World War*. Paperback edition, Glasgow, 1970.

——. *A History of British Trade Unionism*. 5th edition. London, 1992.

——. *A Short History of the Labour Party*. 9th edition. Basingstoke, 1991.

Phillips, Gordon. *The General Strike*. London, 1976.

——, and Noel Whiteside. *Casual Labour: The Unemployment Question in the Port Transport Industry, 1880–1970*. Oxford, 1985.

Pimlott, Ben. *Hugh Dalton*. London, 1985.

——. *Labour and the Left in the 1930s*. London, 1977.

——, ed. *The Political Diary of Hugh Dalton, 1918–40, 1945–60*. London, 1986.

——, ed. *The Second World War Diary of Hugh Dalton, 1940–45*. London, 1986.

——, and Chris Cook, eds. *Trade Unions in British Politics*. London, 1982.

Pollard, Robert A. *Economic Security and the Origins of the Cold War, 1945–50*. New York, 1985.

Potts, Archie. 'Bevin to Beat the Bankers: Ernest Bevin's Gateshead Campaign of, 1931', *Bulletin of the Northeast Group for the Study of Labour History*, 11, 1977, pp. 28–38.

Price, Richard. *Labour in British Society, an Interpretive History*. London, 1986.

Pugh, Martin. *The Making of Modern British Politics, 1867–1939*. New York, 1982.

Reynolds, David. *Britannia Overruled: British Policy and World Power in the Twentieth Century*. London, 1991.

Richter, Heinz. *British Intervention in Greece: From Varkiza to Civil War*. London, 1986.

Roberts, B. C. *The Trades Union Congress 1868–1921*. Cambridge, Mass., 1958.

Ross, Graham, ed. *The Foreign Office and the Kremlin: British Documents on Anglo-Soviet Relations, 1941–45*. Cambridge, 1984.

Rotter, Andrew. 'The Triangular Route to Vietnam: The United States, Great Britain, and Southeast Asia, 1945–50', *International History Review*, VI, 1984, pp. 404–23.

——. *The Path to Vietnam: Origins of the American Commitment to Southeast Asia*. Ithaca, 1987.

Rubin, Gerry. *War, Law and Labour: The Munitions Acts, State Regulation and the*

223

ERNEST BEVIN

Unions, 1915–1921. Oxford, 1987.

Ryan, Henry Butterfield. *The Vision of Anglo-America: The US–UK Alliance and the Emerging Cold War, 1943–1946.* Cambridge, 1987.

Samuel, Raphael. 'The Lost World of British Communism', *New Left Review*, 154, 1985.

——. 'Staying Power: The Lost World of British Communism, Part 2', *New Left Review*, 156, 1986.

Saville, John, 'The Ideology of Labourism'. In *Knowledge and Belief in Politics: The Problem of Ideology*, ed. Robert Benewick, et al., London, 1973, pp. 213–26.

——. *The Labour Movement in Britain.* London, 1988.

Schneer, Jonathan. *Ben Tillett.* Urbana, 1982.

——. *George Lansbury*, Manchester, 1990.

——. *Labour's Conscience: The Labour Left, 1945–51.* London, 1987.

Shlaim, Avi. *The United States and the Berlin Blockade.* Berkeley, 1983.

——. *Collusion Across the Jordan: King Abdullah, the Zionist Movement, and the Partition of Palestine.* New York, 1988.

Sked, Alan, and Chris Cook. *Post-War Britain: A Political History.* Harmondsworth, 1984.

Skelley, Jeffrey, ed. *The General Strike, 1926.* London, 1976.

Skidelsky, Robert. *Politicians and the Slump: The Labour Government of 1929–1931.* London, 1967.

Smith, Harold. 'The Problem of "Equal Pay for Equal Work" in Great Britain during World War II', *Journal of Modern History*, LIII, December, 1981, pp. 652–72.

——. 'The Womanpower Problem in Britain during the Second World War', *Historical Journal*, XXVII, 1984, pp. 925–45.

Smith, Raymond. 'A Climate of Opinion: British Officials and the Development of Soviet policy, 1945–7', *International Affairs*, LXIV, 1988, pp. 631–47.

——, and John Zametica. 'The Cold Warrior: Clement Attlee Reconsidered', *Interrnational Affairs*, LXI, 1985, pp. 237–52.

Stavrakis, Peter J. *Moscow and Greek Communism, 1944–1949.* Ithaca, 1989.

Stephanson, Anders. *Kennan and the Art of Foreign Policy.* Cambridge, Massachusetts, 1989.

Stephens, Mark. *Ernest Bevin: Unskilled Labourer and World Statesman, 1881–1951.* Stevenage, 1981.

Summerfield, Penny. *Women Workers in the Second World War: Production and Patriarchy in Conflict.* London, 1984.

Supple, Barry. *The History of the British Coal Industry.* Vol. 4: *1913–1946: The Political Economy of Decline.* Oxford, 1987.

Tames, Richard. *Ernest Bevin.* Aylesbury, 1974.

Taplin, Eric. *The Dockers' Union: A Study of the National Union of Dock Labourers, 1889–1922.* New York, 1986.

Taylor, A. J. P. *Beaverbrook.* London, 1972.

Thane, Pat. *The Foundations of the Welfare State.* London, 1983.

Thompson, F. M. L., ed. *The Cambridge Social History of Britain.* Vol. 3: *Social Agencies and Institutions.* Cambridge, 1990.

Thorne, Christopher. *Allies of a Kind: The United States, Britain, and the War Against Japan. 1941–1945.* New York, 1978.

Thorpe, Andrew. 'Arthur Henderson and the British Political Crisis of 1931',

224

BIBLIOGRAPHY

Historical Journal, XXXI, 1988, pp. 117–39.

———. *The British General Election of 1931*. Oxford, 1991.

Tiratsoo, Nick, ed. *The Attlee Years*. London, 1991.

Tolliday, Steven, and Jonathan Zeitlin, eds. *The Power to Manage? Employers and Industrial Relations in Comparative Historical Perspective*. New York, 1991.

———. *Shop Floor Bargaining and the State*. Cambridge, 1985.

Tomlinson, Jim. *Public Policy and the Economy Since 1900*. Oxford, 1990.

Tsoucalas, Constantine. *The Greek Tragedv*. Baltimore, 1969.

Tsuzuki, Chushichi. *H. M. Hyndman and British Socialism*. Oxford, 1961.

———. *Tom Mann*. Oxford, 1991.

Turner, Ian. 'Great Britain and the Post-war German Currency Reform', *Historical Journal*, XXX, 1987, pp. 685–708.

Waites, Bernard. *A Class Society at War: England 1914–1918*. Leamington Spa, 1987.

Warner, Geoffrey. 'The British Labour Government and the Atlantic Alliance'. In *Western Security: The Formative Years: European and Atlantic Defence, 1947–1953*, ed. Olav Riste, New York, 1985, pp. 247–65.

———. 'The Labour Governments and the Unity of Western Europe, 1945–51'. In *The Foreign Policy of the British Labour Governments, 1945–1951*, ed. Ritchie Ovendale, Leicester, 1984, pp. 61–82.

Watt, D. C. *How War Came: The Immediate Origins of the Second World War, 1938–1939*. New York, 1989.

Weiler, Peter. *British Labour and the Cold War*. Stanford, 1988.

———. 'Labour and the Cold War: The Foreign Policy of the British Labour Governments, 1945–1951', *Journal of British Studies*, XXVI, 1987, pp. 54–82.

Wheeler, N. J. 'British Nuclear Weapons and Anglo-American Relations, 1945–54', *International Affairs*, LXII, 1986, pp. 71–86.

White, Stephen. *Britain and the Bolshevik Revolution: A Study in the Politics of Diplomacy, 1920–1924*. New York, 1979.

Wiebes, Cees, and Bert Zeeman. 'The Pentagon Negotiations March 1948: The Launching of the North Atlantic Treaty', *International Affairs*, LIX, 1983, pp. 351–63.

Williams, Andrew. *Labour and Russia: The Attitude of the Labour Party to the USSR, 1924–34*. Manchester, 1989.

Williams, Francis. *Ernest Bevin: Portrait of a Great Englishman*. London, 1952.

Williams, Philip M. *Hugh Gaitskell: A Political Biography*. London, 1979.

Williamson, Philip. 'A "Bankers' Ramp"? Financiers and the British Political Crisis of 1931', *English Historical Review*, XCIX, 1984, pp. 770–806.

———. *National Crisis and National Government: British Politics, the Economy and Empire, 1926–1932*. Cambridge, 1992.

Wilson, Trevor. *The Myriad Faces of War: Britain and the Great War, 1914–1918*. Cambridge, 1986.

Winter, J. M. *The Great War and the British People*. Cambridge, Massachusetts, 1986.

Wittner, Lawrence. *American Intervention in Greece, 1943–1949*. New York, 1982.

Wolfe, Joel. *Workers, Participation, and Democracy: Internal Politics in the British Union Movement*. London, 1985.

Woods, Randall Bennett. *A Changing of the Guard: Anglo-American Relations, 1941–1946*. Chapel Hill, 1990.

ERNEST BEVIN

Wrigley, Chris. *Arthur Henderson*. Cardiff, 1990.

——, ed. *A History of British Industrial Relations. 1875–1914*. Amherst, Massachusetts, 1982.

——, ed. *A History of British Industrial Relations*. Vol. 2: *1914–1939*. Brighton, 1987.

Young, John W. *Britain, France and the Unity of Europe, 1945–1954*. Leicester, 1984.

——. *France, the Cold War, and the Western Alliance, 1944–1949*. New York, 1990.

Zametica, John, ed. *British Officials and British Foreign Policy*. Leicester, 1990.

——. 'Three Letters to Bevin: Frank Roberts at the Moscow Embassy, 1945–46'. In *British Officials and British Foreign Policy 1945–50*, ed. John Zametica, Leicester, 1990, pp. 39–97.

Index

Abyssinian crisis, 88
Acheson, Dean, 169, 181, 183, 186
Advisory Committee on Colonial Development, 72
Africa
  EB's desire to develop as centre of empire, 175
Anderson, John, 113
anti-Semitism, EB's, 75, 170-1, 215 n.16
Attlee, Clement, 77, 140, 144-5, 159, 164, 174-5, 184, 187
  challenges EB's cold war policy, 160-2
authoritarianism, EB's, 35-6, 191

Baldwin, Stanley, 40, 42-3, 45
  capitalizes on Lansbury's resignation, 91
Balfour Declaration, 170
Beaverbrook, William Maxwell Aitken, 1st Baron, 106
Berlin blockade, 178-9, 214 n.126
Bevan, Aneurin, 93, 127, 142
  criticises Defense Regulation 1AA, 127
  criticises Labour's foreign policy (1930s), 95
  warns about rearmament, 182
Beveridge, Sir William (later Lord), 107
  EB dislikes, 16, 140
Beveridge Report, 139-40
Bevin, Diana Mercy Tidboald, 1-2
Bevin, Florence Townley, 4
Bevin Boy scheme, 118
Bidault, Georges, 166
Black Friday, 25-6
  see also Miners' Federation of Great Britain; strikes; Triple Industrial Alliance
Bowley, A. L., 28
Bristol Socialist Society, 5-6
Britain, economic and social conditions, 36, 39, 80, 148
British empire
  EB's support for, 147-8, 150, 175, 186
  obstacles to continuation, 148-9
  supported by US, 169

  see also Africa; imperialism; Indochina; Indonesia
Brussels Pact, 177-8
busmen, *see* London Busmen's Rank and File Movement
Butler, R. A. (later Lord), 139
Byrnes, James, 146, 152-4

Canteens Orders, 129
capitalism, 49-50
  EB believes can be transformed, 19-20, 41-2, 48, 189
  EB decides is permanent, 48, 189
  EB supports when regulated, 17, 57-9, 69-70
  interwar crisis of, 39
  see also corporatism; direct action; labourism; socialism
Catering Wages Act (1943), 133-6
Chamberlain, Neville, 95, 97, 98
  fails to mobilise women for war work, 113
  forced to resign, 102
  squanders time preparing for war, 100, 103-4
Churchill, (later Sir) Winston Spencer, 100, 106, 108, 114, 119, 139, 140, 142, 144, 146, 148, 155, 158
  forms Coalition government, 102
citizenship, 135
  EB supports expanded definition of, 27-30
  expanded by Second World War, 103
Citrine, Sir Walter (later Lord), vii, 35, 40, 43-4, 48, 79, 80, 89, 96, 100, 124, 189
Clark, Colin, 65-6
class collaboration, 32, 48, 134-5, 190
  EB's relationship to, 47-50
  EB supports at Shaw Committee, 29-30, 31
  see also corporatism; Mond-Turner talks; trade unions
class conflict, 17-18, 23-4, 31-2, 46, 108, 126
  EB's early belief in, 10-12

227

ERNEST BEVIN

see also direct action; strikes; trade unions

Clay, Harold, 48

Clayton, William, 167, 168

coal mining industry

EB's difficulties with (Second World War), 118-19

post-First World War crisis and, 25, 39-40

provokes General Strike, 49

Second World War, 117-19

see also Bevin Boy scheme; Black Friday; General Strike; Red Friday; strikes

cold war

crystallisation of (1946), 155-6

onset, 147-62

Western responsibility for, 154-5

see also Germany; Greece; Marshall Plan; NATO

Cole, George Douglas Howard, 54, 64, 71

Cole, Margaret, 66

Committee on Finance and Industry (Macmillan Committee), 55-9

confirms corporatist path for EB, 58

confirms value of mixed economy to EB, 55

exposes mysteries of government to EB, 57

platform for J. M. Keynes, 55

shows incompetence of bourgeoisie to EB, 57

shows need to EB to support industry, not finance, 56-7

communism, 165-6

Eastern Europe, 163

Germany, 159-60

Greece, 157-8

Third World, 148

Communist Party of Great Britain (CPGB), 6, 125-6, 128

relation to Labour Party, 81

Spanish civil war, 94

see also Joint Production Committees; London Busworker's Rank and File Movement; National Unemployed Workers' Movement

Conditions of Employment and National Arbitration Order (Order Number 1305), 119

Conservative Party, 46, 62, 102

see also Baldwin, Stanley; Chamberlain, Neville; Churchill, Winston; Tory Right

corporatism, 189

basis of industrial relations in Second

World War, 121-2

defined, viii

EB supports at Shaw Committee, 31

failure of (1930s), 79-80, 98, 189

necessitates opposition to militancy, 81

realization in Second World War, 100, 112, 103, 105, 142-3

see also Catering Wages Act; Committee on Finance and Industry; Dock Labour (Compulsory Registration) Order; Mond-Turner talks; Shaw Committee; shipbuilding and shiprepairing industries

Council of Action, 21

used by EB to justify opposition to USSR, 76, 156

Council of Foreign Ministers (CFM)

London (1945), 152

Moscow (1945), 153-4

Paris (1946), 160

Paris (1947), 176

Coupon election (1918), *see* elections

Cripps, Stafford, 78, 89, 180-2

attacked by EB, 90

crisis of 1931, 59-63

EB's role in, 60-2

Cyrenaica

British claims to, supported by US, 169

EB desires control of, 152, 161

Czechoslovakia, 95, 177

Daily Herald, 26, 79

Dalton, Hugh (later Baron), 35, 61, 77, 88, 90, 92, 96, 118-19, 141-2, 144-6, 161, 172, 187

opposes EB's policy in Greece, 164

Deakin, Arthur, 122

Defence Regulation 1AA, 127-8

Devonport, Lord, 11, 15-16, 30

direct action, 19-24, 46

EB's view of, 19-20

rejected in 1930s, 80-1

see also class conflict; corporatism; strikes

Dixon, Sir Pierson, 147, 153, 161-2

Dock Labour (Compulsory Registration) Order (Dock Scheme), 131-3

Dock, Wharf, Riverside and General Labourers' Union (Dockers' Union), 8, 10, 13, 26-7, 32

see also Shaw Committee; strikes

dock workers, 13-14, 131-3

decasualisation, 132

see also strikes

228

INDEX

Eastern Europe, 149, 154, 163, 167
Economic Advisory Council, 54
economic orthodoxy, 54
Edward VIII, 192
egotism, EB's, 35, 67-8, 142-3, 191-2
elections
    1918, 19
    1931, 62
    1945, 144
Emergency Powers (Defence) Bill, 105-6
empire, *see* British empire
Essential Work Order (EWO), 108-9, 118
    facilitates growth of trade unions, 123
    see also labour supply policy; shipbuilding
        and shiprepairing industries
Europe, 148-9, 194
    division of, and Marshall Plan, 167
    EB fails to join, 180-1, 182, 187
    EB seeks closer cooperation with, 176-7

Factories Acts, 128
    EB clashes with Herbert Morrison over,
        130
Factories (Medical and Welfare Services) Or-
    der, 129
Factory and Welfare Board, *see* welfare·
Factory and Welfare Department, *see* welfare
Fascism, 80
Federation of British Industries, 22, 51
finance, 49-50, 168-9, 189
    EB sees imposing crushing burden on
        economy, 56
    EB sees underlying different crises, 62-3,
        98, 101
    EB's view of nefarious influence, 20, 47-8,
        51, 56, 75, 120
    see also anti-Semitism; capitalism; eco-
        nomic orthodoxy
First World War, 13-19
    EB supports, 13-14
    effect on EB's economic views, 17
    gives working class new claim on society,
        29
France
    EB seeks closer ties with, 150
    needs defence treaty to allay fears of
        Germany, 177-8, 180, 182
    see also Europe; Indochina
full employment, EB's support for, 141, 190,
    194
    see also right to work; social security;
        unemployment

General Council, 40, 42, 44, 47, 53

    crisis of 1931 and, 60-2
    EB chairs, 92
    EB helps to create, 22
    see also General Strike; Red Friday; Mond-
        Turner talks; Trades Union Congress
General Strike, 38-46
    EB overestimates results of, 45-6
    EB's role in, 42-5
    General Council calls off, 44
    General Gouncil fails to prepare for, 42
George VI, 145, 192
Germany, 14, 159-60, 178
    EB defends policy in, 165
    Marshall Plan and, 166
    see also Berlin blockade; Potsdam confer-
        ence
gold standard
    EB rejects, 56-7
Gosling, Harry, 33
Greece, 157-9
    Attlee's criticism of British policy in, 161
    British withdrawal from, 164

Henderson, Arthur, 86, 96
    crisis of 1931 and, 61
Hoare-Laval pact, 91
Hobson, John Atkinson, 58
Hodges, Frank, 25

imperialism
    EB supports imperial development
        (1930s), 72, 96-7
    see also India; Indochina; Indonesia; Middle
        East
Independent Labour Party, 13, 66
    EB's opposition to, 63-4
India, 67, 148, 162, 175
Indochina, 150, 181
    see also British empire; France
Indonesia, 151
    see also British empire
industrial relations (Second World War), 119-
    24
    EB's plans for postwar, 130, 133-5, 136-8
intellectuals, 165
    EB's distrust of, 64, 66-8, 165
    see also treachery

Joint Consultative Committee (JCC), 105,
    119, 137
joint production committees (JPC), 124-6
Jolly George, 20
Jones, Jack, 35, 36

229

ERNEST BEVIN

Kennan, George, 154, 166, 168
Keynes, John Maynard, 54-5, 58, 60, 101, 141
  economic ideas supported by EB, 73, 141
  warns of postwar economic disaster, 151
Korea, 183-4

Labour, Ministry of, 103, 128, 204 n.9
labour discipline, 29-30, 37, 133
  see also corporatism; Dock Labour (Compulsory Registration) Order; trade unions
Labour government of 1929, 54-5
  see also crisis of 1931
labourism, 69, 147, 189-90
  defined, vii
Labour Left
  clash with EB in 1930s, 76-8
  crushed by EB, 164-5
  oppose EB's foreign policy, 156, 164
  oppose Labour's foreign policy (1930s), 89, 92
  Spanish civil war and, 93-4
Labour Party, 60
  domestic policy (1930s), 68-78
  EB's relationship to, 92, 53-4, 70, 139
  foreign policy (1930s), 86-97
labour supply policy (Second World War), 104-8, 112-13
  see also coal mining industry; women (Second World War)
labour theory of value, 28
Lansbury, George, 26, 96
  crushed by Bevin, 89-91
Lloyd George, David, 16, 21, 23, 24, 102
Location of Industry Bill, 141-2
London Busmen's Rank and File Movement (RFM), 83-6
  see also; class conflict; Communist Party of Great Britain; labour discipline; trade unions
Lord President's Committee, 113, 116

MacDonald, J. Ramsay, 54, 59-62, 70
Macmillan Committee, see Committee on Finance and Industry
Marshall, George, 168
  see also Marshall Plan
Marshall Plan, 165-67
  EB's role in, 166-68
May Committee, 59-60
Middle East, 161-2, 171
  British need for oil from, 163, 165
  EB defends policy in, 164-5
  EB sees as replacement for India, 175

US reliance on Britain in, 169
  see also British empire; imperialism; Palestine
militancy, see class conflict; direct action; strikes; trade unions
Miners' Federation of Great Britain (miners' union)
  1921 dispute, 25-6
  1926 dispute, see General Strike
mining industry, see coal mining industry
Ministry of Labour, see Labour, Ministry of
mobilisation (Second World War), 103-13
Molotov, Vyacheslav M., 167
Mond-Turner talks, 46-52, 189
  see also class collaboration; corporatism
Morrison, Herbert (later Lord), 74, 128, 130, 140, 142, 144
  EB's dislike of, 74, 208 n.141

National Confederation of Employers' Organisations, 22, 51
National Council of Labour, 70, 92, 98
national government, 62
National Industrial Conference, 23
National Joint Advisory Council (NJAC), 101, 105
National Transport Workers' Federation (NTWF), 11, 14, 15, 25-6, 27, 32-3
National Unemployed Workers' Movement, 82-3
  see also Communist Party of Great Britain
NATO, see North Atlantic Treaty Organisation
new unionism, 9-10
  see also trade unions
nonconformity, 2, 4, 7
  relation to EB's trade union work, 8-9
Norman, Montague, 57, 60, 101
North Atlantic Treaty Organisation (NATO), 181-2
  EB sees as greatest accomplishment, 185
  origins, 176-8
nuclear weapons, 174
  US, based in Britain, 179

Order Number 1305, see Conditions of Employment and National Arbitration Order

Palestine, 170-4
  EB's sympathy for Palestinians, 171
paternalism, EB's, 30, 97, 192
patriotism, 29
  EB's in First World War, 14
  EB's when Foreign Secretary, 146-7, 193-4

230

INDEX

Pentagon talks (1947), 169
Port and Transit Executive Committee, 16
Potsdam conference, 146, 159
 see also Germany
Production Council, 104, 106, 107

Ramadier, Paul, 176
rank and file, *see* dock workers; London Busmen's Rank and File Movement; strikes; trade unions
rationalisation of industry, 50
rearmament (1950-51), 184
reconstruction (Second World War), 130, 134-43
 EB uses to avert postwar crisis, 134-7
Red Friday, 40-1
Registration of Employment Order, 113
religion, *see* nonconformity
Restriction on Engagement Order, 107
right to work, 6-7, 141, 194
Roberts, Frank, 155
Russia, *see* Union of Soviet Socialist Republics
Russia Committee, 156
Russian revolution, 21

Samuel, Herbert, 40, 42, 44
Sargent, Orme, 146, 149, 158, 159
security, *see* social security
Shaw Committee, 26-32
 effect on EB's career, 32
shipbuilding and shiprepairing industries, 109-12
shop stewards' movement, 17, 124-6
 see also joint production committees
Simon, Sir John (Viscount), 101, 139-40
Smith, Herbert, 25
Snowden, Philip (later Viscount), 54-5, 59-62
Social Democratic Federation, 5
socialism, 13-14, 69, 74, 190
 EB's early, 5, 7, 9-10
 EB's influence on Labour's, 70-4
 Labour's corporate, 68-78
 Second World War, 142
social security, 135, 194
 EB sees as worker's right, 7, 190
 EB uses war to advance, 108
 see also Beveridge Report; citizenship; right to work
Society for Socialist Information and Propaganda (SSIP), 63-8
 EB accepts radical programme of, 64-6
Soviet Union, *see* Union of Soviet Socialist Republics

Spanish civil war, 93-6
 EB's response to, 94-5
state
 EB's belief in neutrality of, 51, 190
 EB's relationship to, in First World War, 16
 EB sees need to change, 65-6, 141
 EB's view of relation to economy, 54, 58-9
 EB's view of trade union relationship to, 79, 98, 189
 see also corporatism; Mond-Turner talks; trade unions
sterling crisis (1947), 168
strikes
 busmen, 85-6
 coal miners (1921), 25-6
 coal miners (1926), 42-6
 dockers (1912), 11-12
 dockers (1923), 36-8
 Second World War, 127
 see also Black Friday; direct action; General Strike; London Busmen's Rank and File Movement; Red Friday; trade unions
syndicalism, 12, 186 n.9

Tillett, Ben, 13, 14
Tory Right, 107, 108-9, 120, 121, 134, 139
Trade Disputes Act, 46
trade unions, 9-12
 EB's belief in, 38, 53, 188
 EB believes can transform society, 13, 41-2, 48
 EB desires acceptance of, 31
 EB opposes unofficial movement, 36-8, 43, 84, 122, 124
 EB sees organisation as vital, 12-13, 15-16, 18, 21-3, 32, 33, 35, 41, 78
 EB supports militancy, 31-2
 EB supports official leadership, 21, 43, 94-5, 122
 EB's view of, as disciplined army, 35, 86, 188
 First World War and, 14-16
 Second World War and, 100-1, 121-4, 126
 see also corporatism; General Council; Trades Union Congress; Transport and General Workers' Union
Trades Union Congress (TUC), 14, 49-50, 82-3, 126
 EB aids reorganisation of, 22-3
 see also General Council; Joint Consultative

231

ERNEST BEVIN

Committee; National Joint Advisory Council; National Unemployed Workers' Movement

Transport and General Workers' Union (TGWU), 11-12, 33, 32-8, 53, 79-80, 188
EB's influence on structure, 33-4
see also corporatism; trade unions; Dock, Wharf, Riverside and General Labourers' Union; London Busmen's Rank and File Movement; strikes

treachery
EB sees disagreement as stab in the back, 35-7, 65, 165, 191
see also intellectuals

Treasury
crisis of 1931, 60
see also capitalism; finance

Trevelyan, Sir Charles, 67

Triple Industrial Alliance, 12-13, 23, 24-6
see also Black Friday; General Strike

Truman, Harry S., 154

Unemployed Workmen Act, 6

unemployment
EB's early opposition to, 6-7
EB's plans to overcome (1930s), 71-2
TUC response to, 80-3
see also Britain

Union of Soviet Socialist Republics (USSR), 146, 149, 152, 153, 154, 157, 160, 162, 163, 166, 167, 176-7, 179-80, 183

United States
British dependence on, 149, 152, 162, 163-4, 168, 172, 173, 181, 182
controls alliance with Britain, 162, 168, 169, 173-4, 186
EB seeks independence from, 174-6
opposes Britain in Palestine, 172-4

pressures Britain to rearm, 183-4

unofficial trade union movements, *see* Communist Party of Great Britain; London Busmen's Rank and File Movement; strikes, dockers (1923); trade unions

Wages Councils Act, 137-8

wages policy (Second World War), 119-22

Wardlaw-Milne, John, 109

Warner, C. F. A., 155-6

welfare, 128-30
see social security

White Paper (1944), 141

Whitley Councils, 18

Williams, Robert, 15, 23, 26

Wise, Frank, 66

Woman Power Committee (WPC), 114-15

women (Second World War), 113-17

Wood, Kingsley, Sir, 120, 122

work discipline
EB supports, 29-30
see also corporatism

working class
EB's ambivalent attitude toward, 29-30, 35, 73, 133
EB appreciates talents of, 16, 30, 57, 98-9, 191
EB believes has right to full citizenship, 27-8
EB resents exclusion of, 30-1
EB sees as saviour of England, 98-9, 102-3
unrest after First World War, 19
see also direct action; right to work; social security; work discipline

workplace democracy, 50, 188

World War I, *see* First World War

Yalta agreement (1945), 154-5

Zionism, *see* Palestine